Techniques of training

Third edition

TECHNIQUES OF TRAINING

Third Edition

LESLIE RAE

Gower

First published 1983 as *The Skills of Training*
Second edition 1991
This edition published by
Gower Publishing Limited
Gower House
Croft Road
Aldershot
Hampshire GU11 3HR
England

Gower
Old Post Road
Brookfield
Vermont 05036
USA

British Library Cataloguing in Publication Data

Rae, Leslie
Techniques of Training. – 3Rev.ed
I. Title
658.3124

ISBN 0–566–07629–2

Library of Congress-in-Publication Data

Rae, Leslie.
Techniques of training / Leslie Tae. — 3rd ed.
p. c m.
Rev. ed. of: The skills of training. 2nd ed. 1991.
Includes bibliographical references and index.
ISBN 0–566–07629–2 (pbk.)
1. Employees—Training of. 2. Training manuals. I. Rae, Leslie.
Skills of training. II. Title.
HF5549.5.T7R25 1995
658.3'124—dc20 94–47428
CIP

Typeset in Times by Raven Typesetters, Chester and printed in Great Britain
by Hartnolls Limited, Bodmin, Cornwall.

Contents

Figures

Preface

The first edition of this book, under the title *The Skills of Training*, appeared in 1983, twelve years ago. Many trainers are so immersed in the practical business of training that they do not realize that time is passing and, more importantly, other things are happening. During this period two important changes in my own training life occurred; during my employment with the Training Agency (previously Manpower Services Commission) I ceased to be principally a direct trainer and training manager and became the Agency's first internal consultant and Advisor on Training and Development. This change was more than titular and it meant that more than ever before I had to be aware of virtually every opportunity, technique and training method available so that my advice could be based on knowledge. The second change was that I completed my contract with the Training Agency and extended my previously part-time external management and trainer training consultancy into a more or less full-time commitment. Again my horizons had to widen even further and take account of the training needs of organizations as varied as engineering, retail trade, shipping, scientific instruments, construction, banking and so on.

I very quickly realized that training and development had *not* stood still since 1983, and although the original edition of the book still contained descriptions of and references to the main arms of training, changes both large and small were occurring continually. This edition contains both comments on new developments and some extensions to the original material, suggested to me in a number of cases by trainers who had read the book and said 'Why don't you . . .?' To those trainers who said that to me, please read the new edition and see that I have!

The decade which has taken us into the 1990s has seen the development of a much more active and corporately acceptable training and development function. A number of surveys have shown that, although the amount of training undertaken is still far less in the UK than in many other 'first world' countries, it is increasing and that the organizations who invest in training are those in the forefront of achievement. The role of the trainer has changed from a straightforward one of delivering training events, to

- consultant and adviser on training and development
- human resource development (HRD) adviser
- designer and writer of holistic training packages rather than 'simple' training courses
- designer, writer and user of a variety of forms of open and distance learning
- an increasing role as facilitator rather than trainer.

The interaction between the training department, line management, senior management and the trainee clients has increased, with all parties taking a much greater interest and being more involved than hitherto.

The second edition incorporated additions and amendments suggested by readers and colleagues. This edition is similar in this respect and some of the additions relate to the concept that a new trainer should have at least an awareness of a number of techniques, which, if not immediately necessary, would soon be requirements. In discussions about what the 'average' new trainer should know, participants frequently asked two questions about the trainer's role: what aids to the trainer's performance were available, and what techniques were available to help the trainer *prepare* to face the learning group?

Clearly the answer to the first question must be the wide range of audio-visual-electronic aids that most trainers have recourse to.

The answer to the second question is wider in scope and, in addition to the attainment of personal presentation skills, must lie in the preparatory work for the presentation, training session, discussion or whatever form of training is introduced, that is, primarily the training design format and tools and the trainer's *aide-mémoire*.

Unfortunately, a very large number (the majority?) of new trainers entering their role are told:

- you will be taking over such-and-such a training session/ course(s)
- the brief that you should (must?) follow is this printed set of sheets or manual
- you will be using the visual aids and handouts listed in the brief, at the stages indicated, and in the order of the session/ course – the ones you will use are provided.

Though this formula appears to afford little opportunity for flexibility, happily each trainer is an individual and few will approach the role in exactly the same way, whatever the injunctions laid upon them. Also, few organizations allow no flexibility whatsoever in the delivery of the training, other than a natural insistence on the extent and veracity of the content. Even under what appear to be quite rigid conditions of performance, the new trainers can start to personalize their training approach as they develop and feel sufficiently confident to stray from the 'party line'. To do this effectively they must have at least an awareness of the range of techniques and resources at their disposal; hence the inclusion, in this edition, of new material on these two key topics.

The original Appendix has been extensively revised for this edition and now gives details of book series containing titles related directly to training, selected films and videos, and selected training activities. Many of the older book references have been deleted and those retained, with the addition of more recent books, have been transferred to the end of the chapters to which they most closely relate. I do not claim that my list of references and recommended reading is complete, but I feel it is sufficiently representative to lead trainers, both new and experienced, to useful information including paths to other sources. I apologize to any author whose works I have not included. This was not intended as a slur on their works; it would be merely my sin of omission.

At the risk of being accused of being sexist (which I am not), the generic 'he' etc. is mainly used in the book to avoid the ridiculous plurals, an over-use of he/she and the boring repetition of 'the trainer'. Consequently 'he' should also be read as 'she'.

Leslie Rae

Introduction: training in the 1990s

The principal changes in training and the role of the trainer that I have observed in recent years have been the greater emphasis on 'development' as opposed simply to training functions, more time and resources allocated realistically to the function, and the public statements by researchers, heads of large and small organizations and educationalists giving more substance and credibility to training and development. It is widely agreed that organizations who take training seriously, and apply time and other resources to its provision, are more likely to succeed than those who engage in less or no training, or merely pay lip service to it.

Two significant changes have begun, which 'trainers' have been urging for many years. Training is being seen more and more as the responsibility of management itself, and of the individual for his/her own training and development. Line managers have become more directly involved in training, in many cases becoming trainers, occasional trainers, guest trainers, coaches and mentors, in addition to assisting with assessment centres, quality circles, employee self-development groups and so on. Techniques in open learning have developed so that facilities are much more readily available for individuals who wish to further their own development.

TRADITIONAL TRAINING APPROACHES

Two techniques were generally available – 'tell 'em' or 'sit 'em with Nellie'. The 'tell 'em' approach was usually employed in group training and with the trainer/instructor standing in front of the 'class' and talking *at* them until they appeared to know (not necessarily understand) what was required. The alternative, principally for individuals (although a small group might be treated at the same time but in an individual way), was 'on-the-job training', sitting beside 'Nellie'. Nellie in these days was usually a skilled operative, beside whom the learner sat or stood, watching the operation until he/she felt he could do it. Then he was on his own. In more enlightened establishments, a separate machine might be made available for the learner, with the trainer (who probably was an operative doing his own job in any case) detailed to keep an eye on the learner.

Training in supervisory and people-management skills and technique skills was virtually non-existent. Managers were for the most part left to work their way up the hierarchical tree, picking up whatever skills they could as they did so.

The 1939–45 war contributed much to the revised attitudes to training with the demands for speedy, efficient and effective training of large numbers of people in a very wide variety of jobs. Psychology, pre-war a rather neglected and suspect subject, had shown itself capable of effectively selecting people and jobs and advising on training methods. Consequently people began to take notice when the psychologists said that telling alone did not produce learning. Probably the first development of this was the introduction of the 'tell, show, do' approach, rather than any of these standing alone as a training method. The combined approach utilized naturally all the learning senses, since research (and observation) had shown that learning was more powerful and produced a stronger likelihood of retention and recall if all the senses were used. Of course, none of this was new, having been 'known' for centuries, but now it was introduced on a wider scale.

THE START OF THE EXPERIENTAL ERA

The next element of learning research which was translated to training was the postulate that people might learn more easily by 'hands-on' practice, not in the 'on the job and get on with it' environment, but in one which supported learning and was supportive in itself. This meant effectively away from the job, in more special surroundings, usually on a training course. By this stage group training and group development attitudes had come of age and the practical and experiential nature of group activities seemed to offer a Pandora's box of training aid. The experiential approach was embraced with such enthusiasm that the earlier, almost total 'stand up and tell 'em' method was almost completely rejected in favour of the new 'give them something to do and they'll learn from it' approach. Training events changed from being totally boring, didactic, non-learning events, to totally enjoyable, active, game-playing, experiential happenings where learning could not be avoided.

Some time, however, was necessary for the realization that perhaps total learning, including learning by different types of people, was not achieved by either 'classroom' or 'experiential' techniques alone. The pendulum had swung too far in the opposite direction. Trainers observed during their training events that some people, some of the time, and for certain aspects of learning, responded more favourably to particular approaches, whereas they appeared to need other treatment for other aspects of learning. Not only that, but different people seemed to vary in the basic ways they learned.

Consequently, the development over the past 15 years or so has been for enlightened trainers and educators to offer a balanced mixture of techniques and approaches – input or lecture sessions, discussions, group activities, case studies, simulations, one-to-one interactive role-plays, films, videos, visual aids and so on. There are, unfortunately in some ways, still many trainers who rely almost solely on lecture sessions. This may be because they

- are unaware of other techniques
- are not now capable of performing other techniques
- find other approaches are not relevant
- are told that the corporate body/training manager decrees the methods used.

The ability to present a session is no longer the criterion of trainer skill. A trainer must learn to identify the learning preference signs, or to administer and discuss the relevant tests; he/she must be familiar with a range of learning techniques and be able to apply them; and must be ready to switch approaches when a different one is obviously required. Above all, the training programme of most events must be flexible. This flexibility demands a much wider range of skills – not just knowledge or a single skill – than ever before. Learners in the 1990s are aware, often unconsciously, of their varying demands and are becoming more insistent on training which becomes learning, rather than something which has to be endured.

These remarks apply equally to in-company trainers and external consultants who enter an organization to provide special training or training which for some reason the company cannot offer. No longer is it possible, if it ever really was, for a 'standard' training course to be brought into the company – training must be tailored to the learning needs.

CHANGING CONCEPTS OF TRAINING

The concept of training through courses alone is becoming a sign of a non-flexible approach and hence limited effectiveness. Learning is being considered as an individual need, to be approached on an individual basis. If the organization has a number of people with a truly identical need, the corporate, group training approach may be the most effective and economic answer. But increasingly the unique needs of an individual are being identified and voiced. How does this affect the role of the trainer? It may mean that they will rarely be called upon to present group training courses, but rather take on the role of information gatherer and provider, adviser, mentor, consultant, one-to-one trainer, expert in ways of achieving learning objectives and so on. As suggested earlier, the traditional skills of training will still be needed but in a wider context. However, the other more demanding skills will be more important. As more senior managers, spurred on by the comments of the authorities advocating professional qualifications for management (Constable and Handy in Britain particularly), become interested in their own education, training and development, they should be looking to the trainer to be the organization's expert in helping them. If this help is not forthcoming, the credibility of training will diminish, with a commensurate reduction in the training section budget!!

The modern trainer, then, will need more new knowledge and broader skills than ever before to perform this extended function.

FLEXIBILITY, REACTIVITY, AND PRO-ACTIVITY

So where does the trainer appear in the organizational hierarchy?

What are the spheres of his influence? Two words sum up the overall requirements of the modern trainer:

- flexibility
- pro-activity

Flexibility has already been discussed, its feasibility being based on extensive knowledge and skills applied to many different methods and techniques. Knowledge alone is not enough; it must be backed by understanding to a level where skill in practice is achieved. Unfortunately to achieve, or even approach, these levels of skill, the trainers must be involved in extensive training and re-training themselves. This may be seen as an incursion into the 'practical working time' of the trainers when they could be 'doing real work in front of a class' – the view of many organizations employing trainers. Consequently this view has to be changed.

Reactivity has been the traditional stance of the trainer who reacts to the demands of line managers, potential trainees and the organization, and often to the methods requested/demanded by these clients. This reactivity is what has restrained the trainer in the organizational hierarchy. He has remained in a subordinate position and role in the organization, highly sensitive to the varying economic climate. When the economy enters a low period, there is often a reduction in or constraints on training. In fact these are the times when training becomes even more important, but from his position in the hierarchy, the trainer can do nothing.

THE 'TOUGH' TRAINER

A 'tougher' trainer approach is needed to secure the proper place of training in industry and commerce. The trainer must become 'pro-active', instead of waiting for 'orders'. Rather than always being told what to do, the trainer should be sufficiently aware of the organization's needs, often before they become evident, to come forward with realistic, improving proposals which cannot be ignored.

Whatever the outcome of the debate over trainer and training development, one change is underway – the strengthening of the relationships between the trainer, the client, the line managers and the trainees. The needs of all these elements are having to be taken into account, and a strengthening of the training function is developing as a result.

THE TRAINING QUINTET

The forces intent on defining the modern trainer's role are:

1) The Organization, represented principally by the Board, the Senior Management Group or those responsible for strategic decisions;
2) Line Management who are both direct recipients of training and clients of the training organization with subordinates to be trained;
3) the Training Manager who is responsible for the operation of the Training Department;
4) the Training Officer on whom the task of training people falls;
5) the Trainee or Learner who is the direct client of the training department.

ORGANIZATION

The organization, usually in the form of senior management, states the overall training requirements, in terms of the developing needs of the organization. Various developments in the medium and long term will suggest training needs. The traditional approach has been to let the training section know when (and not until) the need arises. What is suggested here is to bring training and development into discussions about future developments at the earliest possible stage. This sounds easy to introduce, but in many cases it represents a fundamental change of attitude to training and development by senior management, who in the past have not taken it too seriously. However, given ample warning of changes in prospect, the training section can ensure that any action necessary is planned in good time, and thus more effectively. I shall return to this theme later when discussing the role of the training manager.

LINE MANAGEMENT

Although the support and early activity of senior management is important in indicating future needs and reinforcing existing approaches, it is probably the active involvement of the line manager which is critical for success. The trainees are direct employees of the line manager and need his or her support to determine individual, as opposed to corporate needs; to encourage the satisfaction of personally identified or management identified needs; to ensure that the needs are met in the most appropriate manner and at the relevant time; to support actively the trainees on their return from or completion of the learning event, and to ensure that development is a continuing process rather than an isolated event. The manager will have to be aware of the wide range and complexity of learning opportunities available, and thus will need to work closely with the trainer.

Once the initial decision that training is required has been made, the line manager can discuss with the trainer the ways in which the needs can be met, and agree which will be the most appropriate approach.

Before the trainee embarks on the training the line manager must discuss the final details with him and agree objectives related to the training, to the individual and to the organization, both local and corporate. A date must be agreed on which the line manager and trainee will meet soon after the trainee's return.

There will need to be mutual trust between the manager and the trainer. The manager will be placing a great deal of reliance on the trainer who in turn will need the manager's support. Thus the cornerstone of the training quintet must be mutual trust with cooperative support.

Following the training, the line manager must meet again with the trainee to discuss what has occurred, what action plans have been made, and to arrange future support and action. Again at this stage, the trainer can become involved for at least part of the discussion, particularly when the line manager encounters problems with which he cannot deal.

THE TRAINING MANAGER

The training manager will need to work very closely with the trainer, and in many instances he may be one and the same person! However, the main aspects of this role will consist of:

- agreeing training principles and programmes with the other members of the quintet
- supporting, in a managerial role, the trainer, and ensuring that sufficient resources will be available
- participating in investigatory and research projects which will extend the range of learning facilities
- negotiating or discussing any problems in the early stages with line management to ensure that the quintet is working together.

But above all, the training manager is the link between line management and the trainer. He represents the training viewpoint and, more particularly, knows the conceptual and functional needs of training and development at the top decision-making levels of the organization. This assumes that the training manager is in a position in the organization to wield a reasonable amount of power. Unfortunately many are not in this position, but to ensure that the value of training in the organization is recognized and given the status it deserves, a more pro-active approach must be taken by the training manager. On too few occasions, training, represented by the training manager, is invited to the first meeting of a working group, at whatever level in the organization, when new corporate projects are initiated. This early involvement, to ensure that potential training needs and activities are taken into account, happens only very rarely. The training department is usually asked to provide something which is impossible at a later stage, but could have been planned relatively easily with forewarning.

Budgetary proposals for training, and negotiating those, are the responsibilities of the training manager, particularly if these costs can be directly related and linked to the operational budgets.

The role description suggests that the training manager is the linchpin, necessarily having a keen interest in all aspects of training and development, but also coordinating the interests and requirements of the other members of the quintet.

THE TRAINER

Many of the trainer's activities within the relationship are the traditional ones of developing the content and format of training courses, events and individual sessions; performing the activities, and validating the training event.

However, these are the reactive aspects of a trainer's role, whereas like the training manager, he should be more pro-active. The trainer, likewise, must become actively involved at an early stage in the discussion about and determination of training needs and requirements: who should be trained, when, in which specific areas, where, and so on. In the past it has been more common for the trainer to be *informed* about all these elements and be required to react accordingly. Or alternatively, little advice or help was forthcoming and the trainer was expected to pursue these investigations with little or no line information or support.

In a realistic partnership with line management, both the line manager and the trainer can and should be jointly investigating job and people requirements and identifying training needs. Line managers can be further involved in developing course objectives and constructing the training programme. The line manager brings in the expertise of job knowledge, and the trainer supplies the training and training programme expertise. At a later stage, the line manager, perhaps with tuition from the trainer, can take an active part in the training programme itself. This inclusion of 'real' line managers can often add credibility to a training programme.

In many ways the traditional role of the trainer stops when the training has been completed. But in the increasingly cooperative partnership advocated here there should be a continuing role. The debriefing activity by the line manager with the trainee has been stressed and, although this must remain the responsibility of the line manager, part of the debriefing – advice on implementation, further or other learning and so on – can be enhanced by the involvement of the trainer. It may be, provided the resources are available, that the trainer might become actively involved in the continued learning at work. Much of this will depend on the resource availability of the trainer and care must be taken that the managerial responsibilities are not simply passed to the trainer to reduce the manager's work load, or to relieve him of tasks he doesn't like.

Another area which can be contentious in the discussion of roles is evaluation, the long-term assessment in cost-value terms of the training and training programmes.

One argument runs that evaluation is simply a continuation of the training event and its validation and consequently is the responsibility of the trainer to follow through.

The counter-argument is that improvement in cost-effectiveness occurs within the line operation and consequently it is the line manager who should be responsible for carrying out the evaluation.

There can be no doubt that the line manager is best placed to assess by observation and the analysis of production results the long-term success of the training and any improvements which may result from it. However, the line managers may not have the time or the skills necessary to be able to assess performance in this comparative way; the trainers may be better equipped.

The most effective solution will be complete cooperation between the trainer and the line manager – as in so many cases. A typical method of evaluation could be the sending of follow-up questionnaires by the trainer to both the trainees and their line managers, followed by clarification and diagnostic interviews which will serve to confirm the views of each. The line manager will be in a position to observe the trainee in a more intensive and extensive manner, but the trainer's observations may be more objective. If a full practice of validation and evaluation has been followed, control groups will have been included in the evaluation programme. The trainer will be in the better position to continue the contacts with these groups, as well as again keeping in constant touch with their line managers. Consequently we have the cooperative instances of the trainer providing the expertise in training follow-up and the line manager the expertise in operational improvement assessment.

THE TRAINEE

Last in the training quintet, but far from least, is the trainee, without whom the whole exercise would have no value. We have seen that each role holder participates at different stages of the learning process. The trainees are not excluded.

When the concept of the training is being formulated, the potential trainees are involved in activities related to identifying the needs of the task and the level of competence of those performing or planning to perform the tasks – the determination of training needs. It rarely happens in practice, but the ideal would be for the trainees to be directly involved in the planning of the training itself. After all, the trainees are the recipients of the training and their participation in its planning should help to ensure that the eventual training is acceptable and maximizes the learning possible. More effective training has been achieved in recent years by the introduction of planning workshops, short events during which the potential trainees study and research together, with the trainer acting as a facilitator, to produce a realistic framework on which the actual programme can be based. Similar workshops could be, and are held with groups of line managers for the same purpose and the resulting proposals, when linked with the training expertise of the trainer and the training manager, can result in very effective programmes.

Another trend which involves the trainee more than previously is one in which the training events, rather than being trainer-led as they have tended to be for many years, are more trainee-led. In this reversed approach, the trainee is given the opportunity to determine the content and level of the programme, rather than have this imposed, however well intentioned, by the trainers. Here time is allocated at the start of the training event for the necessary planning to take place. This, of course, is a less effective approach than the pre-course workshop technique discussed above, but it is a useful alternative if workshops are not possible or acceptable. Many trainers, of course, resist this change because the 'power' of the event leaves their hands, a power which has been part of their traditional role. The trainer, however, must be prepared to accept the lead from the trainee and offer a flexible event in which the balance of power has changed.

In similar ways, the trainees can be involved in the validation of the event and the evaluation of the development programmes. Traditionally the pre-training event tests, the interim validation measures, the end-of-course validations and the long-term evaluation approaches have all been constructed by the trainer, or on rare occasions by the trainer and line manager jointly. These measures have then been imposed on the trainee without question. More realistic and effective responses are likely if the trainees themselves are given a more prominent role in the decisions about these validation measures. Again it needs time, but it can be worthwhile, for example if the trainees produce the end-of-course questionnaire or method which they as the recipients would find most acceptable and useful.

TRAINER TYPES AND ROLES

Both training and the trainers who provide it come in such a variety of forms and styles that it is difficult to identify them precisely. Identification is based to a large extent on subjective self-analysis, but is nevertheless worthy of consideration and discussion.

Two attempts at definition are shown in the grids evolved or described by John Townsend; and Roger Bennett, Alan Jones and Andrew Pettigrew.

The Townsend grid is based on three dimensions – trainer competence, teaching skills and concern for the learner. These three factors combine to identify eight styles:

- the Humble Expert – high competence, high concern and low teaching skills
- the Professional Trainer – high competence, high concern and high teaching skills

At the other end of the scale are:

- the Oblivious Incompetent with low competence, low teaching skills and low concern
- the Arrogant Charlatan with high teaching skills, low concern and low competence.

In between, with varying mixtures of the three factors, are:

- the Boring Lecturer
- the Directive Instructor
- the Endearing Bumbler
- the Shallow Persuader.

The different types are shown in Figure I.1.

A rather more serious and scientific inventory was developed by Roger Bennett, Alan Jones and Andrew Pettigrew. They produced a quadrant framework demonstrating four predominant types of trainers. The quadrant is produced by comparing at the extreme ends of the vertical axis:

- organizational *maintenance* orientation

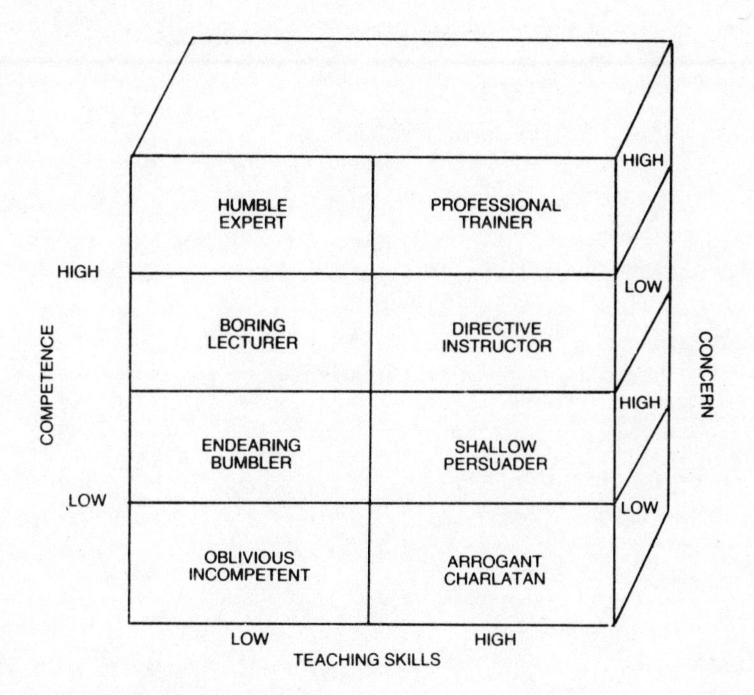

Figure I.1 The trainer grid
Source: John Townsend, JEIT, vol 9, no. 3, 1985.

- organizational *change* orientation

and on the horizontal axis:

- *traditional* educational orientation
- *interventionist* orientation

The quadrant produced in this way is shown in Figure I.2.

The four predominant trainer types are contained in the quadrants. The 'Caretaker' is positioned in the quadrant bounded by organization maintenance orientation and traditional educational orientation. The 'Evangelist' is found at the other side of the framework bounded by organizational maintenance orientation (but introducing innovative approaches) and by interventionist orientation. The 'Educator' is contained within organizational change orientation and traditional educational orientation. Finally the 'Innovator', a type nearer the suggested ideal proactive, highly skilled adapter, is contained in the quadrant bounded by interventionist orientation and organizational change orientation. Obviously again there are shades within these types.

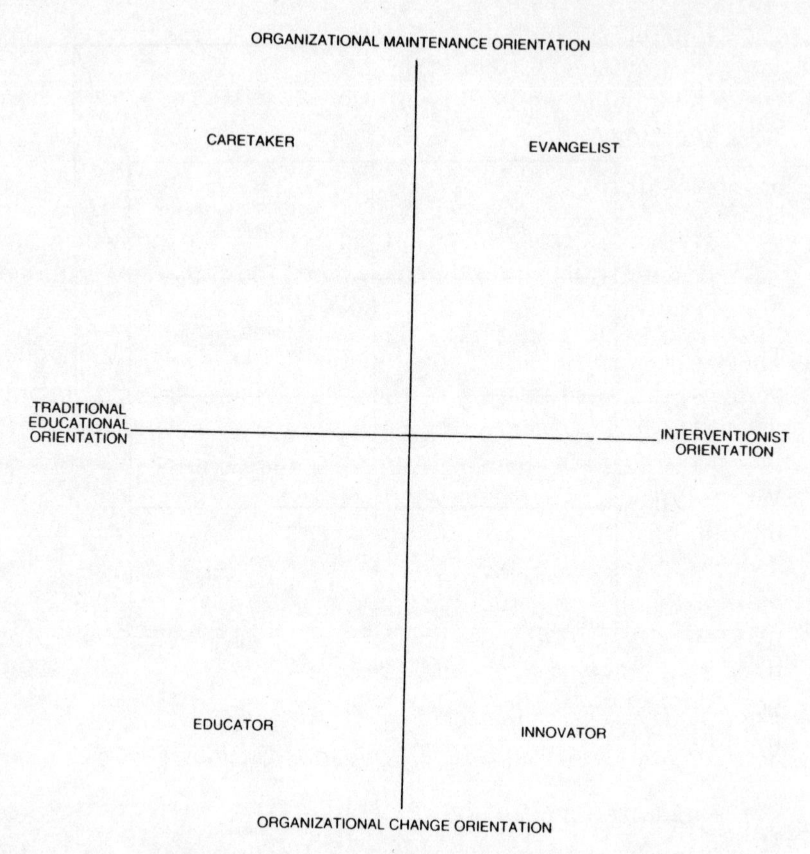

Figure I.2 *The training quadrant*
Source: MSC/ITD, *Guide to Trainer Effectiveness.*

There will be, for example, extreme Innovators who want to introduce so much change that what is intrinsically a good approach will fail through human reaction to extremes of change. On the other hand, the extreme Educator might similarly fail through rejection by learners because they seek more variety, innovation and less 'education'.

The trainer who is to succeed, in any *one* situation, must be able to assess that situation and determine the appropriate behaviour and methods. The factors involved in this pro-active approach will include:

- the organizational culture and traditions
- the environmental flexibility or rigidity
- the nature of the training

- the trainer 'tool kit' available
- the trainer's personal style
- the trainer's ability to perform in ways foreign to the basic preference;

but above all

- the learning preferences of the learners, constrained as necessary by the above, but only when the constraint cannot be removed.

These role identifications are valuable in two ways. One is obviously in the identification of the role of the trainers as people, their likes and dislikes, preferences and areas of avoidance. But the 'roles' can also be applied to the other side of the equation. Which type of trainer role or style is required by the organization, the training content or the different types of trainees themselves? These aspects must be assessed in order to provide the most *appropriate* training approach, one which should prove to be the most effective for the occasion. Within the approach identified the trainer has available a vast range of options, options which become the trainer's toolkit of techniques, methods and 'skills of training'.

REFERENCES AND RECOMMENDED READING

'What Makes for an Effective Trainer'. R. Bennett and T. Leduchowicz. *JEIT Monograph*, vol. 7, no. 2, 1983.

'The Effective Trainer'. R. Bennett, *Journal ITD*, vol. 3 no. 4, 1983.

'Making Training Interventions More Effective'. J.A.G. Jones. *JEIT*, vol. 6, no. 6, 1982.

Guide to Trainer Effectiveness. Manpower Services Commission/ITD 1984.

'Training and Development Roles in their Organizational Setting'. A.M. Pettigrew, G.R. Jones and P.W. Reason. *Journal ITD*, vol. 3, no. 6, 1983.

'The Trainer Grid'. John Townsend. *JEIT*, vol. 9, no. 3, 1985.

The Lone Trainer. Mike Saunders and Keith Holdaway. Kogan Page, 1993.

Managing Training. Sunny Stout. Kogan Page, 1993.

Assessing Trainer Effectiveness. Leslie Rae. Gower, 1991.
Handbook of Training and Development. Edited by John Prior. Gower, 2nd edition, 1994.

1 There is more to training than you think

Some years ago there was little problem in defining training and training methods, and the atmosphere in which these were conducted. If you were invited, instructed or nominated to attend a training course you knew exactly what to expect, what your reactions would be and you might have had a personal theory about the learning you would or would not achieve. This sense of pre-knowledge would be enhanced when you received your course joining instructions, which included a detailed programme showing the exact time of each event during the day and how long each would last, a title for each event and the name of the speaker. Also included with the instructions would be a curriculum vitae of the trainers, tutors or instructors and the speakers involved in the course. To complete the comprehensive package, domestic information would be given including such vital information as whether you would be expected to dress for dinner or that lounge suits would be acceptable wear during the day. An important element of the information was the detailing of the set course objectives which decreed that by the end of the course students would 'know about –', 'understand the –', and 'be aware of –'. One aspect that was noticeably absent, either in the course materials or in the pre-course thinking of the participant, was any consideration of the participant's personal objectives for the course and discussion of these with the participant's boss. My own experience of this during this unenlightened era was my boss saying to me a day before the course, 'Have a good holiday and don't forget to come back'!

Once on the course one's anticipations were quickly realized. The programme was followed almost to the minute with speakers delivering each lecture with varying degrees of skill and demonstrating a remarkable ability to stand for an hour and a half or so covering a blackboard with apposite statements and wielding several colours of chalk in a professional manner. Usually the end of the session was marked by the speaker dusting away a substantial layer of chalk dust from his black or navy blue suit. There were, of course, enlivening occasions when the speaker left several minutes at the end of his lecture to demand questions from the group. Commonly these came hesitantly and often sympathetically from one member, probably nominated by the group, who felt that someone should resolve the embarrassing silence that descended. The session time being complete, the programme moved on to its inexorable conclusion with a further array of speakers delivering other lectures.

The end of the course was often marked by a session to review the course, during which (for the first time) the students were encouraged to speak. Naturally, one of the students had been appointed by his fellows to propose a vote of thanks to the organizers and the speakers; then everybody went home.

The learning outcome of an event such as this was difficult to assess, not only from the level of impact the training method had made on the students, but from the follow-up, or lack of it, that occurred. Again to quote my own experience, I happened to meet my boss in the corridor some weeks later and was greeted by 'Oh, I wanted to have a word with you about that course you went on. How did it go?' Me – 'Well, it wasn't too bad'. Him – 'Good. Now about that project you are involved in . . .'.

There can be no doubt that some of these events were instructive and enjoyable, but many people have rather sour memories of them which have clouded their subsequent attitudes to training. One of the major problems in validating training, particularly management training, is the determination of what course participants have learned, and perhaps even more important, how much of that learning do they put into practice when they return to the real world of work? A considerable amount of research has taken place into such topics as how people learn, and how much learning do they retain and over how long a period. The indications on the latter two aspects are rather alarming as they suggest that about a third is retained over an immediate period and even this low amount decreases with time. This must also be linked with the training method since less effective methods will produce less initial learning and a resulting greater reduction of retention with time.

TELL, SHOW, DO

A tried and tested instructional technique, particularly for training in more procedural matters, has been 'Tell, Show, Do'. 'Tell' on its own has been suggested as the least effective form of training, certainly if too much material is included. It requires a very high degree of motivation and commitment on the part of the learner for the discipline of sitting listening intently to everything that is said. It also demands a high level of interpretative skill to unravel a description in words alone of an object or event that is difficult for a skilled presenter to describe. A common activity used on instructional techniques courses to demonstrate this difficulty is for one person (or group) to describe in words to another person (or group) a fairly common object. The results are frequently humorous but inaccurate and demonstrate the point well. I have heard a hairbrush described in such a way that the result comes out as, among other representations, an elephant holding a toothbrush in its trunk.

The addition of 'Show' increases the learning capabilities and this can take a variety of forms. If one is discussing a typewriter, the most effective visual aid is the typewriter itself. It acts as a visual description of itself, and the tutor, having described the constituent parts, can show these parts *in situ*. In the classroom, visual aids of many types – OHP slides, newsprint illustrations, 35mm slides – can support and consolidate the spoken word, enliven the teaching session and maintain the interest of the students. All these factors create a more realistic approach to the subject and rather than the students having to rely on the spoken word alone, they can see the point or the form being completed in observable, progressive stages. In this way two senses are involved and the learning and retention rate normally increases.

However, the use of verbal and visual aspects keeps the learning at an intellectually relatively passive level. No major demands are made on the student other than a self-imposed listening discipline. During the verbal and visual descriptions, a lowly motivated student can sit and appear to be listening intently, yet be thinking about anything other than the subject under discussion.

The only answer in this case is to include the 'Do' aspect of training. The classical approach, after the verbal and visual description of the learning subject, would be to involve the students in a practical activity in which they would perform the operation to be learned. This activity would obviously be dependent on the subject under discussion, and could be the completion of a procedural form, the entry of a simple programme into a computer system, or the practising of an interview technique. The practical application of a skill in a training event must still involve the trainer who, at this stage, will be monitoring the developing skill of the student and correcting and guiding as the activity progresses. In this way the student is put in the position of having to practise the learning that he should have achieved in the more formal part of the training.

This tripartite approach has been practised for some years now, but inevitably (and fortunately) attempts have been made to improve the approach. Considerable research has taken place into how people learn, and this has suggested that the 'doing' aspect of the cycle is by far the most powerful factor. Some trainers have taken this to a considered logical conclusion and have produced training events that are almost completely experiential events. It is interesting to compare one of these events with the formal training course described earlier.

Some time prior to the training event, the intending participant receives his joining instructions in a similar way to his parallel of some years past. However, these instructions tend to be minimal and are often restricted to the dates of the course, the location and, on occasions, an indication of some general behavioural objectives. Sometimes, in contrast to the earlier course, a particular point concerning informality, including dress, is made. No programme or detailed syllabus is included, for reasons that become obvious at a later stage. If there is some mention of a programme it is limited often to the statement that the training (or learning) day starts at 9am and the day will be taken up with practical learning events or activities.

One encouraging aspect often found as part of the instructions is the requirement for the participant to consider, prior to the event, his or her personal objectives for wanting to attend the course and any specific learning that must be achieved. The participant is encouraged to take these personal objectives to the boss to discuss and agree, if the boss has not already arranged a meeting for this purpose. In this way, the boss is directly involved in the training and at the very least the meeting confirms that the subordinate should actually attend the course. Pre-course briefing meetings of this nature can take a number of formats, from a copy of the original 'have a good time' to an in-depth assessment of why attendance on the course is essential; a clarification of the participant's personal objectives; a discussion about the needs of the employing organization related to those personal objectives and those of the course, and a commitment by both to look at the results of the training and, in particular, their application. Even if only these minimal topics are discussed, the seal is set on the boss's interest and involvement in the training of his staff.

The day of the course arrives and our participant duly presents himself, to be greeted by the trainer, tutor or as is more common in this type of training atmosphere, the person who describes himself as the facilitator. Our hero has by this time realized that he has little awareness of what is to happen, and depending upon the particular individual's personality is aggressive, apprehensive, concerned, nervous or simply suspicious. In all probability he has not previously experienced a training event of this nature and on occasions fails to find a secure staff even in the introductory stages of the event. He is probably expecting a relatively formal opening session in which the participants are required by the trainer to introduce themselves to the group, or even chat to their neighbour.

However, even this is not to be, for the facilitator, after greeting the group, asks them to determine among themselves how they wish to perform introductions, if indeed they wish to do so. Consequently, during the opening minutes of the course the ground rules are laid and course members realize that they have to involve themselves directly in the process of the event. The results of this immediate self-determination can be many and varied, but often when I have been involved in such a process, either as member or facilitator, the introduction system agreed is more structured and formal than if the method had been decreed by the tutor. This can be a significant indication of the attitude of the group at this stage, since by falling back on known methods the group is saying that it wants to be safe and is not yet ready for risk-taking.

Once the initial trauma is over, the group is again shaken to the foundation of its beliefs and experience as to how training should proceed. Instead of being allowed to settle back and allow the tutor to launch into an informative session and propound the principles of this and that, the group is asked by the facilitator a number of questions and also to make a number of decisions, such as

- what objectives does the group wish to set for itself for the course?
- what does it want to do to achieve these objectives?
- how will it go about achieving them?
- what parameters will it give itself?
- how will it measure the level of its success?
- what role does the group wish the facilitator to take, etc?

Most groups reel under this onslaught as previous training experiences have not prepared them to have to take decisions about their own learning. But as time goes by they settle down to determine and practise their own fate, guided or assisted in an unobtrusive and non-prescriptive way by their friendly, but remote, facilitator.

At the end of the event the group will have experienced many learning situations, which to a large extent have been managed and controlled by themselves. Because of this direct involvement it is generally considered that the learning will have been more realistic and acceptable than if they had played a passive role and the events had been structured and controlled by a trainer. Evaluation of the event is likely to be more open and meaningful, since by the terminal stage the group will have few inhibitions about saying what it really feels.

When the individual participant returns to work, because of the pre-event contract made with the boss, a fruitful discussion is more likely to ensue, and the boss will be deeply involved in helping the individual to translate the learning of the event to the work situation.

The training event just described and the one cited at the beginning of the chapter can be considered as almost the opposite extremes of a training approach spectrum. Between these extremes are many variations weighted to different degrees to either end of the spectrum. Unfortunately, although a considerable amount of research has taken place into what may be the most effective methods of training, there is no absolute answer. However, the trainer at whatever training involvement level should have available a wide knowledge of the options open and, if wise, will try to tailor each type of event to suit the demands of the training need. In this way, a trainer who is responsible for a wide range of courses could have six or seven different styles of courses, rather than one approach only which he uses throughout.

BARRIERS TO LEARNING

If the trainer is to make available the most effective opportunities for people to learn, he must be aware of the many problems he has to overcome. He must be able to select the most appropriate method for the individual or group with which he is involved and the nature of the training in question. There is little sense in producing an unstructured, behavioural approach for a group of new entrants who are required to acquire basic skills in working procedures. Selection will also depend on other factors related to the vagaries of human nature.

There exists in all of us a variety of barriers to learning, and unfortunately a number of people who are presented for training demonstrate one or more of these barriers. Few experienced trainers have not encountered the student who arrives at the training course having been sent against his will, and/or has come with the attitude that training is a waste of time and has learned nothing on previous courses he has attended, and/or shows verbally and non-verbally that he is determined to learn nothing. In fact, by his attitude, he challenges the trainer to teach him if he can. Even well-motivated trainees who start by wanting to learn can develop a negative attitude as a result of unhelpful experiences. Commonly recounted is the attitude of themselves or their boss that trainers are isolated from real life, are full of new-fangled, unworkable ideas and that trainees will learn only by doing as the boss does – in the same way that he learned from his boss and so on.

The trainee can have specific internal barriers which must be overcome before real learning can take place. Human memory can be short and our capabilities for retaining certain skills are uncertain. A child has a subconscious motivation to learn and, if nurtured properly during the formative years, will react favourably to teaching and will develop personal learning skills. These skills, if not maintained, can become rusty or cease to operate altogether. If this has happened to an individual who, after years of being in a learning wilderness, is placed suddenly in a learning situation, there will be problems of adjustment whatever the trainer's skills and methods. It is only after the trainee has re-learned how to listen to new ideas and concepts and weigh these against his existing ones, and how to interpret a mass of data instead of being told what the issues are that learning will be possible. Even the simple activities of once again sitting in a classroom, however well disguised, taking meaningful notes which he will be required to use as the course progresses, and expressing his views in an articulate manner within his group, may all be little-used skills which will hinder the learning process.

These reduced basic skills which are, in many ways, prerequisites to learning can also be linked with the trainee's view of the trainer. Comparison can be made with other trainers in the individual's experience – parents, school teachers, foremen, supervisors or managers. If these experiences have been bad, the trainer must overcome the resulting negative feelings before the trainee is in a frame of mind to learn. Unfortunately, many trainers do not recognize this barrier; this is indeed difficult if the feelings are not immediately expressed. Some, however, hinder progress by using jargon with the result that the trainee switches off at an early stage.

There is another danger of which the trainer must be aware, particularly in the case of inarticulate people, or, even more commonly, those who by the simple act of coming into a strange group are very concerned about how they will be received by the rest of the group. If these feelings exist, and there are few new groups at the start of a course in which they are not present in many of the members, risk-taking will be low for fear of exposure to ridicule. The trainer can help or hinder these attitudes: helping by recognizing the syndrome and adjusting the training accordingly, hindering by placing the course members in situations where inadequacies are exposed or highlighted. Trainers must recognize the power they can wield and must use that power to help the learners to progress.

Considerable research has taken place into the problems of adult learning and it is beyond the scope of this book to go into them deeply. Readers are referred to the standard books on the subject, for to ignore the problems of learning is to adopt an egoistic approach to training, in that the trainer considers he is so skilled that he can advance learning against any adversity. This is the recipe for failure.

BARRIERS IN TRAINING

One barrier that deserves special mention relates to the nature of the training and the learner's reaction to what occurs. A comment that is far from rare on many training courses, and not always as a result of the training approach, is that an activity in which the trainees are required to participate is 'only a training exercise', 'isn't real life', and when significantly 'I wouldn't have done it that way back at work'. Many of these comments, and particularly the last one, result from rationalization and defensiveness when success in an event has not been complete. They are most difficult charges to refute as the events are taking place in a 'training centre'; the activities to produce the desired results must be artificial to some extent, and in most cases, success or failure does not have a real-life profit or disciplinary action other than internalized feelings of success or failure, or the expressed or implied praise or criticism of the trainer or fellow members of the group.

The only way to reduce the impact of these criticisms is to ensure that the training is as 'real' as possible within the constraints that must exist. Case studies must be taken from real situations and not doctored to satisfy the inclinations of the trainer; problems too must be real and as far as possible common in the trainee's working situation. Practice interviews should preferably be with 'real' people who will act reasonably normally, rather than with fellow trainees who will act out roles. It will not always be possible to satisfy these criteria but any measure of approach to realism will be worthwhile. By far the most effective, whenever it is appropriate, is to use activities or interactions that have occurred on the course or have arisen in extra-curricular activities. One of the most fruitful and active discussions that took place on one of my courses arose from a chance remark made by a course member during a bar session at 3am. Some discussion took place at the time, but the subject arose naturally the following day and the previous remarks acted as a catalyst to produce a full discussion.

LEARNING METHODS

Another aspect of research of which the trainer must be aware and which will have an effect on his training approach is that which relates to the preferred or actual methods by which people learn. Burgoyne and Stuart conducted this type of research and suggested a ranked order of major sources of learning of managers:

1) doing the job, picking up skills *en passant*
2) non-company education
3) living – life experience of success and failure away from work
4) in-coming education – deliberate training interventions
5) self-learning
6) doing other jobs
7) media influence
8) parents
9) innate learning.

It will be seen from these rankings that direct training, although not too low in the list, is far from being of supreme importance.

My own advice to those involved in the training and development field is

- in spite of all the barriers and possible pitfalls, be ambitious and adventurous but be aware of your own limitations
- consider all the options available
- tailor the course to suit the training needs and the needs of the individual
- be aware of the possible problems that can be created by the trainer and the trainee
- produce an off-the-job training course only if there is no other way of satisfying the training need.

IDENTIFICATION OF TRAINING NEEDS

Whatever training activity is decided upon, it will only be effective if a serious attempt has been made to decide exactly what training is necessary.

The first stage in this process is the identification of the training gap, the gap between the requirements of the job and the deficiencies in skill of the worker. There must therefore be a complete understanding of the job requirements. What tasks, skills, knowledge and attitudes must the worker have to perform the job satisfactorily? The answer to these questions can be determined only by an in-depth survey of the job – the task or job analysis.

A typical approach is to observe the job carefully and systematically as it is being performed to identify all the steps involved. An effective worker can also be questioned in order to supplement the observations. Similarly, an identified poor performer can be questioned to discover the problems he finds in doing the job.

An apparently straightforward job can sometimes be found to require a number of skills and aspects of knowledge that are not immediately evident, and possible areas where training needs may exist can come to light.

Let us look at the initial stages of a job analysis of a hotel receptionist.

1) Receptionist observes person entering hotel reception area and approaching reception desk (observation skills necessary particularly to identify non-verbal indicators of anger, stress, nervousness, etc.).
2) Receptionist greets guest (acceptable manner necessary demonstrated in both verbal and non-verbal behaviour).
3) Receptionist enquires guest's requirements (interactive skills and clear questioning techniques necessary to elicit information efficiently and in an appropriate manner).
4) Guest states requirements (skills on part of receptionist in listening and understanding information given). Guest may enquire whether accommodation is available.
5) Receptionist responds by clarifying nature of accommodation required (skills of questioning in an acceptable manner).
6) When the guest clarifies and receptionist understands, receptionist either gives information from memory, or checks position in records (manual, mechanical or computerized).
   The skills or knowledge necessary at this stage will depend on the system in operation.
   And so on . . . .

An analysis of this nature will identify the skills, knowledge, attitudes and tasks involved. When this information is available, observation can indicate at what stage or stages there is a performance deficiency and the nature of this deficiency. If the performance deficiency has an effect on the success of the job, we have identified a training need.

There are of course a number of approaches to the identification of training needs. The one cited depends to a large extent on direct observation of specific tasks, but less obvious and direct needs can be approached in other ways.

THE CRITICAL INCIDENT TECHNIQUE

This technique, used to identify and analyse the training and developmental needs of individuals or groups, involves the experiences of the trainees, taken from their careers. Virtually every experience in a person's life and career can be a source of learning, but some events are critical incidents in the learning process and have particular influence on us. Concentration on these incidents can produce more understanding of their effect and can point to learning needs or themselves form part of the learning process.

A number of approaches can be used in the technique, but typically the individual or group is invited to describe details of an incident that has changed their life or attitudes, or the most difficult problem they have had to deal with. Often the individual finds it difficult to articulate the incident, either through lack of awareness of any significances, difficulty in expressing his/her feelings, or simply as a result of the passage of time since the event. The trainer/interviewer can assist this process by probing the incident with questions of a 'who, why, what, where, when, with whom' nature.

If a number of incidents emerge from the discussion, it may be that a pattern is disclosed from which significant training needs can be identified. A similar approach to a group can reveal a number of common problems and training needs which can then be satisfied by some form of training. One fairly typical side-effect of a series of interviews with either individuals or groups can be the identification of the training needs of others than the interviewees, from the comments made relating to the incidents discussed. For example, a number of individuals reporting a common, bad experience when receiving job appraisal interviews will suggest that there may be an organizational training need in the conduct of interviews of this nature.

THE REPERTORY GRID

This is another investigatory method that looks in a structured way at the attitudes and values of individuals so that the results can be analysed and training needs concluded.

For an interview or series of interviews, a number of elements are selected as representative of the area of interest for which the investigation is being conducted. These elements could be concerned with, for example, the management training needs in staff relations, and would include in this case a counselling interview, a grievance interview, a discipline situation, a correction interview, an appraisal interview, a selection interview and so on. The elements can be written on separate index cards and three cards selected. The interviewer obtains the views of the interviewee about the subjects on the three cards in terms of any commonalities or differences. This process is repeated using all the cards in overlapping sequences and the interviewer builds up information about how the interviewee views the subjects. These views, which can show weaknesses of attitude or approach, are referred to as the constructs. The results are plotted on a grid, the elements against the constructs, and from this a pattern of skill/knowledge or lack of it emerges.

STANDARDS OF COMPETENCE

Trainers have often asked themselves or their colleagues, 'How well should I be doing in my job? I know *what* I have to do, but *how well* does my boss expect me to do it? How well am I doing it? I expect he'll tell me at my appraisal interview, but that might be too late.' Or, as the manager of trainers, 'I know what so-and-so should be doing; I know how they seem to be doing it; but *how well* and *to what extent* are they doing it? And how am I supposed to know?' This type of information is important if trainers are to train to a standard that is known to them and their bosses and there is a method of assessing these requirements. The level must not be decided by the trainers or their bosses, but should be levels which can be validated by reference to national standards and are transferable to almost whatever training role the person might be called upon to perform.

It was with this uniformity of approach in mind that the national system of competence standards was born. A number of organizations had already started to produce their own lists of skills and tasks, but this was far from a uniform approach, which would be necessary to establish national standards. Also few had even attempted to assess the possibility of skill levels. However, a British government impetus for a national approach was given in 1986 with the stated intention of having national standards for all occupations. Reports produced by such experts as Handy and Constable supported this intention; they strongly advocated the pursuance of professional qualifications by British managers, in which they compared unfavourably with most advanced nations.

The then Training Agency was charged with the responsibility of carrying forward a competences project and, in partnership with the Management Charter Initiative, of classifying management competences on a generic basis applicable to any management post in any industry.

This project proceeded apace and the approach soon developed over a wider range of occupations than management. Three factors aided this programme. The first was a decision to construct the standards from working practices actually in operation within industries and using the industries themselves to identify the competences. The second was the decision to use functional analysis rather than other approaches to define the standards – another method had been in operation for some time in the USA. The third was the formation of Lead Bodies which ranged over all sectors of industry and commerce and which were formed to develop industry-based standards of occupational competence. The Lead Bodies were also charged with formulating and approving the framework of National Vocational Qualifications (NVQs), the qualifications based on the competence standards. The Lead Bodies became in effect the executive arm of the National Council for Vocational Qualifications (SCOTVEC in Scotland), the accrediting bodies which approve qualification proposals submitted by the Lead Bodies.

Organizations accredited by the Lead Bodies award NVQs (SVQs in Scotland) – these are the Awarding Bodies and include such organizations as the Institute of Personnel and Development, City and Guilds, RSA, BTEC and professional bodies among others.

An S/NVQ award from one of the Awarding Bodies can be attained by individuals either on their own or from organizations in a variety of ways. Individuals, either singularly or in organizations, can seek the awards directly with the Awarding Bodies or via organizations or educational establishments which are accredited as centres by an Awarding Body. Organizations following this path for the candidates from their organization can eventually become accredited centres themselves when they satisfy criteria set by the Awarding Bodies. In this way the organization can then assess its own employees for the NVQs rather than through a third party.

An example of one approach through this system concerns a large organization with which I was associated as a consultant. The organization decided to 'dip its toes' into the NVQ pool by supporting a project of a pilot group of twenty trainers to seek the Training and Development Lead Body (TDLB) NVQ awards. The services of an accredited centre were contracted. The pilot group included one person appointed as VQ manager who was trained in these duties by the accredited centre. It was also agreed that up to about nine of the candidate group, in addition to seeking the NVQs Levels 3 or 4 would also seek Assessor certification. A further aim was to try to have the candidate-assessors certificated as quickly as possible so that (a) they might support their certification by assessment practice on their colleagues who were candidates for the NVQ awards and (b) the organization might as quickly as possible become itself an accredited centre. The latter action would of course eventually reduce costs and permit a larger number of staff to follow the NVQ award system.

The pilot group which started in September 1994 is now progressing along the lines described above, working towards the revised standards.

THE STANDARDS

So much for the general approach to standards and NVQs, but what do they actually consist of? Again there are some differences between the Lead and Awarding Body approaches, but a broad standard pattern exists:

- A Key Purpose
- Key Areas (these may be divided into Areas and Sub-Areas or some other division)
- Units of competence (the levels at which NVQs are assessed)
- Elements of competence

- Performance Criteria
- Range Statements.

As most readers of this book are likely to be in the training area or have an interest in this area, let us use the TDLB standards and NVQs to describe the details of the system.

The first draft standards framework was published by the TDLB in July 1990 and the definitive standards were produced in 1992. Candidates have worked towards an NVQ award from these standards since that time within the proposed three Levels of TDNVQ:

Level 3 (roughly equivalent to the training officer role)
Level 4 (roughly equivalent to the senior training officer and staff control functions or the training manager)
Level 5 (roughly equivalent to the training director or HRD manager/director role).

As a result of the candidates who have already studied for awards and the increasing interest in training and development and in professional award support for those involved, the TBLB has received a considerable amount of feedback on the nature and usability of the standards. Concern was expressed about the ambiguous and sometimes incomprehensible language used in the standards as well as the ambiguity of some of the applications. In response to this concern, and in order to make the standards more acceptable and usable by more people in the interest area, the TDLB decided in early 1994 to review the standards and submit a revised framework to the NCVQ and SCOTVEC. Their intention was to launch the new qualifications and standards in Spring 1994, but because a more fundamental review was requested by participants in the early part of the review, it was decided to extend the review and finalization was put back to the end of May 1994. Eventually agreement was reached on the consequences of the review and the new standards were published in the autumn of 1994.

THE TRAINING AND DEVELOPMENT STANDARDS OF COMPETENCE

KEY PURPOSE

The *Key Purpose* is a statement of the role being discussed, in this case the training and development role, and it sets the scene within which the standards are constructed. For the training and development role the Key Purpose is:

> Develop human potential to assist organizations and individuals to achieve their objectives.

AREAS

From the Key Purpose general statement we can identify broad areas of work which lead to its satisfaction. In the TDLB standards there are five *Areas*:

A Identify training and development needs
B Plan and design training and development
C Deliver training and development
D Review progress and assess achievement
E Continuously improve the effectiveness of training and development.

KEY ROLES

The *Key Roles* define in rather more detail the Areas listed above, and in the TDLB standards each area contains from one to four *Roles*:

A – A1 Identify organizational training and development requirements
A2 Identify learning requirements of individuals
B – B1 Design training and development strategies for organizations
B2 Design training and development programmes
B3 Design and produce learning materials
C – C1 Manage the implementation of training and development

C2 Facilitate learning with individuals and groups
D – D1 Monitor and review progress
D2 Assess individual achievement
D3 Assess individual achievement of competence
E – E1 Evaluate the effectiveness of training and development within an organization
E2 Evaluate the effectiveness of training and development programmes
E3 Improve own training and development practice
E4 Contribute to advances in training and development.

UNITS OF COMPETENCE

It will be apparent that the competence of an individual cannot be assessed from the wide statements listed above. To enable the assessment, the Key Roles are further divided into the building bricks of competence standards and NVQs: the *Units of Competence* which are then further divided into *Elements of Competence*. From the tests available to assess competence in the Elements, a build-up to Unit competence is possible. It is by demonstrating competence in the required Units that NVQ awards can be made.

Each Key Role contains a number of Units. As an example, the Units in Key Role B3 (Design and produce learning materials) are:

Unit B31 Design, test and modify training and development materials
Unit B32 Design, test and modify information technology (IT) based materials
Unit B33 Prepare and develop resources to support learning.

ELEMENTS OF COMPETENCE

Even the Units are not sufficiently detailed to enable a realistic assessment of competence in the function to be performed. Consequently each Unit is further described in terms of elements which describe the detailed aspects of the function. The Units vary in having from two to five Elements each.

As an example, the Elements contained in Unit B31 quoted above are:

Element B311 Agree requirements for training and development materials
Element B312 Design training and development materials
Element B313 Test the design of training and development materials
Element B314 Modify and produce training and development materials.

You will see that the range of Elements shown above describes the progressive involvement in that particular competence, from agreeing requirements to producing the end result.

PERFORMANCE CRITERIA

The Units and Elements define what is included as functions in the competence standards. The *Performance Criteria* define what an assessor must look for to determine whether these functions are being carried out satisfactorily – the test of effectiveness.

Each Element has a number of associated Performance Criteria, ranging from five to ten or more criteria. If we look at, for example, Element B312, the eleven Performance Criteria for this Element are:

Unit B31: Design, test and modify learning materials
Element B312: Design materials to support learning
Performance criteria:

a) The agreements made with clients for materials are clarified and explained to all those involved in the design process
b) The specific aims and objectives of the materials are clearly identified
c) Possible types of materials, media and delivery methods suitable to the subject matter, learning context and duration are selected
d) Possible design problems are identified and realistic ideas for overcoming them are generated
e) A range of design options are developed and a preferred option selected which meets all specified requirements
f) Materials from external sources are adapted and used within the constraints of copyright law
g) Guidance and instructions on the correct use of the materials are precise and clear
h) Designs are discussed with all relevant people at critical development stages

i) Final design option selected conforms to the agreements made and meets all specified learning requirements
j) The language, style and format of the materials is appropriate to the learning needs of users
k) Materials are designed within the agreed timescale and resources.

In addition to the Performance Criteria listed, notes are included in the Element giving guidance on the type of evidence – performance and knowledge – required to satisfy the criteria. For the Performance Criteria described above the evidence required is:

PERFORMANCE EVIDENCE

Records and notes of discussions and agreements on requirements
Finished learning materials
Notes of discussions concerning the development of the design.

KNOWLEDGE EVIDENCE

Principles of design
Methods of differentiating materials to promote achievement of objectives
Ways to introduce, promote and negotiate materials with clients
How to design materials to support training and development
How to assess which learning materials are most suited to clients
Common design problems
Examples of good design
Current relevant debates concerning the design and use of training and development materials
Copyright requirements
Equal opportunities legislation and good practice
Principles of non-sexist and non-racist language.

RANGE STATEMENTS

To complete the standards and the guidance on what is required to assess them, a final section is included in each Element – the *Range Statement*. Not every trainer performs the functions described in the standards. The Range Statement guides the assessor when considering the range of contexts and applications in which a competent person would be expected to achieve the Element. In the B312 example, the Range Statements include:

2) Purpose of materials: to support learning, for assessment and review
4) Materials used by: practitioners, learners
6) Guidance and instructions cover: completion instructions, information on learning processes and so on.

These items from the Key Purpose to the Range Statements describe *all* the competences that are found in the training and development function. Obviously one role holder cannot be required to demonstrate or perform all the items: some 5 Areas, 13 Key Roles, 29 Units and more than 100 Elements. The standards form the basis on which NVQs are built.

TRAINING AND DEVELOPMENT NATIONAL VOCATIONAL QUALIFICATIONS

Following the identification of the standards involved in the function, the next stage is to use these standards to describe NVQs at different levels for groups and individuals performing different roles within the training and development function. The TDLB has developed three levels of NVQ – Levels 3, 4 and 5 – and the Awarding Bodies offer NVQs at these levels based on the units of competence. Each level requires that certain Units and parts of Units should be demonstrated by the candidate before an NVQ can be awarded. Units are awarded on a Unit-by-Unit basis until the required selection has been assessed for competence.

The NVQs determined by the 1994 review of standards consist of Level 3 Training and Development, Level 4 Training and Development (Learning Development), Level 4 Training and Development (Human Resource Development) and Level 5 Training and Development. Each of these NVQs requires candidates to satisfy Unit award in determined selections which currently are:

Level 3 Training and Development – 7 core plus 3 optional (from 12 options) Units
Level 4 Learning Support – 7 core and 5 (from 19) options

Level 4 Human Resource Development – 7 core plus 5 (from 19) options
Level 5 Training and Development – 7 core plus 5 (from 10) options.

LEVEL 3 TRAINING AND DEVELOPMENT NVQ

This will be the NVQ award that will be sought by the majority of trainers with a principally direct training role. The Units required for the award of the NVQ consist of:

CORE UNITS (7)

A22	Identify individual learning needs
B22	Design training and development sessions
B33	Prepare and develop resources to support learning
C21	Create a climate conducive to learning
C23	Facilitate learning in groups through presentations and activities
E23	Evaluate training and development sessions
E31	Evaluate and develop own practice.

OPTIONS (3 TAKEN FROM A LIST OF 12)

C22	Agree learning programmes with learners
C24	Facilitate learning through demonstration and instruction
C25	Facilitate learning through coaching
C27	Facilitate group learning
D11	Monitor and review progress with learners
D21	Assess individuals for non-competence based assessment systems
D32	Assess candidate performance
D33	Assess candidate using diverse evidence
D36	Advise and support candidates to identify prior achievement
E32	Management relationships with colleagues and customers
MCI SM2	Contribute to the planning, monitoring and control of resources
MCI SM3	Contribute to the provision of personnel.

The competence of the NVQ candidates such as that described above will be assessed by a qualified assessor who will follow the competence standards requirements described earlier. If a candidate does not satisfy part of the requirements, training can help to develop his or her knowledge and skills and the candidates will then be able to practise their skills until they are able to demonstrate competence. In this manner, training and education can complement the practicality of the NVQ competences, the ability to perform the function to the required level of competence remaining the unique criterion for the award of the NVQ.

Additional or separate Unit requirements are provided for standards of competence in Assessment and Verification and include Units D31, D32, D33, D34, D35 and D36, the combination depending on the award sought.

TRAINING FORMATS

Once the training needs of an individual or group of individuals have been defined, a suitable training event can be identified or constructed. The various techniques discussed in the remainder of this book can be and have been employed in a variety of training events with different aims and objectives. The skills of the successful trainer can be identified by his ability to decide which methods will be most appropriate for the training need and his skill in carrying them out. The new trainer, manager-trainer or training manager who may be required to produce a training event will be best advised not to be too adventurous in his choice of approaches, as many of them require high degrees of skill. At this stage we can look generally at the variety of overall approaches; all the more specific techniques and methods are described in more detail later.

Although self-instructional, computer-assisted action learning and similar approaches are becoming more commonly employed, the vast majority of learners still come together in groups for a training event.

The most common of these events are usually described as *courses*. Courses can vary enormously, being organized internally for company staff or externally for mixed groups; their duration can vary from one or two days to several weeks; there can be a participant mix of a group of peers, hierarchical levels, stranger, cousin or home groups. The degree of structure can range from a formal, highly structured event to the completely unstructured format of the sensitivity T-Group. The atmosphere can be very formal or completely informal. The trainers can be tutors (i.e. teachers), or facilitators (i.e. help agents) in the learning process. But it is in the content that courses can vary the most. They can consist of lecture-type sessions throughout; lectures interspersed with activities, case studies, films, audio-visuals and so on; completely unstructured activities, part-structured and structured activities, or either structured or unstructured activities alone, or virtually any permutation of the methods and approaches that will be discussed later. A course can be an enjoyable learning experience or a boring failure.

The traditional course is a tutor-centred event in which the aims and objectives are decided beforehand by the trainer and the methods of achieving these objectives are controlled by the trainer. In recent years the learner-centred approach has come into prominence. The degree of learner-centredness can vary from the learners designing their own learning methods to achieve the set objectives or they can be responsible for providing the whole event, from objective setting, through structuring and achieving the learning, to evaluating the experience. Few learning groups, however, have the capability to construct the whole event, so the best product is usually when there is effective collaboration between the learner and the facilitator.

At the opposite end of the spectrum is the *conference*, although this is not always identified by the participants as a learning event. However, an accepted aim for a conference consisting of people for the same or similar professions or with similar interests, is that they go away knowing more than when they arrived, even if this is only what the chairman expects of his employees in the coming year. Conferences can be simply a series of lectures or can be enlivened by small-group discussions or workshops.

Seminars are conferences on a smaller scale and utilizing a greater degree of involvement of the participants. A further difference from the conference is that the seminar usually concentrates on a single theme, whereas the conference can contain a wide range of topics. The format of the seminar typically follows a sequence of lectures by experts or specialist speakers with subsequent syndicate or small-group activities, and plenary sessions where a report is made on the results of the syndicate discussions. The seminar can often be described as a *symposium* and it is difficult to differentiate them absolutely. Some seminars/symposia follow the pattern described above, but either seminars or symposia can be a succession of specialist speakers following a single theme or closely related topics.

Workshops are usually more clearly defined as training events and normally involve a considerable amount of practical participation by the members. The workshop can have a single topic of theme or a number of related topics. But the principle difference is the absence of 'expert' speakers and, usually, formal sessions. Any inputs that occur are by the facilitator at the request of the workshop members or by the workshop members themselves. Quite often the members decide how the workshop will be run and what the terminal objectives will be. The emphasis is on 'doing', either in the production of plans for operation on return to base, or the practical production of materials, methods, programmes or activities for use back at work.

The members of the workshop, if they themselves are trainers, may return with sets of newly constructed exercises that they have tried out on their colleagues during the workshop; new or modified training sessions that they have had the opportunity to try out, or complete training programmes or events. Managers may go home with actual work problems solved or at least possible solutions, or new methods of approaching their problems.

One recent workshop started by everybody involved posting up around the walls of the room topics that they wished to discuss or learn about, and topics that they could and would provide training in, whether in the form of inputs or activities. The trainer, who was the workshop organizer, also took part in this sharing of skill and knowledge, and the event produced maximum learning in the most informal and enjoyable manner.

VIDEOS IN TRAINING

Although training videos are most commonly used when groups are being trained, and are usually combined with trainer input, they are also used in other forms of group training and also self-development. There are a number of variations in their use although on many occasions the basic approach only is used.

The traditional approach to showing a video is based on two pre-existing attitudes. Before the advent of video cassettes, films were the moving pictorial medium used in training. Because the film was transported through the projector by means of holes at the side of the film moving over sprockets, projectionists tended not to want to stop the film in its progress too frequently. The sprocket holes could become torn or distorted, and the passage and quality of the film suffered. Consequently the projectionist (trainer) tended to run the film through without interrupting its passage. In addition, people as audiences had become accustomed to the 'accepted' way of watching a film, from beginning to end without stopping.

When videos, a stronger and more compact form of film, were introduced, the traditional approach to the film was transferred to video showing, i.e. continuously with no interruptions, whereas the mechanism for stopping a video tape does not have the same problems as that of film. Even the production of videos tended to compound this attitude – if a video intended to be played continuously is interrupted, the interruption appears abnormal. Obviously, there will be many occasions when the training video is played through, but trainers must not fall into the habit of thinking that this is the only option, and video producers must not produce videos in this format alone. Fortunately some video producers are now introducing variant types, thus encouraging the adventurous use of this new medium.

Use in self-development Few videos can, or are intended to, stand alone, even when used as a self-development instrument – you cannot question a video about aspects you do not understand, or discuss with it your disagreement of a point. If the video for home/office consideration does not include it, the issuing trainer must ensure that there is some supporting material. This can take the form of questions and activities intended to ensure that the viewers think about what they have seen, rather than simply view. If, for example, the video is about time management and part of the video deals with clearing the desk of non-essential work and setting up priority and non-priority files, an activity following the video might be to invite the viewer to perform these functions. Or, a list of questions might come with the video, intended to:

- allow the viewer to self-test his or her knowledge about what has been seen
- consolidate the information in the video, even if it means that the video has to be viewed again to answer the question
- require the viewer to seek out further information which will support and reinforce the video material.

The main intention *must* be that the viewer does not switch off his mind once the video has been switched off.

Use in group work The first use of the video when a group is involved is similar to that described above for the individual. The video is played through in one sitting – most take about 20 minutes. This sitting can be a special occasion when the video alone is to be used, or as part of a trainer's input session. Whichever is the case, there must be some action following the showing of the video. This would seem to be common sense, but I have encountered one organization which, in one of its branches, had a resident trainer who 'trained' by showing a video in the rest room at lunchtime. The video was shown – that's all! There was no discussion, no questions or any other action following the showing, not even 'What did you think of that, folks?'

A video used in conjunction with an input session can:

- introduce the material of the session, the trainer's input reinforcing the simple messages contained in the video
- introduce material which would otherwise have been introduced by the trainer (in this way, variety of presentation and a different face and voice maintain the trainees' interest)
- form a summary of what has been considered in the session, either during it or at the end.

In all these uses, and particularly the first two, something must happen after the video has been shown. Usually the trainer will initiate a discussion about the material contained in the video. If it is used as an introduction, it is good way of discovering how much the trainees already knew about the subject, by questioning them about the impact made on them. If it is used as part of the session, a full discussion must follow; otherwise the video could be seen as an unimportant diversion. Many trainers find these discussions difficult to start or to maintain. At least two options are available which can ease this process:

- The trainer leads the discussion by the use of appropriate questioning until the discussion takes on a more natural form. Some questions will always be held back in case the discussion falters before it has reached a natural ending. Such questions could include:

  'What did you see as the major learning points brought out in the video?'
  'Why did you see them in that light?'
  'How do you feel about points a, b, c etc?'
  'How do you feel about the way Joe reacted in situation x?'
  'Would you have reacted in any other way? If so, how?'
  and so on.

  If the group is reacting naturally and easily, there should be little difficulty in producing a useful discussion in this way.
- If the trainer finds it difficult to start a discussion a questionnaire can be used, based on the content of the video and related to the topics the trainer wants the group to discuss. The group is asked to complete the questionnaire as individuals, so that each person reflects on at least some view on each point. These self-expressed views can then be used in a discussion in which the trainer finds out what the individuals have written. It is often found that when people have written something down first, they are much more likely to say something than if they have to think and talk on demand.

Interrupted videos A developing use of the video, although not of course a completely new technique, is that of interrupting the video during its play. However, these interruptions must be deliberate and purposeful. In order to use this technique, the trainer must be very well versed in the content of the video so as to stop it at exactly the right moment – reliance on the footage or rev. counter of the video player can be risky and can sometimes vary from one machine to another.

There are two ways of interrupting a video. The first is to stop at a point immediately before a part of the action and ask a question of the group:

'What do you think is going to happen now?'

'What should happen now?'
'If you were in this position, what would you do now?'

The video can then be continued until the outcome is evident and the video can again be stopped to check out the previous discussion against what was shown. Some videos now being produced either pause at this point or actually stop and pose one of these questions. However, any video can be treated in this way, the trainer having decided at which critical points the action has to be stopped, and what questions have to be asked.

The second approach again stops the video, but in this case after the action of that part of the video has been completed. The questions in this case will follow the pattern of:

'How did you feel about the way that this situation was handled?'
'What would you have done in that situation?'
'What alternative approaches were possible in that situation?'

In both these instances it is intended that there should be some form of discussion. The ways of circumventing any possible difficulties have already been discussed and are relevant here.

There are problems with this interruptive technique. Because the viewing of videos and films is traditionally continuous, there may be reaction among the viewers, and if it happens too often the reaction of 'Oh, not again' may occur. If you are going to stop the video at intervals, it is advisable to let the group know that this is going to happen before you start, and you must ensure that you are stopping only for really important reasons. At least one video producer is attempting to get round the problem in a rather novel way. The company produces a package which contains two videos. One is in the traditional format, intended to be viewed straight through. The second initiates the discussion by showing short scenarios based on the learning points of the traditional video. Supporting handbooks are also included suggesting the questions which can usefully be asked at each 'trigger' scene and also activities which can follow or take the part of these discussions.

Another approach to help the trainer in the use of videos is provided by at least one other company. When the learning points are reached, the action is suspended and captions are superimposed. The trainer then has the option of initiating a discussion there and then, or waiting until the end. Handbooks again support the video and suggest ways of presenting it in addition to extending the learning points in a textual form.

One other variation on the theme of interruption is action by the trainers themselves to ease the information from video to discussion. Many training organizations have equipment which allows them to edit existing videos and perhaps add blank stretches of video tape with 'voice-over' instructions at the relevant points. The trainer leaves the video with a small group, asks them to play it and obey the instructions they will find appearing at intervals throughout the tape. The group then takes part in an activity to, for example, produce an analysis of the video, its learning points, or perform some other related activity. While one group is taking part in this small-group activity, unattended apart from perhaps occasional visits by the trainer, the trainer is taking some other action with another group or groups from the main training group. None of these activities is difficult although care has to be taken when editing the original video in case irreparable damage is done. Alternatively video consultants can be used to perform these operations at a relatively small cost.

The corporate video Another developing use of videos, although not specifically for training purposes, is in corporate communication. Before the relative ease of the production of in-company videos, when it was necessary to circulate information around an organization, particularly one with widespread work units, two main methods were used. One was in the written form – reports, news-sheets, memoranda and so on. The dangers of this form are well-known and well established – failure to actually read the material, misunderstanding due to the writing and reading of words, time for copies to circulate and so on. The other form has been described, at worst, as the 'mushroom' method, or more correctly as team briefing, succession meeting methods. In this approach, the corporate message originates at a senior-level meeting. The participants of that meeting then hold meetings with their subordinates and pass on the message; these subordinates in their turn hold meetings and so on down the chain. The main problem is that from the original message, the messages passed down can become successively selective or contain increasing errors and/or omissions, depending on the skills of communication of the meeting leaders. Such techniques as team briefings help to avoid some of these errors and omissions, but the danger is always present. The modern alternative, which is used increasingly, is the corporate communication video. Even with relatively inexpensive and unsophisticated equipment videos can be made and copied for circulation to key points in the organization. The members of the organization are brought to these key points to see the video – in this way all see and hear exactly the same message. Obviously, not everybody will immediately understand all the message and a leader will have to check understanding and answer questions raised by the video – there will always be some.

Interactive video Interactive video (IV) is one of the more recent developments in the use of video in training. It can be described as the blend of audio, visual, textual and computer media to produce a training medium, usually used on an individual basis – either as a self-development instrument or in a trainer-monitored environment.

A separate, special video disc, rather like a 'grown-up' audio compact disc, contains both still and moving images and is played on a special video disc player. This player is linked to a computer into which is inserted a text and graphics programme. Both parts are usually controlled by one keyboard or mouse, although there can be several variations.

A common use of IV is for the system to produce a scene from which questions, either spoken or produced as screen text, are posed. Quite often the questions are offered with multi-choice responses, the user choosing one of these by selecting a key. If the answer is correct, the scene moves on to the next problem, but if incorrect or not the 'best' answer, the user can be told why the answer is 'wrong' and either given the correct response or invited to try again. This procedure continues to the end of the video disc programme.

The benefits of IV are not only in the use of a range of effects, but also that the learning can proceed at the learner's own rate, returning to earlier stages to repeat them or skipping areas where the knowledge presents no problems. It also has the advantage over the straight computer programme in that the human element is present, albeit on video – people can work better when the user can relate in some way to the programme (either negatively or positively).

There are, however, disadvantages. These are common to all video/computer uses when the medium is used by a self-developer in isolation. If the user does not understand whatever may be presented or is happening, there may not be immediate recourse to another source of explanation – trainer, experienced peer, book or other resource. Similarly, if the user does not agree with the choice decided by the programme, there is no opportunity to discuss, argue or disagree with the programme, unless the other resources mentioned above are available.

Equipment for IV use is still developing, and although the initial battle between video disc and video tape (a less costly product) is not complete, the market strongly favours video disc. Many of the advances will be technical in nature, but some may include additional facilities, such as those for the user to modify the programme. In the future artificial intelligence may be applied to IV: this would permit much more interactivity than the present forced reaction, but the commercial application of AI would seem to be distant. In the meantime, the existing state of the art offers an alternative, attractive method of learning, particularly in the area of self-learning and self-development.

CONCLUSION

Responsibility for training involves difficulties and hard work. There are few, if any, rigorous guidelines as to what type of event to organize and how it should be constructed; to try to answer this is to try to answer the question 'how long is a piece of string?' The training approach can be an overkill, like taking the motorway from one junction to the next over 15 miles, when a perfectly good road exists with a length of only five miles. The aim of the committed trainer must be to build up a wide-ranging toolkit of ideas, techniques, methods and approaches into which he can dip and extract the most appropriate. He must himself experience as many training experiences as he can and learn from these – the mistakes as well as the good features. He will soon learn to plagiarize in the best possible way, but there are many dangers in simply copying the style or approach of another, seemingly successful trainer.

The new trainer, full or part-time, the manager-trainer or training manager, should acquaint himself with as many approaches and methods as he can and, above all, develop the skills to use them.

REFERENCES AND RECOMMENDED READING

The Identification of Training Needs. T. H. Boydell, BACIE, 1971.

A Guide to Job Analysis. T. H. Boydell. BACIE, 1970.

The Critical Incident in Growth Groups. Arthur M. Cohen and R. Douglas Smith. University Associates, 1976.

Training and Development Handbook. Edited by Robert and Craig. McGraw-Hill, 1976.

Encyclopedia of Management Development Methods. Andrzej Huczynski. Gower, 1983.

Adult Training. Edited by M. Howe. Wiley, 1977.

The Training Directory. Kogan Page and BACIE, Annual.

Helping Others Learn. Patricia H. McHagan. Addison-Wesley, 1978.

Developing and Presenting Staff Training Courses. Peter R. Sheal. Kogan Page, 1989.

Managing the Manager's Growth. Valerie and Andrew Stewart. Gower, 1978.

Training Resources. Parke Sutton and the ITD, Annual.

Management Development and Training Handbook. Edited by B. Taylor and G. L. Lippitt. McGraw-Hill, 1975.

Guide to Training for Managers and Trainers. John M. Cheyne. Insurance Industry Training Council, 1987.

The Trainer's Desk Reference. Geoffrey Moss. Kogan Page, 1993.

Training Methods that Work. Lois Hart. Kogan Page, 1991.

Teaching Hard, Teaching Soft. Colin Corder. Gower, 1990.

The Theory and Practice of Training. Roger Buckley and Jim Caple. Kogan Page, 2nd edition, 1992.

NVQs, Standards and Competence: A Practical Guide for Employers, Managers and Trainers. Shirley Fletcher. Kogan Page, 1991.

Competence-Based Assessment Techniques. Shirley Fletcher. Kogan Page, 1991.

Designing Competence-Based Training. Shirley Fletcher. Kogan Page, 1991.

The NVQ and GNVQ Assessor Handbook. Ros Ollin and Jenny Tucker. Kogan Page, 1994.

Training and Development NVQ contacts:
Training and Development Lead Body, PO Box 28, Rugby, Warwickshire CV22 7UH.
Tel. 0788 577503 (for Helpline and general enquiries).

2 The lecture

The lecture is probably one of the oldest training methods and used correctly can be a powerful training device. Unfortunately it is open to abuse and can be used badly or can be inappropriate. The demands on both the lecturer and the audience are great and it is usually because these pressures are ignored that the lecture method fails and training based on lectures has gained such a bad track record. Things can so easily be wrong or go wrong, such as

- the lecturer has low skills in the art of public speaking
- the lecturer has prepared his material badly and it may not all be relevant
- the lecturer presents his material in an unorganized way
- the lecture contains too much, too complex material to allow ready assimilation
- the audience is asked to do no more than appear to be listening and thus is allowed to be completely passive.

A lecture with some or all of these faults, or more, can be boring, frustrating or annoying to the audience and, unless the lecturer is completely unaware of his effect on the audience, gives little satisfaction to him. On the other hand, if the poor techniques are corrected, the lecture can be instructive, enjoyable and satisfying to all. Unfortunately, for the lecture to be the success it deserves, virtually every possible wrecking factor must be absent. One side of the equation is the lecturer using effectively every skill of his trade, but if the problem is on the other side of the equation – the audience – then the skills of the lecturer can be wasted.

To ensure the success of a lecture the audience must be committed and motivated. Without this, even the most highly skilled speaker will find his words falling on stony ground. We are more used to thinking of the lecture as a public event organized by somebody with a particular interest so that the vast majority of the audience will be present through their personal choice. Here is the motivation to attend, listen, analyse and consider, particularly if the audience has had to pay to attend.

In a training event we cannot be sure that these criteria will be satisfied. Our student audience may range from those with no interest in the subject who may have been compelled to attend, through those with some interest but who require a kindling of this interest to make them completely involved, to those with a strong interest and desire to learn as much as they can. The motivation behind the latter group can be varied and might include a need to learn to support or even advance their own careers, fear brought about by the consideration that their boss wants them to learn this subject, or even that their peers or subordinates are more knowledgeable, or a change of job may demand new knowledge. Even with this group, the event must be handled with skill to ensure that their needs are satisfied. The middle group can react either way depending on the skill of the lecturer but only a superb lecturer with a charismatic approach has any hope of achieving anything with the first group.

A lecturing technique that is quoted many times is to work on the principle of telling them what you are going to tell them, telling them, then telling them what you have told them. This is a sound and respectable principle that can be translated into training terms as an introduction to the subject, the subject itself and a summary. An approach of this nature will not solve the problems discussed earlier, but at least those who are listening can fully understand what has been discussed.

ADVANTAGES AND DISADVANTAGES OF THE LECTURE

When these principles are accepted, understood and managed as far as possible, the lecturer has made every effort to produce an efficient presentation. In this form it can be a powerful tool for learning. Obviously it has its more appropriate applications, and these can include

- the general introduction to a subject
- where there is a need for descriptive learning

- the input of completely new material
- possibly in the early stages of a course when the group is not yet sufficiently mature to learn through participation.

Equally there are occasions when it is completely inappropriate, namely

- when group members have demonstrated their need to be active
- when the subject is familiar to members and learning from each other's experiences is likely to be more productive
- where the course objectives are concerned more with human relations and behaviour than with procedural operations

When the atmosphere is right the lecture still has advantages and disadvantages, although it must be admitted that some of the advantages are suspect if real learning is to take place.

ADVANTAGES OF THE LECTURE

The lecturer is in full control of the material It is his decision as to what aspects of the subject are presented and, having prepared his material he can conduct his lecture along these lines and refuse any diversions. The problem is, of course, whether the material he is presenting is what the audience wants. But, taking this stance and approach, he has taken a prescriptive decision about what they want, what they should want, or, at the basic level, what they are going to receive, i.e. what the speaker himself wants to talk about.

The lecturer is in full control of the time In the more traditional highly structured courses time is at a premium. If a session extends beyond its allotted time, there is interference with the time available for the next session, with a possible knock-on effect throughout the day. The skilled lecturer will have divided his material into 'must know', 'should know' and 'could know', which he can adjust as the session progresses in order to finish exactly on time. The common complaint of a more liberal session speaker is that he was unable to get through all his material because the audience (following his earlier invitation) kept interrupting him with questions or raising points about what he had said. It follows that the speaker must determine his strategy of maintaining his time and material, or accepting that if he plays the session in a more informal way, he is not going to have time to ensure that all his material is used. This comes back to the decision of whether to produce what the *speaker* wants or what the *audience* wants.

All material is covered in a logical order The lecturer has prepared his material in advance and, in order to simplify the learning, will have arranged his material in such a way that the audience can follow the logical presentation, one point leading to the next. When this aspect is considered in relation to the control of time, the lecturer has ensured that he includes all his materials in the most effective way possible. One of the most interesting lecturers I have attended was also the most confusing. The lecturer presented eight or nine point none of which was related and each were treated independently. As a result, after the lecture I remembered the final subject and part of the penultimate one, but of the rest everything was forgotten.

A safe approach The lecturer is in complete control of time, material and presentation, and, provided he has some degree of capability, knows before the start of the session that all should go reasonably well. He will have presentation 'butterflies' at the start, and rightly so, but that is all the concern the session should give him. This is particularly so for new or inexperienced trainers who need to have as much as possible going for them. The controlled or mechanical approach can rarely be the most effective, but it is certainly better than the tyro trainer falling on his face by trying too soon a too adventurous approach.

Easy trainer replacement Again, this is not an advocated procedure, but on occasions accidents or illnesses occur and another trainer has to step in to take the same session with the same material. If the lecture is well prepared, any notes can be handed over, preferably giving the reserve trainer some time to acquaint himself with the format and the contents. As an absolute, final resort, the notes can even be read to the group.

Student safety This is one of the suspect advantages, although there is a benefit in protecting a group at some stage in its development. In the pure lecture approach, the lecturer is the only person present who is taking an absolutely active role; as discussed earlier, the activity or passivity of the group is in the hands of the group or individual, depending on the motivation.

DISADVANTAGES OF THE LECTURE

Any method or approach that has advantages will also have some disadvantages, and the considerate tutor will take account of these. Some of the disadvantages will become evident in the following cases.

The presentation is ineffective Above all, the lecturer must be an effective presenter. It is easy to say that interesting material will provide its own commitment, but even the most important, interesting and useful facts, opinions, views or feelings will negate their own value if they are presented in a boring, uninteresting way. The listener should be as skilled as the speaker, and many communication courses look closely at listening skills. These skills are aimed at helping the listener to take full advantage of what is being presented, to think about the material content rather than the way in which it is being presented, to discipline one's thinking by, for example, note taking, to consider the extension and implications of what is being said, and so on. The theory of this is excellent and some disciplined course members will practise these skills.

However, a group having to listen to a boring, inept speaker may not have had the benefit of this training and may switch off at an early stage. Result – little or no learning.

Repetition is encouraged Most trainers work, or should work, on the basic principle that every group appearing in front of them is different, has different needs and will react in a different way. But there is the danger that if a trainer produces a lecture that is well balanced and effective, he will be reluctant to make changes and risk the possibility of failure. So he continues to provide the same lecture over and over again, trapped in a rut of apparent success. However, he can become blind to the changing needs and attitudes of his audiences and become less and less effective.

The audience is passive This has been discussed earlier, but it must be emphasized since not only is the audience encouraged to be passive, but it may not wish to be so. A cultural change has been occurring over recent years in that course members no longer want to be passive, but wish to be involved as much as possible with the training event and control of their own learning.

Lack of feedback This is perhaps the main disadvantage. If the audience is not involved positively and, above all, verbally in the training session, the speaker receives no feedback on how his material is being received. Certainly some apparent feedback is given in the form of non-verbal behaviour, but this must be treated as highly suspect for non-verbal behaviour is notoriously inconsistent. A look of concentrated attention could be just that, but it could be merely a facade to cover other thoughts. A smile could suggest encouragement, but could otherwise disguise a malicious intent. Without real feedback the trainer has no knowledge not only of how his material is being received, but also whether learning is being achieved with a reasonable chance of retention. The absence of results of this nature means that the time spent in the 'training' may have been wasted, and even though this may not be so, the trainer will never know or will discover it too late.

The style of lecture discussed so far suggests the specific approach of the lecturer appearing, delivering his material and finishing at the allotted time. The simplest form of this approach is the after-dinner speech, many of which are very successful, but have limited value in training.

MAKING THE LECTURE LIVE

The simple lecture form, however, can be improved to become a more effective training approach. The basic modification is to make the verbal approach live rather than rely on the speaker's oral skills alone. The trainer should have the facilities to achieve this at his fingertips and modern methods offer a wide range of aids to the speaker. Some of these will be described in detail later and many of them transform the lecture into a completely different type of event. The aids can be summarized as:

- overhead projector and slides
- 35mm transparency projector and slides
- films
- chalkboard, flipchart or newsprint
- audio cassettes
- audio-visual packages
- video cassette recordings
- demonstrations, both behavioural and with practical teaching aids.

TIME FOR QUESTIONS AND DISCUSSION

The least sophisticated, though very effective, way of moving the lecture on to be a living event, is to involve the audience.

Once again there are a number of ways in which this movement can be achieved:

- leave time for questions and discussion at the end of the talk
- allow interruptions for questions during the talk
- allow interruptions for both questions and discussion during the talk.

Perhaps the least effective is the method of allowing a period of time at the end of the talk for questions and/or discussion. This, at least, gives the members of the audience the opportunity to participate, to clarify points of doubt, to express views of disagreement with what the speaker has said, or to build on the speaker's ideas. The speaker retains all the measures of control discussed earlier since he can arrange his material so that it is contained within the time allocated to the pre-question period. He can assess to some extent how well his contribution has been understood from the nature of the questions posed. The modification affords the speaker a low level of risk in view of the limited time that would normally be allowed. Certainly the speaker runs the risk of having some of his views challenged, but again time is the limitation and the risk is low. The principal danger is that at some stage during the talk, at least one individual may disagree violently with something the speaker has said. From that point in the talk he will probably not be listening, awaiting only the end of the talk and the question time.

Rather more effective, but also of more risk to the speaker, is an invitation given by the speaker for the audience to interrupt at any time to ask questions rather than retain these until the end. These can be questions of clarification or requesting the speaker to expand on a particular topic to make it more relevant or more clearly understandable. There has to be, of course, a good measure of rapport between the speaker and his audience, otherwise the audience may fell inhibited in questioning or may feel that there is a danger of interrupting the speaker's flow. The greatest risk, however, is to the speaker, and this concerns his control of time and material. The control is taken out of his hands and into those of his audience. He can restrict the flow of questions, but this must effectively defeat the purpose of opening out the lecture into something more meaningful than a straight lecture. There is a positive aspect as far as the speaker is concerned: the questions that come will give feedback to the speaker on the understanding of the material he is presenting, and also show that at least part of his audience is not asleep.

The most effective approach to the lecture method of training is undoubtedly a progression from the question invitation just described to, in addition, giving an opportunity for discussed disagreement with any points made, or general discussion about topics raised, at any time during the session. The control of time and material is consequently lost to the speaker, for, if discussion occurs, so much time can be used that by the end of the session the speaker has covered less than half the material he intended to introduce. Unless the session concerns procedural matters that must be explained, the failure to include everything is of little concern. The session has been active, the audience has been involved in a positive manner, and, most important as far as learning is concerned, the session material has been on topics and to the depth required by the audience. The discussion can be directed to some extent by the speaker who can pose leading questions, but the approach still retains many risks. Many schoolboys know the favourite game of leading teacher away from the subject; the speaker has to be skilled and experienced to control the persistent quibbler or the mini-discussions that can arise within the group. But this is all about being a trainer and one who feels that these risks are too great should stay with the straight input or 'questions at the end' methods.

The choice of approach must be that of the trainer/speaker and will depend on his preferred style, skill and experience. The attitude of the audience and other factors, such as its composition, must however be borne in mind in deciding the approach, for after all these are the people who matter most.

SIZE OF AUDIENCE

The size of the audience can be very important in selecting the most appropriate approach. Any speaker would be taking on an almost impossible task in attempting a participative session with an audience of 100 or more. He may tend to play safe with the straight input or even invite 'questions at the end'. The latter method can produce the problem that many speakers have experienced – the embarrassing silence at the end of the talk when the invitation is extended. The silence can continue to such an extent that all that is left for the speaker to do is to get up and go. Unfortunately one cannot assume that this silence means that no individuals in the audience are wanting to raise points; they can themselves be subdued by the size of the event.

USE OF BUZZ GROUPS

Some years ago I was invited to give a talk to a group of scientists. My briefing from the organizer was that I would be expected to speak for about an hour with time for questions at the end, any aids I required would be available, but, although I was told that the audience would be large, I was not told how large. What I was told, however, was not to expect many questions at the end, not because they would not be interested in what I had to say, but the cultural atmosphere inhibited questions (they were afraid to show ignorance in front of their peers or seniors!).

This was not my normal or preferred type of situation but I regarded it as a challenge and considered deeply how to make it a memorable event. The basic approach decided upon was to include as much controversial material as possible to encourage participation at the end – not too controversial though, to avoid being attacked by an alarming collection of intellect.

One method of which I had heard but had not used occurred to me and I decided to try it. After a welcome pre-talk meeting with the organizer I was conducted on to the stage to face at least 200 of these 'frightening' people. The talk was given, and at the end instead of inviting questions I suggested, with some trepidation, that before putting myself forward for questions, they were required to do something. They were asked to pull their chairs into groups of 10 or 12 and discuss what had been presented. They were also asked to produce questions they wished answered, within the groups, and questions would be responded to when raised by a spokesman from each group. The noise of 200 chairs being shuffled was tremendous and the auditorium soon looked as if a small explosion had occurred. After this initial noise, the noise level became even greater for 10 minutes or so (a welcome respite) as 20 groups or so released the thoughts of the previous hour. When they were finally called to order, the questions came fast and furious and, I seem to recall, only came to an end when the caretaker arrived and asked if we were going to be there all night.

The jargon term for this technique is 'buzz groups' and I have used such groups on many occasions since then, usually with similar effect. A single group of any size can be manipulated in this way, although there can be some constraints imposed by fixed seating; this can sometimes be overcome by asking the people to turn round to the row behind in sections, or to have them move bodily and produce standing buzz groups. Although the technique has been described in terms of large groups, it can be equally effective in smaller groups of say eight or 12 upwards. Such small groups are operated in the same way, preserving for the individuals the anonymity of the buzz group spokesman. This anonymity is the key factor of buzz groups and they can be particularly valuable at the start of a course when views are less likely to come into the open than later in the course when the individuals are no longer strangers.

Whatever the participative or passive approach, the success of the lecture method falls principally on the skill of the presenter and the input part of his presentation. A number of books exist on how a speaker or trainer can improve these skills. To describe the techniques in detail would be out of place here. However, the basic principles can be summarized as

- prepare fully
- consider the use of aids
- present in as effective a manner as possible

- use the aids efficiently
- obtain feedback on effectiveness and revise approach as necessary.

REFERENCES AND RECOMMENDED READING

A Training Officer's Guide to Discussion Leading. A.I.B. Debenham. BACIE, 1968.
Effective Presentation. Anthony Jay. British Institute of Management, 1970.
A Guide to the OHP. Len Powell. BACIE, 1961.
A Guide to the Use of Visual Aids. L. S. Powell. BACIE, 1961.
Lecturing to Large Groups. L. S. Powell. BACIE, 1966.
The Skills of Communicating. Bill Scott, Gower, 1986.
Effective Speaking. Cristina Stuart. Gower, 1989.
Tips on Talking. BACIE, 1960.
How to Communicate. Gordon Wells. McGraw-Hill, 1978.
The Floor is Yours, Now. Video, Gower, 1987.
The Audience is Yours, Now. Video, Gower, 1992.
How to Talk so People Listen. Sonya Hamlin. Thorsons, 1989.
Running an Effective Training Session. Patrick Forsyth. Gower, 1992.

3 Self-development

In contrast to the tutor-based, formal and highly structured lecture approach is an individual's attempts to achieve learning through some form of self-development. In the worlds of training and consultancy, many words have been spoken and written in the definition of development. Probably the simplest description, although not a purist one according to some, is that self-development is an all-embracing term. It can include self-instruction, self-learning and distance learning, but not the learning-community concept or groups engaged in development. In this description I prefer to consider self-development as a generally individual effort as opposed to learning in a group. This is not to deny that an individual who attends a self-development group, whether for skill development or for psychiatric reasons, is attending for personal developmental reasons. It is the means to this end that I wish to distinguish.

BLOCK TO SELF-LEARNING

Possibly the most difficult barrier to self-learning is the individual himself, principally for the same reasons discussed earlier when training overall was being considered. The initial criterion for self-instruction to succeed is the determination that a developmental or training need exists and that self-instruction is the most appropriate path. Some people have the critical ability to analyse their own needs; others require the intervention of a second party – this may be the individual's boss or an intervening development adviser. The entry of the adviser may be as a specific approach, or the result of the organizations's career development or appraisal scheme. Whether the need is shown from self-analysis or with the aid of another, there must be motivation. This is more likely to be present if self-analysis has occurred, as this action in itself demonstrates motivation.

Let us assume that motivation is present, or at least has been encouraged. The next barrier involves the ability of the individual to direct himself and his learning in a sufficiently disciplined way. Those who cannot discipline themselves, but still have developmental needs, can follow the group approach to learning.

Discipline may not be enough. The learner may have left school some time previously and may have lost any skill in self-study that he possessed. If the learner finds extreme difficulty in learning without others to lean on, he will become disillusioned with this form of learning and move away from any learning at all. Others have an innate need to learn in other ways; some need to have aspects explained to them by another real person (perhaps because of a learning laziness, perhaps because of psychological or physiological reasons); others look towards the medium of a well-produced film whereas others need to talk problems through with their peers.

Even if our motivated, self-disciplined, capable individual has decided that self-instruction is the most appropriate vehicle to satisfy his needs, there is still the procedural decision to take – which form of self-instruction will be the most effective one to follow?

LEARNING BY READING

The simplest form of self-instruction is the written word, such as a book that can be read at leisure and convenience. This form of learning can be private and at a pace determined by the learner. These are advantages, but of course there are disadvantages. The main one is that reading a book is essentially a passive activity and this very passivity can lull the reader into thinking that he is really reading whereas his eyes are taking in the words only. Most reader learners find that the reading can be made more effective if they are involved in a more active mode. Without involving others in a discussion about what has been read, which is the natural extension of individual reading, probably the most effective progression is some form of extraction or note-taking activity. Students at school, college and university are accustomed to this activity and use their notes to avoid having to read the textbooks again fully. Extracting requires, however, that the reading is at much more than the superficial level, for if key concepts or facts are to be identified and extracted, the reader must obtain a good grasp of what is being read.

A useful activity in assisting people to make a start in the extraction process is to ask them to review a magazine article of some substance that has already been reviewed by a capable reviewer. Once the review has been completed this can be compared with the expert review, not for differences in style or presentation, but to see whether the essential facts have been extracted by the learner. A similar exercise can give practice by the extraction of key elements from a report, as for example briefing documents for one's boss.

Extraction in the form of note-taking can be a valuable process, but the production of a sheaf of notes can be daunting. Even more so is having to read and re-read these notes to recall facts and views. Many students have failed in their studies because, faced with almost as many notes as the original text, they have not bothered reading them because the task is viewed with horror. Adult course participants are faced with the same problems on returning from courses with extensive textual notes of the sessions plus the almost inevitable stack of handouts, each consisting of several closely printed pages. The usual destination of both of these, unfortunately, is, at best, the desk drawer, whence they are rarely retrieved and read.

PATTERNED NOTE TAKING

Tony Buzan introduced a method of note taking intended to avoid the mass of words contained in the usual pack of notes; it is known as patterned notes, mind maps or spidergrams. The basis of the technique is that the brain does not work in a completely logical way, for instance in a vertical format starting at the top of the page and working down to the bottom, reading from left to right. The mind is much more chaotic, but within the apparent chaos a pattern can be identified. In traditional note taking the layout is of the vertical pattern, usually containing reasonably well-produced sentences or perhaps quite long phrases. Such notes can take up a lot of space, contain a considerable number of words, and have to be read for recall.

The patterned note takes us away from this regular, logical format and produces a record in a pattern that replicates the working of the mind. Because the note is directly related to the individual producing it, the patterns can take a variety of forms and to another person can be unintelligible and almost indecipherable. This is perfectly acceptable as notes are intended for the use of the note taker only in most cases.

A variety of formats can be used, the criterion being that they are meaningful to the note taker. Colours can be effective, as can symbols enclosing parts of the note, e.g. the key part of the note can be enclosed in the shape of a key. Arrows from one part of the note to another can link similar or related subjects. Symbols such as asterisks, exclamation marks, question marks and so on will highlight important parts of the note.

The most important aspect, however, in the construction of the note is the identification and summary of the key elements of the medium that is being noted, using words that are meaningful to the note taker. These key words or short phrases act as triggers to the memory and recall the more detailed aspects of the particular point.

Patterned notes of this nature, in addition to acting as an extraction record of a publication, can be used in a variety of other ways, including.

- recording a talk, lecture or training session
- recording a discussion
- preparation for the compilation of a report
- initial stages in the preparation of a talk or training brief
- actual brief for a talk or training session
- reminder notes for the stages of an exercise or activity.

A further use, employed in this particular instance, is in the preparation of an article or book. Before starting this book, I prepared a patterned note relating to the complete structure of the book, then patterns for each chapter. The patterned note for this chapter is shown in Figure 3.1.

A further advantage of this method of note taking is that the complete pattern of the talk, report or, as in this case, chapter, can be seen at a glance, usually on one page. Changes can be made easily and the relationship of one part with another can be seen readily.

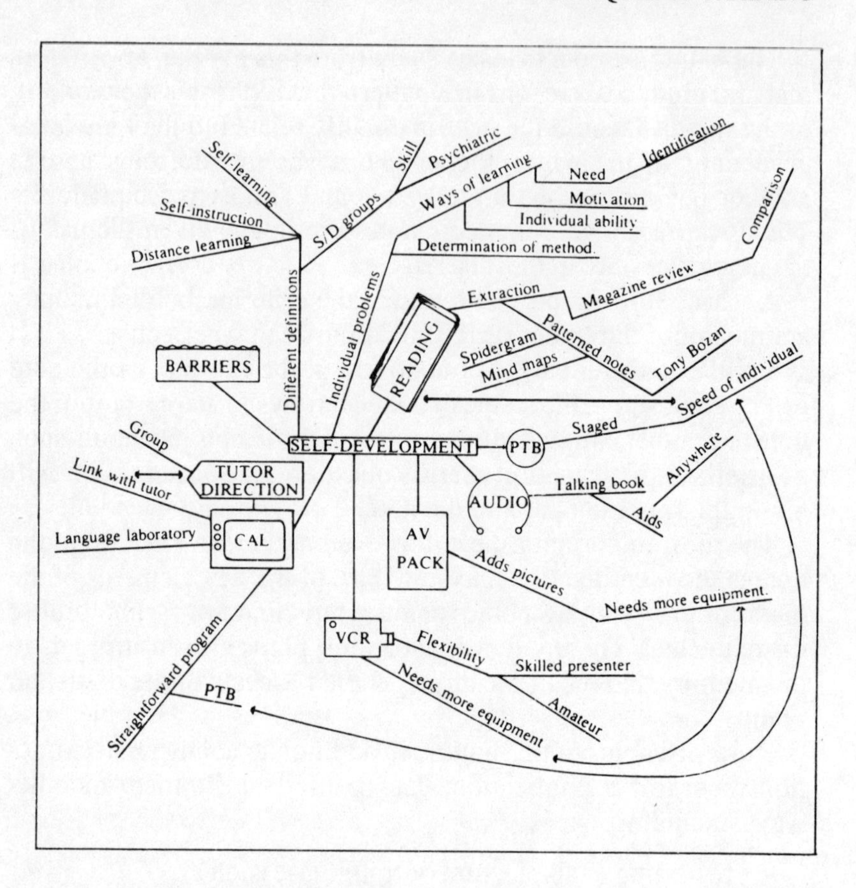

Figure 3.1 A patterned note

THE PROGRAMMED TEXTBOOK

A different form of book from the straightforward book of text is the programmed textbook (PTB). The PTB was designed especially for learning purposes and in particular for self-instruction. PTBs are most valuable in training in the more straightforward and procedural matters, including technical subjects. As with any other form of pure self-instruction, meeting other people is not necessary, but it is difficult to conceive behavioural training being conducted in a programmed textual mode.

The typical form of a PTB is the progression through the incremental stages of, say, a procedure or operation. When each new aspect or stage has been described, the reader is asked questions on the text. Commonly, alternative responses are given from which a choice has to be made. If the correct response is chosen, the reader has his choice confirmed with a reiteration of the basic information. If, however, the wrong choice is made, the learner is shown why it is the wrong response and is referred back to the part of the text where the correct information is given. The alternative choices are again offered and when the correct choice is made the reader passes on to the next stage, and in this manner progresses to the end of the PTB.

Problems can occur, of course, and in the extreme these could be fatal to learning by this method. The learner may stumble at a particular stage which may be complex and difficult to assimilate, even when the text is broken down into the smallest, simplest steps. He may be unable to grasp a concept or fact even with the simplest explanation in words or diagrammatic form possible, and so is unable to progress beyond that stage.

Such a difficulty suggests the danger of a learner trying to work through the PTB in complete isolation. If an insuperable difficulty arises, it is valuable if the learner has recourse to another source of information or help, such as an expert in the subject or a trainer skilled in both training and the subject. The problem can be resolved and the learner returns to the PTB. An interruption of this nature can, of course, be unsettling for the learner even with recourse to the aid, which can take time. The wise trainer or adviser who is helping the self-learning individual will ensure that effective back-up is readily to hand.

As an apparent contradiction, the self-learning facility of the PTB can be combined with a training course. Rather than use a traditional training method for a particular subject, the individuals in a group can work through the PTB under the watchful eye of a trainer. Used in this way the PTB aids training by taking advantage of one of the major helping facilities of this approach. A learner works through the PTB at his own pace, and as almost everybody has a different learning pace, no pressure is placed on the slower learners in the group. In the more traditional training methods an average approach has to be sought, one which allows the slower learners to keep up, yet keeps the faster learners still interested. This is difficult, as few groups are homogeneous as far as learning speed and skill are concerned.

The PTB has the same advantage as the conventional book in that it can be read almost anywhere, but, apart from the technical difficulty described, the barriers to learning discussed under conventional book learning apply equally to PTBs

AUDIO CASSETTES

The more modern approach to learning through reading is to use an audio cassette – the talking book. Lectures, demonstrations, exercises and so on can be recorded on audio tape either by a professional recording unit or by the training organization. In the former case, the cassette is usually on sale to everyone and is produced from material that has a general application. In-company productions can be custom-made and related, if necessary, to the specific nature of the job or organization.

Generally available cassettes can be purchased by an individual for his own use or by an organization for distribution as needed on a library basis. The locally produced unit is usually held on this library basis and is made available to students throughout the organization.

A considerable range of cassettes is now available and can be a useful source for the self-developing student who may not have the time to sit and read a book, or may have reduced or absent vision. Given a portable cassette player, the availability of the cassette is even greater than the book, as it can be played, for instance, in the car as the learner drives to and from work – a very effective way of using time normally wasted sitting in a traffic jam.

The principal disadvantage at one time used to be the necessity of having a cassette player, but these are fairly common household objects nowadays and a combined car radio-cassette player is now replacing a car radio alone.

There are problems in the use of audio cassettes for self-learning purposes. Essentially they can be considered to be simply the verbalization of the printed word and consequently have the same problems as books alone. Or they can be considered as a basic form of lecture without the visual aids or the opportunity to discuss the subject with an expert.

Although not completely relevant to the use of the audio cassette in self-instruction, it may be useful to consider at this point their other uses. When the lecture was being discussed, the use of aids to vary the presentation was commended. The audio cassette can be such an aid and may be usefully introduced as a pre-event study, during the actual session to vary the presentation, or as a follow-up to the learning event.

As a pre-event aid, for example, the cassette can be used to prepare the students for what may be a complicated learning event, or to provide the initial stages of the subject so that the learning can proceed from a more advanced point. Its use in this way can help to produce at the start of a course a group that is at a common stage of knowledge. The problems that can arise from this type of use may include a failure to carry out the required listening, or the potential students may feel that the subject is too complicated for them to continue the learning.

When the cassette is used during the training event, it can interrupt the solo performance of the trainer in the most appropriate way by introducing a change of pace, voice and presentation medium. It can be particularly useful when an important or complex point has to be conveyed, since the words and logical progression can be planned and recorded in advance for maximum impact. The pressure is also taken off the live trainer, although obviously not the responsibility.

The audio cassette can also be extremely valuable following a session or course to summarize the learning material, to set progressive projects for the student or to guide him into more advanced studies.

The main problem with audio cassettes is the difficulty many people have in sitting listening to words without a face on which to concentrate. Many cassettes are produced with either a transcript of the tape that can be followed as the tape is playing, or work books that require activities at stages of the tape. Such aids act as the missing centre of attention, in addition to making the listening active rather than passive.

AUDIO-VISUAL PACKAGES

An effective centre of attention is provided in the extension of the audio cassette; this is the audio-visual package. In addition to the audio cassette itself and any supporting scripts or work books, the pack includes a number of 35mm transparencies. These slides are intended to be projected at the same time that the cassette is being played. There must be some indication when the slides have to be changed at the correct point of the tape. This can be a cue marking included in the accompanying script, showing at which points the slides must be changed. This ensures that the learner in fact follows the script and listens intently to the tape. Two other methods can also be used to ensure correct slide changing, usually in conjunction with the script cues. The simplest is the addition to the tape of an audible signal in the form of a note. Unfortunately, if the audio-visual pack is being used by a group, the signal is also audible to the group and can become an annoyance. It also means that any error in the slide changing upsets the sequence.

The most effective and least troublesome method of ensuring efficient slide changing is the inclusion on the tape of an inaudible pulse that operates the slide projector automatically. A 1 kHz pulse is transmitted from the cassette player along a line to the slide projector. When producing one's own tapes, the procedure for adding pulses is simple if the relevant equipment is available. This introduces the principal problem in using an audio-visual package, namely the availability of equipment that is capable of using the inaudible pulse. However, such equipment is reasonably available, either in the form of a linked synchronizing cassette player and projector, or as an integrated system, or a normal cassette player and slide projector plus a separate synchronizer.

Although commercially produced audio-visual packages are available for a variety of subjects or purposes, it is relatively simple for a pack to be produced in-house at minimum cost, to satisfy organizational objectives and needs. Recently I produced such a package with a 25-minute audio cassette, thirty-six 35mm slides and supporting work books on the subject of Behaviour Analysis.

The cost of such a production is minimal. There is the cost of film for slides and the cost of developing and mounting the cost of audio cassettes and the cost of any supporting text or work books. There are also, of course, the implied costs of equipment use, time and personal expertise, but these would normally be available in any training organization. The finished product is not necessarily fully professional, although I have experienced some commercial products which were not up to an acceptable standard. However, a product can be made relatively quickly and for relevant use, whereas there might be some delay in having one made commercially or finding a suitable one on the shelf.

Another advantage of the home-grown variety is that it is quicker and simpler to modify as circumstances eventually change.

VIDEO CASSETTE RECORDINGS

Even more flexible and indeed easier to use than the audio-visual package is the video cassette recording (VCR). Although the VCR is similar in many ways to the audio cassette or the AV package, it has the advantage of combining a variety of techniques:

- a speaker as the main centre of attraction
- visual displays of moving models or other aids
- live demonstrations of techniques, either by the main speaker or supporting role players.

In the same way that equipment availability can be a problem with audio cassettes or AV packages, so it can be with the VCR. However, VCR playing equipment is becoming more common, and trends suggest an even greater availability. Again, VCRs can be purchased as professional productions or can be home-made to satisfy specific training needs. The main danger of which the trainer should be aware is the direct substitution of a VCR lecturer alone for a live lecturer – in most cases the latter has more learning impact. However, the VCR technique allows the use of many more and varied aids than can be crowded into a live training classroom.

Many of these approaches can be included in the term 'Distance Learning' which is usually intended to imply that the learner need not travel to a training centre to receive his training, but will work on the learning events at home or work. It is obviously a synonym for self-learning and instruction and can be viewed as an extension of this, but can also involve a trainer at the centre as facilitator.

CORRESPONDENCE COURSES

Probably the simplest form of distance learning is the correspondence course, in which the learner completes required reading and research, followed by exercises on the stage reached. The learning is controlled by a centrally based tutor who confirms, or otherwise, the student's progress and sends him the next lesson. Original correspondence courses used the written word as the correspondence medium. Modern courses can involve the use of all the media discussed so far, in addition to records, static visuals such as photographic prints, and specific research projects. The zenith of the present stage of distance learning is the Open University, in which there is a considerable amount of home self-study of textual material, linkage with a tutor, research and project work, television programmes specially produced for OU courses and occasional periods on campus with the course tutor. Whatever the level of the distance medium, the basic personal problems still remain, even though there may often be a monetary motivation and contact with the tutor from a distance.

COMPUTER AND LANGUAGE LABORATORIES

What is required to maintain a self-instruction mode is direct and immediate access to a mentor. Computers may be the solution to at least the mentor availability problem.

COMPUTER-BASED TRAINING

During the 1980s the training world has seen a great increase in computer applications to training being offered. Perhaps the take-up has not quite matched the offering because not every trainer or training department has a computer or access to one, and when the technique is applied to self-development through self-learning, the individual may have even less opportunity to avail himself of a computer. However, progress and developments have taken place, and the economic situation has often made organizations consider whether alternative forms of training to those existing may be more viable. The caveat must be given, as in the case of all 'discrete' forms of training, that one approach to training will not suit every learner and even less cost-effective learning may result if one method is introduced to the exclusion of all other alternatives. These remarks certainly apply to computer-based training (CBT) if it is considered on its own as the complete answer to the economics and processes of training.

Although CBT is not the panacea for all training ills, its introduction has perhaps been delayed somewhat for a number of reasons. Computers are usually introduced or offered by enthusiasts and this over-enthusiasm has often frightened trainers and organizations. The widespread use of and familiarity with computers has not been with us for very long – perhaps it still has a long way to go – and trainers may either be frightened of the computer itself; and/or suspicious of its introduction because it may be seen as yet another training approach which will reduce their control of the training situation, or even threaten their jobs.

Many of these fears can be allayed if trainers become more aware of the relative ease of working with computers and applied training programmes, and appreciate the advantages *and* disadvantages of computer systems.

The benefits of CBT The main benefits offered by CBT to trainers are as follows.

1. The trainee does not have to wait for a viable number of trainees to appear before a training event can be mounted. It is therefore almost available on demand. If a new training demand arises, there is often a considerable delay between this realization, the time taken for the training department to construct an effective training programme, the administration to set up and complement the training event(s), and all the other necessary adjuncts of a live training programme.

   If the training is available on a computer program, is suitable for learning by this medium and the learner(s) have computers available, the training can be provided almost immediately, which simplifies matters.
2. In most cases training time is reduced. In group training activities, the trainer has to pitch the training at a lower level than required by a number (often the greater number) of the participants. This has obvious consequences. If the learner is studying as an individual, using a flexible CBT programme, he can pace his progress to suit his own knowledge and skills. This is a common feature of what we can describe as open or self-learning systems whether computer-based or not.

3. The training is taken to the learner, rather than the other way round. The traditional way can cause difficulties of release, cost of travelling and accommodation, replacement while the learner is absent from work and so on. A further advantage, which is linked to the learner's choice of pace, is that the programme need not necessarily be followed in one session or consecutive sessions. The programme structure may allow it to be taken in sections, at intervals on a part-time basis. This in itself could help both the learning and the availability of the learner.
4. There is a higher degree of consistency than with exposure to live trainers. There are good trainers, bad trainers, and those in between; each trainer will present the same material in a different way – some ways will be effective, others will not. Each trainer has a different level of knowledge – if the level is sufficient for the learner all is well, but if it is not problems can arise. Many trainers have different attitudes to the topics for which they are responsible – some may be biased, others have twisted views on the subject and so on. The CBT programme is at least consistent every time it is run – it is hoped that it is consistently 'correct'.

The disadvantages of CBT

1. Problems of availability of the relevant computer or any computer at all have already been discussed. This situation should improve with the installation of a wide range of computers in commerce and industry, but it may still be a problem for some potential learners.
2. If there is a computer program available from the learning topic, it will have only a limited degree of flexibility. This may mean that the learner may have to make considerable jumps in relating the material to his own circumstances, especially if other support is not available.
3. Not every subject can be learned by means of a CBT programme. Many, where the basis is the acquisition of knowledge, or knowledge from which skill can come, are very suitable for CBT application. In general, however, learning areas which have a high degree of human resource interaction are not usually very suitable. In cases such as this, the learning often demands actual interaction

under controlled circumstances with a group of other people, which is not normally associated with CBT. However, and this supports the argument that few training techniques can stand alone, if the CBT programme is linked with a short (short because of the prior learning) training event where the skills learned in theory can be put into practice, there can be a successful marriage of techniques. The use of the CBT programme in prior learning for a training event not only reduces the length of the event, but also helps to ensure that the learners are all at the same learning level.

4. You cannot argue with a computer. Most CBT programmes are inflexible and produce what is from the programme author's point of view the 'right' answer. In many cases this is no problem, but problems do arise for the learners if they disagree with the point made in the programme and/or do not understand the points made, however many times the programme is played. The disadvantages here are the absence of a live group with which to discuss the problems, or the absence of a live trainer with whom to discuss the problem or have its meaning clarified. (This problem can be overcome to some extent if the learner has access, perhaps by phone if not in person, to a trainer.)

The trainer of the 1990s has to accept that there is a CBT application and, whatever the end decision, the trainer should develop an awareness of what CBT is and what it can and cannot do, bearing in mind the advantages and disadvantages described above. With the existing and future programmes, linked as necessary with other forms of learning suited to the subject, the environment and the learner's learning style, the range and success of training can be greatly extended.

The conclusion in the training world at present is that, for certain purposes, in certain circumstances and for certain individuals, CBT has a developing place in training. However, progress in its use is at a crossroads and trainers in general have widely differing views.

First, trainers are at the stage of exploring with enthusiasm the potential of the opportunities available with the new technology. These enthusiasts are principally seeking the most effective range of ways in which technology can make training more enjoyable and enlightening. This group is already familiar with the hardware available and in many cases can compare the different computers, as well as produce an increasing range of software and programs. These trainers use the technology at every opportunity, not only to help the learning opportunities of the trainee, but also to demonstrate to management and other trainers the advantages of the developments. They must, however, be careful that their enthusiasm does not take over completely and make them fall into the trap that CBT is *the* training answer.

Even more trainers are still in the early courtship stages, wanting to develop new personal skills and learning methods for their trainees, but very apprehensive about the new technological advances. The more they learn, the more applications appear. But the addition of this technology to the trainer's toolkit still seems to have a high risk factor for them, apart from the expense. This group can with benefit meet members of the first group and interface with their enthusiasm, at the same time retaining controlled scepticism, and also take every opportunity to see and have hands-on experience of the materials available.

A large body of trainers falls between the first two types, having a strong personal commitment to the use of the technology, although perhaps not to the extent of the first group. However, they are not being allowed to progress by the organization for which they work, perhaps because of:

- doubt by the organization of the value of the methods
- restrictions in the availability of the organization's existing hardware
- the organization's refusal to invest in computers for training and/or company work.

All that this group can do, if its members are really motivated to introduce the technology, is by various means to obtain as much experience as possible with the range of material available so that they can submit a strong case to their organization. They can, of course, move to an organization which is more in tune with the way they wish to work!

A fourth major group is the training world equivalent of the dinosaurs, the Luddites or simple reactionaries, who tend to claim, without any real knowledge or understanding, that the approach is valueless, want to have no knowledge of it, and are obviously hoping that it will simply go away. It may well be that, like many other approaches which have sprung up over the years, it is not the panacea for all training ills. But, go away it will not, and any trainer who takes this ostrich-like attitude is courting disaster for their training and their own careers.

The language laboratory is a natural extension to the completely individual programme. Although the learner is using the programme in a laboratory with a group of other learners, individuality and self-controlled progress are still retained. Each individual is linked to the tutor who can intervene to raise points or to assist with difficulties encountered. The natural extension to this approach is for the learners to have a computer and programme available anywhere in the country, at home, in the office or works, or in a training centre. The computer outputs would be linked to a central computer with which problems could be raised, either completely computerized or with the supplement of a human mentor. The variations on this theme are many, and as computerization develops so will the opportunities for this approach.

Many of the better distance learning approaches involve a number of different methods within the learning. One example of a tailor-made approach is a training package with which I have been associated. This was concerned with a numeracy and statistical appreciation programme, aimed basically at self-instruction but linked with a more involved assistance. The process begins with a self-applied diagnostic test using an instrument designed to cover the widest possible range of knowledge. Once the training needs of each individual have been determined from the diagnostic test, discussion with the learner about his needs takes place. This discussion involves the diagnosed needs, any other criteria that must be taken into account, such as job or organization requirements, in addition to those of the individual, and the possible ways of meeting the needs.

The discussions determined the specific learning needs of the individuals, who were then approached by tailored programmed learning with the constant support of the centre-based tutor. In the case of one group of learners, all located in one city, the guiding tutor was able to pay occasional visits to resolve particularly tricky problems. Many of the self-instructional approaches discussed so far were used, the particular type of approach being decided before the training began. The success of the approach was monitored during the self-instruction and in some instances the method was changed to suit the individual's emerging learning methods.

Once the learners had individually mastered their programmes, they came together for a practical workshop, facilitated by the tutor. This event was used to clarify any final problems, but as all the learners came from one organization, it was mainly used to discuss and plan the practical application of the learning to their work.

BARRIERS TO SELF-LEARNING

A description of some of the possible self-development activities that can take the place of more formal methods of training has been given. However, these activities can never completely replace other approaches to learning in view of the natural barriers that exist. Temporal (in *Management Self-development: Concepts and Practices*) summarizes these barriers as follows:

- Perceptual – the learner may have limited vision as to his personal needs and the resources available
- Cultural – he may have been programmed through past experience to look for traditional training methods
- Emotional-motivational – the learner may have a fear of failure or ridicule
- Intellectual – the individual does not believe learning to be an ongoing activity
- Environmental – risk-taking may not be encouraged in his working climate.

REFERENCES AND RECOMMENDED READING

Effective Leadership. A Self-Development Manual. John Adair. Gower, 1985.

Management Self-Development. T. Boydell and M. Pedler. Gower, 1981.

Use your Head. Tony Buzan. BBC Publications, 1974.

Make the Most of Your Mind. Tony Buzan. Pan, 1988.

The Seven Keys to Super-Efficiency. Winston Fletcher. Sidgwick and Jackson, 1988.

How to Get Control of Your Time and Your Life. Alan Lakein. Gower, 1985.

How to Assess your Management Style. Dr Charles Margerison. MCB Publications Ltd, 1979.

A Manager's Guide to Self-Development. M. Pedler, J. Burgoyne and T. Boydell. McGraw-Hill, 1978.

Interactivity: Designing and Using Interactive Video. M. Piocotto, I. Robertson and R. Colley. Kogan Page, 1989.

The Open Learning Handbook. Phil Race. Kogan Page, 1989.

Management Self Development: A Practical Manual for Managers and Trainers. Manpower Services Commission, 1981.

4 Training at work

'Here's t'new lass, Fred. Put her alongside Nellie to learn how to do t'job.'

The indomitable Nellie has been invoked many times through the ages in the name of training, but nowadays tends to be neglected in favour of more sophisticated approaches. But in almost every case, most of what people learn takes place at work, while they are actually working. It is usually admitted that a training course was interesting and useful and 'taught me something, but where I really learned was when I got back to work and had to do it'. The ideal situation would be to link the training activity with the actual work in the workplace, not the simulated work environment of a training course.

The simplest approach to training at work is expressed in the quotation at the start of this chapter from the northern mill boss to his foreman, when a new girl reports on her first morning of work. There is no doubt that this system worked, although perhaps not as efficiently or as quickly as it might have done, and the evidence is the flourishing textile industry in Britain during the nineteenth and early twentieth centuries when formal instruction was virtually unknown.

At its most basic, the approach involves the learner sitting beside an experienced worker, watching the relevant operations. If 'Nellie' was a helpful person, she would describe what was being done, though rarely why it was being done. The learner would sit in this way until Nellie felt that sufficient had been observed to allow the learner to try. Usually mistakes would be made and Nellie would take over again as demonstrator, then a second attempt would be permitted. The trial and error process was continued until the learner had acquired the basic skills and was ready to go it alone – or go.

The process could be helped if the trainer could also explain to the learner why a particular operation was done and in what way it was, and perhaps some other explanations about where the operation fitted into the complete work scheme. With the introduction of more structured approaches to this type of training, 'Nellie' became respectable.

It would be ideal if trainers skilled in instructional techniques could take the place of all the 'Nellies', but obviously this is out of the question in view of the many operational skills the trainer would have to master. So skilled operatives must be given specific instructional technique skills to become what is generally known as desk trainers. The desk trainer is basically a skilled worker who is allocated to the training function when a trainee arrives.

The advantages of this training approach are many, particularly in smaller organizations without a substantial training department and where new entrants are not too frequent. The training takes place in the real-life atmosphere in which the trainee is destined to work, on work that can be operational rather than mock-ups or simulations. The desk trainer has complete credibility as he is known to be a skilled worker. There are few financial requirements, compared with training courses where additional expenses are certain to be involved.

There are some disadvantages, the main one being that the desk trainer is given the skills of the trainer. Appropriate facilities may not always be readily available. Operational pressures can arise at any time with consequent interruption of the training. When the disadvantages can be overcome, desk training can be very effective, and indeed can be linked with the self-development approaches discussed in Chapter 3. The basic desk-training approach has in fact been discussed earlier, as the Tell, Show, Do method.

Let us consider the case of a newly appointed machinist in a light clothing factory which operates an effective desk-training approach. Once the new entrant has been welcomed by the manager of the department in which she will be employed, a period of induction to the company is commenced. This will vary from one organization to another, but will commonly include a familiarization with the premises and in particular the training/work area; instruction in the company's procedures relating to payments of wages, sickness and other absences and so on. An introduction to safety measures will be included, to be built on during the actual training.

An introduction to the desk trainer and transfer of the trainee from the manager or supervisor to the trainer takes place. A tour of the department is a natural first move, with a full description of the company product, not only for the department's function but the complete assembly, followed by an introduction to the machine that the learner will be operating.

From this point the Tell, Show, Do approach comes into its own. The trainer describes the operation of the machine, gives it a dummy run to show how it works, and then the learner tries the operation several times until she is familiar with it. The process is then repeated with a paper pattern inserted in the machine and the Tell, Show, Do is repeated with this pattern to demonstrate, for example, how a row of stitches is made. The learner practises this operation until the trainer is satisfied, then the training passes on to more difficult stitching, up to the most complex that will be required in the immediate work. Once the required skill is attained on the paper patterns, the process is repeated with scraps of material from the production run. Each new level of skill is presented by the trainer in the established method and eventually the learner is considered sufficiently skilled to move on to production. This will probably not be the full production line, since, although skill has been acquired, speed has not, so in many establishments there is a trainees' corner where the progress of the trainees can be supervised by the trainer until they are ready to progress to full production work.

Although the training described here has been for a practical operation, roughly the same procedure would be adopted for any occupational training – clerical, reception, commercial machine operating and so on. Obviously this approach will work best with operations of a relatively routine, repetitive nature, although the principles can be applied to a high level of complexity.

COACHING

The other main form of training and development that takes place in the work situation is the coaching of an individual by or in association with his boss. As with the less complex desk training, coaching utilizes work and work events as the vehicles for development and occurs principally at the workplace. However, other forms of training can be included in the overall coaching plan, but the main feature of coaching is that it is a real event, using real work and involving the learner's own boss.

Coaching is a multi-purpose approach and can be used for:

- remedial training. Although a member of staff may have received basic training in the skills needed to perform his duties and has had some experience, the required level of performance is not being attained.
- new or extended duties. An individual may be required to extend his skills beyond the normal range or to take on new work and will require progressive assistance to meet these enhanced demands.
- career development. A skilled and efficient worker may be on the point of promotion or may need job enhancement to stretch his abilities and ensure continued job satisfaction.
- consolidation of other training. A training event away from work is not an end in itself and almost invariably requires a follow-through in the workplace to ensure translation of the training to work and the use of the new skills. Often good training is condemned as having failed when the real cause is the lack of opportunity or encouragement to put the training into practice.
- a total learning event. In this case it is felt that sufficient skill exists within the area of work to train an individual rather than send him on a training course.

These are some of the occasions when coaching can be introduced, although it must be admitted that the method is commended more than it is practised. For example, in the last case, it is obviously easier for the learner to be sent on a training course, all responsibility being abdicated by the boss. It may be that coaching is more expensive in resource time than a course, but there can be little doubt that, because of its direct work relationship, its impact can be greater.

COACHING TECHNIQUES

One personal experience as a coach will describe the basic approach to coaching and its techniques. During the time that I was manager of a group of trainers, one of the group was developing in such a way that his skills needed to be extended in other directions in order to round his overall capabilities, prepare him for promotion and stretch him in a way that would also increase his job satisfaction.

The first step was to arrange a discussion with the individual to consider what might be done and agree a method of achieving movement. During this discussion it was confirmed that although he had never shone at formal report writing, this was an area of work that attracted him although he had had little opportunity to perform this type of work. Also if he were to progress in the organization this type of work would be required more often.

All these aspects were agreed, as was the decision to produce a coaching plan to try to satisfy these needs. Terminal objectives were also agreed so that the plan could be reviewed objectively. It was agreed to hold a further meeting a week later. During the interim period both would consider the problem and prepare provisional solutions to be discussed. This second discussion comprised presenting alternative solutions, considering each of them fully, and producing a complete plan of action – the coaching plan.

The agreed plan included as a starting point the attendance of the individual on a training course in report writing that was known to provide the required level of training. However, immediately before attending the course, a pre-course briefing meeting was held to consider together what the trainee should be particularly looking for during the course. This was based on the trainee's personal objectives linked with the particular needs of the organization.

The course was attended and, as previously agreed, a meeting was held immediately to discuss it, the learning achieved, and more importantly, the action plan completed at the end of the course. This action plan was modified by agreement to relate to the specific means of achieving the coaching objectives.

Course follow-up was satisfied by agreement that:

- his tutorial time would be reduced
- reports and papers that I was required to complete as part of my own duties would be passed to him for initial drafting
- the drafts produced would be discussed thoroughly and guidance would be given with the required style and construction

- when he had reached the necessary standard, certain reports would be allocated to him as his responsibility.

Specific review dates, in addition to the continuing discussions on drafts, were also arranged during which progress and problems would be considered, the latter being solved jointly if necessary.

This project was highly successful, but it was assisted considerably by motivation on the part of the trainee and willingness on my part to use a large proportion of my time in helping his development. The motivation and commitment may not, of course, always be present, particularly in the case of remedial coaching. This will mean that the initial discussion will place demands on the coach's counselling, consulting and persuading skills to move the individual to the point where he feels an equal need for development and commitment to taking action.

Demands are also placed on the coach, in addition to the expenditure of his time. He must have both the skills of coaching which include counselling, consulting and persuading skills, and some expertise in the topic involved. However, apart from using the training course expertise, other people with specific skills and experience can usefully be brought in to supplement the coach. He must also have the determination and discipline to see the project through, as nothing could be more disastrous than the coach losing interest before the end of the project. Of course, accidents can occur, with either or both the coach and trainee leaving the work location during the project on transfer or termination.

The trainer or training adviser can have an important part to play in a coaching programme and the working together of the trainer and coach has much to commend it.

At times the boss can be too close to his staff to identify any real problems and the experienced trainer or adviser with his skills in the identification of training needs can be invaluable. The wise trainer waits until he is invited to intervene, or does so with tact. With a welcomed entry, the trainer can suggest the topics for coaching or the methods by which the objectives might be achieved. The potential coach may not have the skills to perform his responsibilities and the trainer can obviously help to train the coach as necessary.

Finally, the trainer can support the coach during the programme as a guide or counsellor when problems arise. Again his interventions must be tactful and preferably by invitation. He is in a position to provide information about special courses that may be necessary and may be the valuable intermediary in obtaining specialists and experts to supplement the coach.

PROJECTS

Similar to the coaching approach is a project programme. In many organizations with a well-defined management structure new appointments are made of people who are identified as having a potential for progress to high management levels – the management trainee. Existing managers or supervisors may be identified as having this or similar potential, but may require long-term development for them to achieve it. Other developmental needs may require a coaching approach, but may need activities of a longer duration than a normal coaching programme. These types of situation call for a special approach which can usually be met by a project assignment programme.

Coaching programmes involve the trainee in performing more routine tasks, albeit not the normal tasks of the individual. In project assignments particular tasks are identified as projects intended to test the trainee and stretch his capabilities. The trainee may be attached to a particular department and given a project related to the work of that department. The task could be a survey of attitudes, methods or procedures, perhaps where there has been the intention to do this task, but its performance has been prevented for some reason. The project could involve the trainee investigating some aspect of the department by looking at the work with a lateral approach rather than being bounded by the existing traditional methods or attitudes.

Project assignment can be a powerful developmental approach, but requires skilful setting up on the part of the training officer responsible for the trainee's development. The trainer must have the full backing of the organization's senior management, which will be reflected throughout the departments in which the projects will be performed. He must also ensure that the departmental management and staff understand the reasons for the project approach: this, in many cases, may place strong demands on his own skills of consulting, persuading and negotiating. The trainee must have ready access to the trainer to discuss problems that may arise and this will introduce the need for counselling and guidance skills on the part of the trainer. Preparation for the start of a project and the trainee's own skills and knowledge must be identified. If the trainee has needs, these must be satisfied before the projects are commenced and a regular review process will have to be initiated.

These aspects of mounting projects for developmental purposes are obviously expensive in time and money, but are fully justifiable when it is remembered that the organization is planning for the future senior management.

Training at work can therefore be conducted at many levels within a organization, not just at the lower, routine work levels. There is strong evidence that many people learn more easily and effectively when their training is linked directly with their work. It also places heavy demands on the organization while it is trying to conduct its operations, which may in some instances be intolerable.

It also appears that for some people an 'at work' approach may not be suitable. Unfortunately, although subscribing to the value of this form of developmental approach, some organizations consider the effort too great and take the 'easy way out' by sending people requiring training on a training course. This may indeed be the answer in a number of cases, but other options should be considered.

REFERENCES AND RECOMMENDED READING

A Manager's Guide to Coaching. D. Megginson and T. Boydell. BACIE, 1979.

Coaching for Results. Leslie Rae. Industrial Society, 1987.

Effective Management Coaching. Edwin J. Singer. IPM Publishing, 1979.

Developing Managers as Coaches. Frank S. Salisbury. McGraw-Hill, 1994.

A Guide to In-Company Training Methods. Leslie Rae. Gower, 1992.

Multi-media Computer Assisted Learning. Edited by Philip Barker. Kogan Page, 1989.

Interactivity: Designing and Using Interactive Video. Michael Picciotto, Ian Robertson and Ray Colley. Kogan Page, 1989.

Coaching, Mentoring and Assessing. Eric Parsloe. Kogan Page, 1992.

One-to-one Training and Coaching Skills. Roger Buckley and Jim Caple. Kogan Page, 1991.

5 Learning in groups

Although many people use non-training course approaches to learning and development involving self-instruction or training at work, probably more people attend training courses for these purposes. The basic training course involves the bringing together of a group of people for a communal approach to learning. The event offered to the group can range over a wide spectrum, which includes at one extreme the basic lecture approach, through a variety of group activities, to the completely experiential group event.

The purpose of this chapter is to describe the more common training approaches that use group association; later chapters will show the more unusual or advanced techniques.

ADVANTAGES AND DISADVANTAGES

The main advantages of calling a group together for training are that:

- it is the most cost-effective method of training a large number of people with a common training need
- other people are present with whom problems can be discussed, experiences exchanged and ideas supported
- a trainer or specialist can present new ideas or techniques to as large an audience as possible.

Naturally there are problems and disadvantages, as well as advantages, with this type of approach and among these should be mentioned:

- the different learning speeds of a heterogeneous group which is normally forced to progress at a compromise rate

- the possibility that not all the members of the group have a similar motivation to learn, and some may not even want to take part in the learning event
- the fact that although many group learning activities require active participation of all members, some may have personal barriers that restrict their involvement. This will minimize the possible learning not only of the members who do not take part, or do so only minimally, but also the remainder of the group.

INTRODUCTIONS

When the course is ready to start, the introductions can take many different forms (see the book list at the end of this chapter). Some of these are simple introductions, but others involve other skills – interviewing, listening, presenting, summarizing, checking understanding, influencing, negotiating, coping with conflict and so on.

One example of these introductions is known as 'Progressive Group Introduction'. The process starts with the new training group being divided into pairs and given the brief to find out as much as possible about each other in *x* minutes. *What* they find out is left to the delegates and no indication is given about any subsequent activity. Many delegates who have attended previous, more traditional courses, assume that they will have to introduce their partners to the rest of the group.

However, instead the pairs are formed into fours and the 'interviewer' has to introduce his partner within that group. So pairs A–B, C–D, E–F, G–H, I–J and K–L in a training group of 12 become three groups of four – ABCD, EFGH, IJKL. Consequently, in each four, all delegates have been introduced to three others.

The next stage produces two groups of six each in which the original pairs are separated and the fours are divided among the groups of six – ACEGIK, BDFHJL. In these sixes, one member will introduce to the others another member *who has been introduced to them (not one they have interviewed).* So in group ACEGIK, A will introduce C, and C, A; E will introduce G, and G, E; and so on.

This process can be shown in summary form.

A introduces B and C	B introduces A and D
C introduces D and A	D introduces C and B
E introduces F and G	F introduces E and H
G introduces H and E	H introduces G and F
I introduces J and K	J introduces I and L
K introduces L and I	L introduces K and J

It will be seen that everybody has been introduced twice, so that everybody else in the group has heard the introduction. But the activity is not only about introductions: it is about listening to others' introductions, practising recall of information, presenting information in an accurate and acceptable manner, interviewing to obtain information, interacting with others, interacting with strangers, possibly leading a group or being an effective member of a group and so on.

The group events to be described will exclude the more passive groups involved in the lecture approaches, but will concentrate on activities that require the group to interact in the learning process. However, one simple group activity was discussed with the lecture approach to large audiences – the use of buzz groups. Of course, buzz groups are not restricted to large groups only and can be valuable in a variety of group situations.

BUZZ GROUPS

The natural follow-up to many group activities is that the trainer discusses the activity with the group members, concentrating on either the task or the process, or sometimes even attempting both. A main aim of the trainer is that the group should provide most of this discussion. But, particularly in the very early stages of a course, the course participants may be unable or unwilling to express themselves openly. It is possible that in these early stages the barriers are too strong to permit individuals to express views which are critical of themselves or others in the group, or the way the group has performed the task. At a later stage in the course this is more likely to happen as open relationships develop. A buzz group can allow an individual to retain anonymity in the group, since the buzz group's spokesperson will express a group view, not an individual one. However, any individual can also express a personal view during the full group discussion, if he wishes to do so.

I have used the buzz group method with as few as six, dividing into two buzz groups of three people. This approach was used following the first activity of an experiential course in which it was necessary to encourage the participants to involve themselves in open discussion at an early stage. During the full group discussion that followed, comments were made on group and individual performance that would have been much less likely if the full group had entered discussion immediately after the activity. In fact, the immediate full group discussion approach had been the norm until that particular course, and buzz groups were introduced because of the group inhibitions experienced. The previous method was never revived.

PROBLEM-SOLVING GROUPS

The traditional form of groups on a course is often known as 'syndicate work'. This is simply dividing the course members into a number of smaller groups or syndicates, for the purpose of considering a case study or engaging in a problem-solving activity. The term 'syndicate' is nowadays synonymous with group and many trainers use either term at will.

It may be useful to consider at this stage the uses for which groups are formed. The usual reason is to provide an opportunity to practise a problem-solving technique that has just been discussed with the trainer. Each group is given the same problem to solve, in which case the plenary, or full group, discussion is based on the different ways the problem was approached or the different solutions obtained. Alternatively, each group may be given a different problem, in which case the plenary discussion will centre around the method of approach. The trainer has options in the stance he can take during the plenary session. He can act as an 'agent provocateur' by having the groups challenge each other's results and methods and allowing them to come to a comprehensive decision – but he must be prepared for and skilled in settling little more than a fight between the groups. He can act as the adjudicator in the differences between the groups, but must anticipate that the members of at least one group will reject his arbitration and his credibility as mentor of the course. Another approach is to try to balance the different views expressed to a common conclusion.

DISCUSSION GROUPS

Division into groups can also be used simply to provide discussion opportunities in smaller associations than the full group. This will allow the quieter members, or those who do not shine in large groups, to have a say. Obviously there must be a reason for the discussion and this could be to allow separated discussions of a common subject, of different subjects with a common theme, to prepare for a tutorial session, or as the follow-up to a session. This last reason is a most valuable one and can be used to ensure that the learning attained during the session does not end with the session, but is continued in a meaningful way. A useful discussion topic when the groups are used for this purpose is for the groups to consider the application of the learning to the participants' work.

BRAINSTORMING GROUPS

Other groups may meet for brainstorming purposes. Brainstorming is often misused as a term for a particular form of activity, but in its correct form it is carried out under very specific rules. The main objective of a brainstorming meeting is for the members to generate as many ideas as possible within the time allotted. This in itself sounds little different from many straightforward problem-solving events, but unlike other approaches, in brainstorming no immediate discussion or evaluation of any idea is allowed. In fact, one of the parameters of power given to the leader of a brainstorming group is for him to stop any discussion immediately. The principle behind this rule is to help in lowering the barriers to lateral thinking among the members. If a member puts forward an adventurous idea which in discussion is denigrated, it is possible that any further meaningful ideas, from that member or any other, may be stifled before birth with the member feeling that he does not want to expose himself to ridicule. The leader also has the responsibility of encouraging the members to produce ideas, and can often do this by putting forward rather wild ideas himself in the hope that this will encourage lateral thinking by the others. Another requirement for effective brainstorming is that every idea, however wild, shall be recorded; if some are not, the originator may feel that his views are being ignored and may not participate further.

Once all ideas have been extracted, the task of the brainstorming group is over. Assessment and evaluation of the ideas can then follow either by the same group or by a different one. Much will depend on the criteria placed on the assessment of the ideas, but full discussion must be encouraged, even on more traditional proposals that have been rejected previously. After all, situations change and what may not have been operable in earlier days may now be appropriate. Nor should the wild ideas be rejected without due consideration, as these on investigation may contain a germ of something worthwhile that can be developed.

Brainstorming is a technique that can be valuable near the start of a course to get the members talking and feeling that they can be open with their thoughts. I have used this approach, linked with buzz groups, to encourage the groups to talk to each other and produce in plenary a combined list of ideas. From this final list the groups can again be formed to evaluate the ideas either with every group considering the full list or each group being responsible for looking at linked sections of the list. In the latter case the linking is decided by the full group. Once this evaluation has been completed, the groups again form a plenary group to reach agreement on final outcomes.

It is often useful for the course participants to be prepared for brainstorming with a practical session on lateral thinking led by the trainer and a description of the rules of brainstorming. An effective exercise can be to ask the group to list individually as many uses they can think of for an everyday type of object, e.g. a paper clip. This will encourage the generation of non-logical uses and ideas, which, once started, will continue when more serious issues are being considered.

LEARNING IN GROUPS

Groups can also be used for the performance of tasks or activities, structured or unstructured, in which the end result may be the completion of the task, or observation and discussion of the interactive processes involved. Some of these activities can be performed by an individual in a self-instruction approach, but many require the interaction of the group to produce learning possibilities.

Two highly structured activities are action mazes and in-tray exercises. The action maze can certainly be performed as an individual event, since it is a particular variation of a programmed textbook, but there is considerable value and learning in the group discussion following the event.

ACTION MAZES

In an action maze, each individual is given an information sheet which describes a technical or interpersonal problem. At the end of this first piece of information, the person is asked to make a decision based on the facts given up to that stage. Usually a choice between a number of actions is given. The particular choice leads the learner to the next piece of information, at the end of which there is a further choice to make. Each learner can proceed at his own pace and his skill can determine how long the individual takes to move through the maze. The individual who has a good grasp of the principles involved can reach the final decision very quickly, having made the correct choices most of the way along. The unskilled learner is likely to make a number of inappropriate choices and will take a circuitous path to the eventual end. The intention of the exercise is that the learners will absorb the correct methods or attitudes from the mistakes they make.

One of the disadvantages of the action maze is with the 'clever' student, who may have read the right books and consequently can give the 'right' answers, whether or not the real reasons for those moves are understood.

IN-TRAYS

In-tray exercises, or as they are sometimes called, in-baskets, also require the learner to make choices, but without the luxury of multiple choices. The material for an in-tray exercise can, like the action maze, be concerned with technical tasks or personal problems, or both problems can be included.

A typical in-tray exercise requires the learner to assume that he has been promoted or transferred to a new position or has just returned from holiday. He is provided with an in-tray containing a number of letters, notes, internal memos, requests, queries and unimportant lists or reports. A constraint is introduced putting pressure on the learner to make decisions about each item in a certain period of time – important colleagues or bosses are going away within a short time, an important meeting to attend, or a visit that has to be made shortly. The skills required of the learner are the abilities to sort out the wheat from the chaff in a decisive manner, taking into account any staff or industrial relations involved.

The follow-up of the in-tray exercise, like the action maze, is a discussion about why decisions were made in that way, a consideration of the effects of some of the decisions and justification of some of the decisions made.

Both action mazes and in-tray exercises are, in my experience, more effective if the maze situations and the in-tray materials are directly related to the organization or job in which the learners are employed.

Other problem-solving and decision-making approaches are common to training courses and many of these can easily be directly related to the work of the trainees.

ALGORITHM OR LOGIC TREE

This is a logic-based approach which can be compared with a computer working through a program. In both the algorithm and the computer program, the decision-making process is reduced to a yes/no response. The algorithm is constructed in the form of a flow chart which is used to facilitate progress through a correct course of action or procedure. At strategic points in the flow chart, questions are posed requiring a yes/no answer. Whichever answer is given, the user is taken along that path, at which stage another yes/no response question is posed. The principal advantage of this technique is that complicated textual descriptions of a procedure can be simplified and presented in a more easily comprehensible form. The algorithm can replace formal training, particularly if the subject is a standard procedure in frequent use, and learning can be achieved through self-instruction. The learner follows the procedure using the algorithm until the process is understood and remembered.

The steps of the algorithm are arranged in a logical progression which has usually been decided by a thorough job analysis. Once

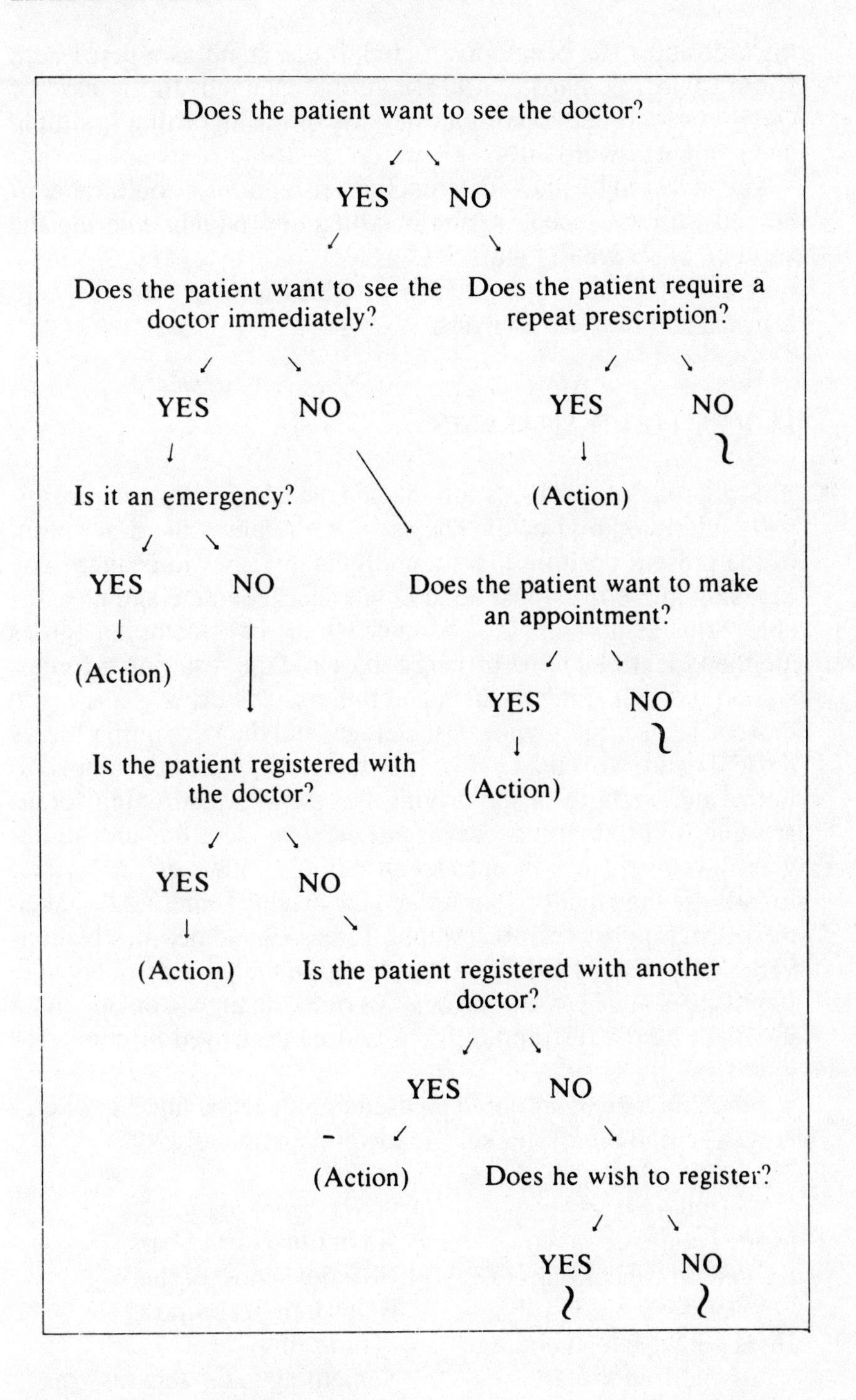

Figure 5.1 An algorithm

the algorithm has been constructed, it can stand as a permanent feature until, perhaps, the procedure is changed. In the case of change, a modification of part or parts of the algorithm is simple and straightforward.

Part of an algorithm for a doctor's receptionist could be concerned with the reception and handling of a patient entering the surgery, as shown in Figure 5.1.

Another specific approach to problem solving introduced to learners is force field analysis.

FORCE FIELD ANALYSIS

This approach to problem solving and decision making was originally advanced by Lewin. The approach requires the description of the present position that the individual wishes to change. The first step, therefore, must be to define in as concrete and measurable terms as possible the change desired. Two factors or forces are then identified – the driving forces and the restraining forces, sometimes called the pushers and pullers. The driving forces are those aspects which will assist change, and the restraining forces those that are working against it. Strategies are then developed to utilize the strength of the driving forces. The restraining forces are analysed so that the weaker ones can be identified and strategies developed to concentrate on reducing their effect further. Efforts are than made to strengthen the driving forces and weaken the restraining forces. Restraining forces can sometimes be converted into driving forces and thus help in the process of change. It may be possible to sell the benefits of the change to an opponent in which case a restraining force will be destroyed or converted into a driving force.

Force field analysis could be used to reduce the number of cigarettes an individual smokes or stop him completely.

Driving forces	*Restraining forces*
Money could be saved	Addiction over *x* years
Decreased cancer risk if he stops	He enjoys most of them
Does not wish to encourage his children to start	Helps him to compose himself
Sweeter-smelling breath	Something to do with his hands

Cleaner air in house
No stained fingers
Wider choice of seats in public places
Not having problems when he runs out of cigarettes
Saves washing up ashtrays
Less hazard when driving car
No need to buy/matches/ lighters/gas

Helps the Exchequer and the tobacco industry in which he has shares
Social gesture to offer to friends
Balances a pint of beer
Might eat more and gain weight if he stopped
Needs a lot of will power

CASE STUDIES

Case studies are similar to the problem-solving activities just described in that they are more effective if they are job-related. They can be simple or complex and can be designed to take a short time or several days, even the length of the complete course which is built around the case study. The group may be limited to the material contained in the written case study or may be required to seek further information either directly from the trainer or by practical research. If the learners have access to computers, in their organization, these could usefully be made available in the training event to help in a thorough consideration of the case material.

A common case study supplies the learner group with all necessary financial, organizational, production, statistical and staffing information relating to the organization and the problem being studied. The group is given a problem or series of problems to solve from this information, ranging from fault-finding and rectification to planning the progress of the company. An extension to the basic case study approach is to divide the course into separate groups which represent pseudo-companies, with individuals given the roles of Managing Director, Financial Director, Sales Director, Production Director, Personnel Director and so on. Each group can be styled an independent company which would be in competition with the other groups, the end results of success being compared between groups with an analysis of the differences.

The pseudo-company extension of the basic case study is often referred to as a business game or simulation and can have many modifications.

Probably the most common group activities encountered on training courses are structured and non-structured exercises. The range of these exercises is considerable and the trainer looking for suitable exercises has a wealth of publications to which he can refer. Exercises can also be constructed by the trainer himself.

Existing exercises provide the trainer with training objectives, materials required, methods to be employed, follow-up discussion aspects, and any briefs for the group. The trainer who is constructing his own exercises is recommended to follow these guidelines to produce an effective exercise, rather than try a 'general consumption' off-the-peg exercise.

STRUCTURED ACTIVITIES

The simple structured exercise requires the group to perform a simple, usually non-job-related task. Typical tasks are the group construction of a jigsaw puzzle, the formation of four-letter words, or mixed-up magazine pages and the like. The actual task is not important as it is only a vehicle for the participants to practise various skills. The skills that can be utilized in these tasks can include all aspects of the management cycle – planning, organization, communication, operation and control.

More complicated tasks can be evolved, the limit being only the bounds of creativity of the exercise constructor. Usually the more complex the exercise, the more skills are required of the participants. One example of a frequently used exercise is to use Lego bricks to build a mast or bridge. Constraints are imposed in terms of the number of bricks used, the height or length achieved and the time taken with penalties imposed on failure to achieve optimum results. The activity can be divided into two phases. During the first phase, the group is required to plan its activity and produce a set of objectives for itself. In the second phase, the group has to put its plan into action and it is during this operation that the group's plan succeeds or falls. The borderline between an exercise or activity and a case study is uncertain, depending to a large extent on the complexity and perhaps the greater job relevance of the latter.

Although the actual performance of the task must itself be

important, more valuable in this form of training is consideration of the process involved. There are different schools of thought on how this may be examined: one supports reliance on self-observation and analysis by the group itself, perhaps with the assistance of the trainer; the other supports the use of part of the full group in observing the performance of their colleagues. The latter method is often referred to as the fishbowl technique – the fish being the participants observed by their peers outside the area of operation and with no verbal contact.

The observers, where these are used, can be allocated observation tasks such as each element of technique – planning, communication, interpersonal interactions, carrying out of the plan and so on. Alternatively, each observer can be detailed to observe individuals of the participating group, particularly the leader. Sometimes a mixture of both approaches can be used. Whatever the method, the intention, following the completion of the task, is to give the participants as much feedback on their performance as possible.

The importance of the role of the observer cannot be overstressed, although allocation to these roles can present problems. If a training event contains a large number of activities, the trainer is normally able to ensure that every course participant takes a significant part in at least one of the activities. However, if it is possible to include only a small number of practical activities, there may be a problem of ensuring this total involvement. If not everyone taking part in the course has the opportunity to play a significant role in an activity, the role of the observer becomes even more important. The observations not only give feedback to those taking part in the activity, but also give the observers the opportunity to see the events in action, observe them closely and analyse the incidents. In this way what is often said – 'The observer sees more than the participants' – becomes a reality. One of the trainer's responsibilities is to ensure that both learning experiences can occur:

- the participants get the most out of the activity and consequently learn from this participation and action
- the observers learn from their observations rather than just being there to 'see'.

These objectives can be achieved by ensuring that the participants are given not only the opportunity to reflect on what they have done, but feedback from the external viewpoint of the observer. The observers must be given the opportunity to reflect on the observations they have made and to comment in a comprehensive and meaningful manner.

The observers must be aware of the importance of their role and the trainer can stress this before the activity by giving them time and support in deciding what they are going to look for, what instruments they can use, whether the task should/can be divided amongst them and so on.

An important element in assisting this role is a set of observational guidelines or a checklist of significant aspects for which they should look. Some of these will vary with the nature of the activity itself, but there will usually be a generic, core set of questions to consider.

A typical observer checklist for use in basic management skills or leadership activity observation is shown in Figure 5.2. This checklist is reproduced from a series of similar observers' checklists collated in *50 Activities for Developing Management Skills, Volume 2* by Teresa Williams (Gower, 1989).

The method of using the checklist is important and again guidance should be given by the trainer. Alternatively, and very usefully, if there are several observers, time can be given to them as a group to confer and decide amongst themselves how they are going to observe, how they might divide the observations amongst them, and how they will present the observations. The division may be related to an earlier division of observation responsibilities before the event, or may be a simple division between them of the aspects of the observation categories. If several observers are available to oversee a group activity which includes behaviour/performance not only of the leader, but also the group members, the observers can be allocated one or two members each.

More sophisticated observational approaches can be used to make the feedback useful, and can include the techniques such as behaviour analysis and closed-circuit TV. The latter can be used either to remove the observers from the presence of the participating group to avoid disturbing them or, with only the trainer as observer, the action can be videotaped for eventual playback to the group.

Many trainers do not use activities as much as would be useful to them. This restraint may be because:

OBSERVATION SHEET FOR BASIC MANAGEMENT SKILLS ACTIVITY

It is your task as observer to record points under the headings below. Do *not* take part in the exercise or voice suggestions or comments, either verbally or non-verbally. The information which you will provide will be very important in helping the whole group to learn points which are directly relevant to the way in which they operate.

How was the exercise explained by the leader?

How did the planning take place?

What targets or objectives were set?

How and when were people organized?

Were all the available resources (people and things) well utilized?

How was the group led?

What motivated people?

Record aspects of communications which were particularly helpful.

What management style was used?

Record anything else relevant to the way in which the exercise was managed.

Figure 5.2 Observer checklist

- the trainer is frightened to stray away from the 'safe' atmosphere of the lecture or input session
- the trainer has had no experience of running activities, and is frightened to initiate an activity; or produce feedback and appraise it
- the trainer is not aware of a relevant and suitable activity
- the structure of the programme is too rigid or there is not time

and the fear held by many trainers inexperienced in using activities that:

- the delegates may not want to play the game.

This last fear, although very real in the minds of many trainers, is in my experience unfounded. I have introduced and seen introduced games, exercises and activities on many programmes, with all levels of delegates, and I have never encountered one delegate who overtly stated that he/she did not want to take part. Many are reluctant before the activity, but usually after the activity they are fully supportive, once they have seen what the activity has been able to produce.

The time factor can be a real problem, but the remedy should be in the hands of the trainer. There is no doubt that many activities eat up considerable time within a course – not only the activity itself, but also, and perhaps more importantly, the time needed after the activity to take feedback and appraise the results and processes. In some activities and groups, the post-activity discussion can take as long or longer than the activity. The time can be an expensive item, but the benefits usually outweigh the costs. Learning by doing and analysing what happened is often much more effective than from formal inputs, or even video and computer programs, principally because of the enjoyment and peer learning pressure of operating in a group. But to satisfy the learning needs of the various delegates with different learning styles, the opportunity must be given, not only for the doing, but also for reflection, analysis and consideration of application to the world of work.

Actual experience of running activities should resolve the other fears in most cases; initial experience can often be obtained by working with another trainer until the trainee trainer feels sufficiently confident to run the activity alone. However, this is not always possible, but should not deter the trainer who wants to add the skills of running activities to his toolkit.

Solving this problem can be linked with the other problem of now knowing about suitable and relevant activities. If the trainer is reasonably skilled in leading discussions, the obtaining of feedback and appraisal should be relatively easy to develop (particularly if some guidelines are available with the activity). Much of the remaining skill in running activities is an intimate knowledge of their content, format and operating instructions. I believe that for every activity to be introduced by a trainer, he/she should have taken part in the activity himself. This participation provides an invaluable insight and can give the trainer practical experience of the problems participants might encounter and the types of feeling which might emerge.

Not too long ago, most trainers relied on their own involvement in others' activities to learn of their existence, or came across a suitable activity in one of the scattered literature sources. More recently, publishers of training books and packages have developed collections of activities for trainers, some under general headings, others within more specific subject areas – stress, self-development, team building, negotiating and so on. Many of these collections have been designed to help the inexperienced trainer in particular. For example, Gower Publishing has initiated a series of ring-binder collections of activities for developing management skills. Some eight volumes have been published in this series so far, each volume containing 50 activities, which the trainer can reproduce freely. But more important, each activity in each volume follows a common pattern designed to make it easier for the new trainer to use.

The activities in these collections are presented in a format which gives the information necessary for an inexperienced trainer to introduce the activity. More experienced trainers need only read some of this information or can use it to modify the activity to suit their particular needs. The basic format contains:

- tutor's notes
- handouts, participants' briefs and so on.

The tutor's notes include brief, but sufficient, comments on:

- the applications of the activity
- a general description of the activity

- the time required for the activity and post-activity action
- the recommended group size
- physical resources necessary
- pre-course work
- advice on conducting the activity
- post-activity discussion guidelines.

With these notes, descriptions and comments, and with all the physical resources either described or provided, a 'strange' activity can be introduced with every chance of success. A matrix is provided in each collection to show at a glance the areas of learning into which the activity falls, and tables indicating the approximate time needed for each activity.

(Full references to publications of this nature are given in the booklist at the end of this chapter – see particularly *50 Activities for Developing Management Skills* in Appendix 4.)

UNSTRUCTURED ACTIVITIES

Unstructured exercises are similar in operation to the structured variety, but no specific task is allocated or the task is not as well defined. The trainer can invite the group to consider what they would wish to do to achieve any learning needs they may have identified. The group is then left to reach these ends by whatever means it decides, to whatever level and in whatever time it decides to take. When the group has reached the end of its self-imposed task, there is no formal appraisal of performance, but commonly the group itself decides to appraise how it went about the event.

There are, of course, various levels of non-structuring and many, particularly in T groups are even less constrained than the one just described. A typical example of this type is when the trainer, having brought the group together, simply leaves them alone either to do nothing or to make their own decisions as to where they progress.

Rather less open is to use the actual process of the group to lead to the next activity, so that the activities arise naturally rather than being planned. On a recent human relations course the group had been given the semi-structured task of producing working guidelines for itself for the next stages of the course. During this discussion the question of the role of the group leader was raised as a specific issue. It had been decided that whenever the group might be performing, a leader should be appointed. From this simple decision, the group decided that the leader's role should be determined in full and specific terms and that this discussion should be treated as a separate event when the remainder of the guidelines had been agreed.

The group does not always decide to follow a pattern such as this, and the course climate must be favourable to encourage it to happen. Obviously it can only be allowed in an informally structured or unstructured course, for a course with tightly controlled methods and objectives would be thrown out of gear by this amount of latitude.

The subject of unstructured activities will be returned to in the discussion on human relations training; it is in this mode of training that non-structured methods are most suitable.

The availability of technology as an aid to training can produce variations on traditional approaches, and the use with groups of prepared mini-case studies on videotape can often assist the learning process. Typical short cameos of incidents can be recorded on VTR and when the need arises can quickly be brought into use. One tape can include a number of cameos lasting about 30 seconds, in which the critical part of an interaction can be shown. The group or groups are then asked to discuss their reactions to what they have seen, either at the technical or emotional level, depending on the circumstances in which the VTR is used. For example, a meeting might be shown when one member makes a contribution of an ingratiating nature to the chairman with the resulting attack by another member 'I might have expected you to come out with something like that!' The group is asked to discuss their reactions to this incident and consider what action they might take as (a) the chairman and (b) the member who made the initial contribution. Discussion could continue on more emotional aspects of what feelings might be on display and how they would feel during an incident of this nature.

MIXING

A common problem experienced by new trainers when faced with a reasonably large group which has to be subdivided to perform tasks in small groups is how to produce the most effective division.

The simplest method is often used by trainers perhaps because they do not have the time or the inclination to use a more sophisticated method. With a group of twelve sitting in the traditional training arrangement of the horseshoe, division is made halfway round to produce two groups of six. This is a simple and quick method, but has some dangers. If the initial seating arrangement has been left to the participants, it is common for friends in a 'cousin' or 'family' group to seat themselves next to each other. When the course is divided simply, the friends can find themselves in the same group. Although this is not necessarily detrimental it could have a disturbing effect on the group and the possibility of learning from strangers from different disciplines may be diminished.

One way out of this difficulty is to produce the two groups by nominating alternate members to each of the two groups: members seated in positions 1, 2, 5, 7, 9 and 11 form one group, members 2, 4, 6, 8, 10 and 12 the other group. If it is necessary to change the groups, various permutations can be worked out in advance to ensure a thorough mixing throughout the course. For example:

	Group A	*Group B*
Activity 1	1, 3, 5, 7, 9, 11	2, 4, 6, 8, 10, 12
Activity 2	1, 2, 5, 6, 8, 11	3, 4, 7, 9, 10, 12
Activity 3	1, 2, 3, 10, 11, 12	4, 5, 6, 7, 8, 9

A difficult decision for the trainer is whether the small groups should be changed following the initial division or whether they should remain the same throughout. Much will depend on the trainer's objectives in splitting the main group in the first place and the learning he hopes will result from the small-group activities. Problems can arise whatever he does. If the groups are kept the same throughout the course the group members

- may achieve a high level of awareness and understanding of each other's behaviour, knowledge, skills and attitudes
- can use this knowledge to make the group working highly effective
- can develop into a team as opposed to a non-integrated group of individuals

but can also

- be a group of low-skilled individuals who achieve little task fulfilment and learn little from each other
- fail to come together as an integrated group and hate the sight of each other by the end of the course.

If, however, the groups are constantly changed,

- the individuals can be exposed to a variety of people in a similar way to that in which they have to interact in the 'real' world
- the skills available to the group are varied and learning can be achieved interactively
- incompatible individuals would not be forced to remain in the same group for the duration of the course.

On the other hand,

- there would be no opportunity for individuals to achieve a high level of awareness of each other
- there would be no team development.

A rather more positive approach to group mixing can be taken by using different forms of selection to the basically haphazard, numerical method described above.

When the training group is composed of members from the same organization a rather more definitive mixing can be made. For instance, a national organization may be split into divisions and regions. If, with a course of twelve members, several come from the same divisions or regions, a natural mix is to separate them and also those with similar areas of work. Normally the course includes both men and women, so a further natural division is to put an equal number of each in both groups, again using the other decisions in addition.

A more systematic approach can utilize behavioural information about the individuals to mix the groups, for part or all of the course. Questionnaires are available to determine different aspects of an individual's behaviour. One may identify the members' learning styles – activist, reflector, theorist, pragmatist – or influencing styles – boss, peer, system or goal-powered – or some similar style identification.

If the learning-style approach, for example, is used, a variety of possible mixes is available. The group may contain a number of each category and these groupings can be used to produce teams in different ways for different reasons. One group could be composed of all the activists and pragmatists, group effectiveness being based on the principle that such a mixture would require the active nature of such individuals to be more reflective in order to get things done. Similarly, the homogeneous group of reflectors and theorists would need to 'do' something in order to be effective in a reasonable time. There could also be a completely heterogeneous mix which would enable each type to balance the others in forming an effective group. Of course, this latter mix might produce a dramatic situation which will require behaviour modification to result in effective decisions.

Similar mixes or 'unmixes' can be developed from the identification of other styles and behaviours. Each method has its supporters and much has been written about the benefits of homogeneous or heterogeneous mixing, but I suggest that each trainer or training manager experiments with different approaches to satisfy his own objectives. In my own training I have tried most methods of mixing, but have come to the conclusion that for certain forms of training the numerical choice approach is as good as any other. However, each trainer should try different approaches to see which ones work best for him.

Perhaps the ultimate in mixing methods is to bring the group together, announce that *x* small groups are required and ask them to produce their own groups. This approach has many advantages and can save the trainer from being accused of 'fixing' the groups or limiting learning by producing incompatible groups. I have found that, although the first voluntary mix revolves around friends, subsequent group decisions voluntarily exclude this type of arrangement.

THE OPEN FORUM

Another problem that trainers often meet is how to close a course. One method is to introduce the open forum as the terminal event, although it can stand alone at any stage during the course. The forum usually consists of the course tutors, supported by some of the guest speakers and senior people of the organization. The purpose is to give an opportunity to the course members to ask questions about aspects of the course material that may not have been completely clarified, to obtain additional information from the senior staff attending, and to make comments about the course itself. The method can vary from a simple request from the chairman of the panel that course members ask questions or make points in a free manner, to questions prepared by the course members beforehand and considered prior to the forum by the panel. In the latter case, the questions can also be allocated to individual members of the panel to answer. The aims of such a forum are praiseworthy, but the result on many occasions can be a stilted discussion; or course members ask questions or make points in a free manner; or there is an embarrassing total silence. One way of circumventing these undesirable situations is to give the course members the opportunity of preparing for the forum in a realistic way. The course is divided into two groups and each group is given specific questions to consider and bring back to the forum to present. These questions can be those leading to a Learning Review discussed later, can aim to produce specific comments on the course and its material, or to produce real questions for the panel. When the groups report back, a spokesman from each group presents the group's views, findings or questions, and the other group and the panel members can take up any points that require comment. At the very least an embarrassing silence is avoided by this method.

REFERENCES AND RECOMMENDED READING

Group Training Techniques. M. L. and P. L. Berger. Gower, 1972.
Making Meetings Work. Leland P. Bradford. University Associates, 1976.
Industrial Relations Training for Managers. C. Brewster and S. Connock. Kogan Page, 1980.
Learning through Groups. Phillip G. Hanson. University Associates, 1981.
A Sourcebook of Management Simulation. Ken Jones. Kogan Page, 1989.
Managing Meetings. B. Maude. Halsted Press, 1975.
Taking your Meetings Out of the Doldrums. Rainman and Lippitt. University Associates, 1975.
Creative Thinking and Brainstorming. J.G. Rawlinson. Gower, 1981.

Creativity at Work. Tudor Rickards. Gower, 1988.
Faultless Facilitation. Lois B. Hart. Kogan Page, 1992.
Interactive Learning Events: A Guide for Facilitators. Ken Jones. Kogan Page, 1988.
Workshops that Work. Tom Bourner, Vivien Martin and Phil Race. McGraw-Hill, 1993.
Meetings Management: A Manual for Trainers. Leslie Rae. McGraw-Hill, 1994.
Let's Have a Meeting. Leslie Rae. McGraw-Hill, 1994.

ACTIVITIES. A number of publishers produce an extensive collection of activities covering a wide range of subjects. These include BACIE (now part of the Institute of Personnel and Development), Connaught Training, Fenman, Gower, Kogan Page, Longman, McGraw-Hill and Pfeiffer; trainers interested in these should write to the publishers concerned for a current list. See also the article 'Activities for Trainers – bane or boon', *Training Officer*, December 1993, vol. 29, no. 10, by Leslie Rae.

6 Preparation for training events

DESIGN

Chapter 5 described the techniques and approaches that can be used when training people in groups. But before these events can take place, an extensive amount of preparation must take place, including a decision on which of the techniques will be used in the event. The type of training, the subject concerned, the culture of the organization, among other factors, must be considered and agreed and all the relevant preparations made – this is the subject of training design.

The new trainer will be introduced to some aspects of existing training that will be capable of modification; the purpose of this chapter is to explore some of these so that the new trainer may be able to change with the agreement of the organization. The areas that the trainers will find that they have eventual permission to modify will include:

- Environment preparation
- Presentational skills – verbal and non-verbal
- Script or brief preparation
- The design, production and use of training aids.

Presentational skills were considered briefly in chapter 2 and you are referred to the numerous publications on these skills for more detailed descriptions and advice. The design, production and use of training aids will be discussed in the next chapter. This chapter considers what the trainers can do to develop their script planning skills and prepare the environment for the most effective training.

PREPARATION OF TRAINING BRIEFS OR SCRIPTS

In many, if not most, cases, a new trainer first encountering the training courses or sessions in which he or she will be involved is presented with:

- a standard brief or script for the session(s) which they will be required to follow
- a set of visual aids and handouts to be used in connection with the session(s).

Delivering training material can be a personal matter and most organizations are willing for the session brief to be modified to take this into account. In fact, many trainers would be psychologically incapable of presenting a pre-prepared brief strictly along the lines in which it is presented to them. With this potential for modification in mind, it is useful for the new trainer to be aware of the ways in which a session brief or script is prepared and used.

There are few trainers, experienced or not, who perform their training without any form of script or brief. New trainers are recommended to have this essential document always with them during their session, of whatever nature.

The next key recommendation of new trainers is concerned with the use of briefs, particularly those in full script form. In their early days, it is certainly important that they have a full script of their session, but it is equally important that they do not use this to read from during the session. In fact, to have a full script at the session is dangerous as its presence might tempt the new trainer simply to read it out.

The effects that reading out the script might have on the session and the learners could include:

- The learners might feel they could just as well have read the text themselves
- Written material read out usually sounds boring unless you are a skilled actor
- Eye contact would be lost with the group
- Non-verbal signals given by the group would not be noticed
- The current place in the script could easily be lost if the trainer was interrupted with questions, had to use a visual aid or the flow of the reading was interrupted in some other way.

PRODUCING BRIEFS OR SCRIPTS

There are four principal methods of producing briefs:

- the traditional, vertical method to plan and make notes
- the headline method of producing a brief
- horizontal planning to plan and use a brief
- the patterned-note, principally to plan a brief, but can also be used as the brief.

THE TRADITIONAL, VERTICAL METHOD OF SESSION PLANNING

The full script method has been commented on above, and although it should not be used during the actual session, it has a valuable place when designing a session and writing the initial brief from which a working brief can be made.

Writing out text in full The text of the script or brief is written out in full, word for word as if it was a report or essay. The wording should be in the style of the 'spoken' word rather than the 'written' word. For example, in speaking we tend to say 'can't' rather than 'cannot' and so on.

Division in paras and sub-paras Dividing the script into paragraphs and sub-paragraphs, each with their headlines, is helpful, not for any grammatical or appearance reasons, but to make the different parts of the text clearer visually. Different colours can be used for alternate paragraphs (or sections) and if the brief is produced on a computer, different fonts can be used to aid this purpose.

Underlining for emphasis One of the necessary actions to be taken with a script of this nature, is to make the different parts as separate and as visually impactive as possible. Underlining, either single or double can be used, particularly **with bold printing** if this is available.

Using colours for emphasis Bold and different colours can be used as another method for producing emphasis in the document. These can be produced by the use of coloured pens if the script is hand-written, or coloured print if typewritten or word processed. In the latter cases, if monocolour only is available, colour can be added by the use of highlighter pens.

Framing for emphasis or isolation

Adding a frame or boxed border, particularly if combined with some or all of the previously described emphasis producers can be very impactive and attention producing. Remember, however, that if too much use is made of any one effect, the impact is lost.

Leaving broad margins

It is helpful to leave broader than normal borders on both sides of the text so that notes can be added – comments made during the session, amendments that become necessary as a result of session comments, directions to reconsider certain aspects and so on, in addition to stage directions such as those described in the next section. Leave plenty of space between paragraphs or sections to isolate them or make the differences more apparent.

Stage directions OHPs, handouts, questions and timings can be added to the margins on each side of the text, or one margin only can be used to make stage direction entries such as:

- when to display which visual aid – OHP, flipchart, audio cassette, video, etc.
- when to issue a named or numbered handout
- the occasion to ask a question
- the occasion to break the group into sub-groups for an activity and so on.

Timings can also be included at stages throughout the text. Do not write actual times – the session may not start at the advertised time and therefore any time will be wrong. Rather, enter the period of time by which the stage in the script should have been reached. If the session is divided into very definite sections, an alternative might be a time period for each section.

HEADLINE PLANNING

Headline planning is an extension and an abbreviation of the traditional full script method of preparing a brief; it involves deleting many of the words in the full script and using a shorthand form only. The method is as follows:

List headlines on A4 sheet Identify the main subjects of the topic and list these as main subject headings. Initially, these can be listed as the thoughts occur and when all have been identified, a logical order can be produced.

Enter inter-heading summarized notes Under each main subject heading, in logical order, enter brief, summary notes of the material you would wish to include under the heading. This will not be your final notes as the material will need to be edited for essential content only.

HORIZONTAL PLANNING

Horizontal planning breaks away from the traditional approach and produces a document, usually on one sheet of paper which can be used both in the planning process and as a headline brief. The planning is in four stages.

Stage 1 First thoughts on the main subject areas should be entered, preferably as single words, as column headings across a sheet of paper placed in the landscape position. These words, or subject headings, need not be complete nor need they necessarily be in order, although this helps in the planning. But other headings may be added as the planning progresses, and the headline brief planning may suggest a different order from the one originally considered.

Stage 2 At the second stage, the trainer considers each subject heading and notes beneath it words or phrases describing the aspects relating to that subject. These are the detailed aspects of each main heading.

He/she continues to add sub-headings until no more can be thought of at that time – others can be added later if necessary.

The headings can then be arranged into the order in which they would be discussed during the session.

Stage 3 At the final planning stage, the stage directions are added. If OHP slides are to be used or handouts issued, a note can be made to this effect.

Priority inclusions can be annotated at three priority levels. Items in the first class – the MUST KNOWS – are essential to the session and the timing must allow for their total inclusion. The SHOULD KNOWS are also important, but may be reduced if time is restricted. The COULD KNOWS are items which although relevant to the session, can be omitted if there is insufficient time. To save space, these priority entries can be abbreviated to M, S and C. At this stage, estimates of the timing can be linked with the prioritization for the main sections. More detailed timing can be included in the working brief.

The variety of horizontal plans is wide – colours can be used for emphasis; certain important items can be enclosed in a frame or block; different-sized lettering can be used again for importance or otherwise.

Lines with arrows can be added to show how items need to be moved for the final version, and so on.

Stage 4 Finally, a fair copy of the plan can be produced, with moves of items incorporated and the entries made clear. This copy can then be used to produce a more traditional script and brief, or can be used as it stands. If used as the brief the stage directions may need to be supplemented or clarified.

Of course, as only headlines are included, the trainer must be completely aware of what needs to be said about each item, but the format has the decided advantage that the brief for one session can be contained on one, or at the most, two sheets of paper. This is very helpful when locating your place in the brief during a session. At a glance, the remaining material can be seen, or the order can be changed without moving pages about.

THE PATTERNED-NOTE METHOD

The patterned-note method of taking notes in the manner suggested by Tony Buzan (see chapter 3) can be used when designing a training session and preparing the session notes. This approach has a number of advantages once the trainer has become accustomed to working in this medium.

At the planning stage, the central box contains the key word for the session being designed. The first branches emanating from this box are annotated with the key words relating to the main subject areas. Again, at this stage in the design process these need not be in order round the centre as the first pattern is usually only an initial working document. Sub-ideas are then added to the main branches to which they relate.

Colours, boxes, symbols (e.g. ?, *, →, ←-----→, ☺, 🗎, 💻, ☞), directions – 'OHP', 'Issue h/o' etc., topic linking lines and so on can be added, particularly in different colours in order to make them stand out.

Once the initial pattern has been completed, the branches and their additions can be moved to their appropriate parts of the pattern, i.e. the order in which the subjects will be presented.

A patterned note is a very personal production, one which can often be understood only by the person who produced it. If necessary, therefore, the notes from the pattern can be converted to one of the more traditional formats. But when the trainer becomes accustomed to patterned notes, and after all it is the trainer who has produced the pattern, it can be used directly as the brief for the session.

One principal advantage, certainly as far as the design pattern is concerned, is that the session design pattern is contained on one sheet of paper; if the subject is complex a sheet of A3 could be used rather than the more usual A4. As a result the whole session can be seen at a glance without having to refer to a number of pages. This advantage can be related to using the patterned note as the session brief itself, although this is a rather more difficult operation. Critical stages, links with other parts of the session, the extent still to be covered at any stage and so on can all be seen at a glance, and no longer can script pages slip out of order.

PLANNING WITH THE COMPLETED DESIGN

TRANSFER TO CLEAR SHEETS OR INDEX CARDS

The purpose of producing a design for a session is to use this design during the actual session. As suggested above, your design document when it has been finalized, ordered and annotated as required can be used directly as your session brief. Or, when the notes have been completed – main subject headings and the contents of each section – transfer these notes to the format you will be using in the session itself. This might be sheets of A4 paper or index cards. The A4 sheets which would normally rest on the trainer's desk or table, should be written in large enough print (not script) to be seen when the trainer is standing beside the table as well as when he/she is seated.

Index cards can be completed with rather smaller print, but this must still be sufficiently clear and large to be easily readable from, for example, a standing position near the table.

COMPLETE BRIEF WITH IMPACT TECHNIQUES

A working brief whether on A4 sheets or index cards will be difficult to use if all the entries are the same. As suggested in the design stage, full use of mixed print (upper and lower case), colour, underlining, boxes, highlighting, marginal stage directions and so on should be made. Err on the side of too few rather than too many as the latter can confuse, especially when you are quickly trying to find your place in the middle of a session.

NUMBER AND TAG EACH SHEET OR CARD

Ensure that page numbers are entered on each sheet or card and punch a hole in the top, left corner of the sheet or card so that a tag can be inserted, holding the sheets together. It is only too easy to drop the set in the middle of a session with disastrous consequences if the sheets are not held together.

There is no golden rule about where the brief should rest during the session. Both paper sheets or index cards can be carried in the hand, or placed on the trainer's table. The former tends to make them more obvious to the learners, but if you need your brief to hand this sighting can be ignored in favour of ensuring that you are able to make your session run freely. Much will depend on whether you are seated, standing, walking about, or a combination of all three. My own method is to have the brief on the side of a small table at the front; as I move about in front of the group, if I have to refer to the notes I can unobtrusively move over to the table and glance down at the notes.

Most new trainers say that they feel self-conscious about using notes and briefs in front of a group. In fact, usually the use of the notes is not as obvious as the trainer feels it is and, as stated above, it is better to ensure an effective and flowing session even if the learners see you using the notes, than to flounder and fail because you do not want to be seen referring to notes.

THE TRAINING ENVIRONMENT

Not only must trainers present the training content in an effective manner, but they also have other responsibilities. Although these may have been carried out by others on their behalf, the trainer still has the final responsibility for ensuring they have been done effectively. If, for example, in the middle of a session, the trainer for whom a set of OHP slides has been produced, discovers that one of the most important slides is incorrect, the trainer must accept full responsibility for this error.

One of these responsibilities relates to the training environment and the wise trainer considers this well before the session or event and again just before the start of the event. The trainer is responsible for setting up the training room or area or otherwise ensuring that it is set up to the best advantage. Here the trainer has powers to a greater or lesser degree: many of the environmental aspects may be permanent features. But there is always something that can be done if the environment is not the most suitable.

THE PHYSICAL ENVIRONMENT

The training session, as with any other task, can only be effective if preceded by considerable planning, design and preparation. The physical environment in which the training is to be held is almost as important as actual skills of presentation, for if this is wrong, even the best training can fail. This aspect of training can be approached from two different levels, depending on the actual practices allowed to the trainer. Some trainers will be able to develop the event from the beginning, others will have many aspects arranged by, for example, their administration section, while others will have no responsibility or authority in the matter.

THE TRAINING ROOM

One preparation detail usually (although not always) open to all the classes of trainer will be the arrangement of the training room. Even when the training event has been in operation for some time and the trainer in question is new to the event, this feature of preparation is still open for change. Of course, there are training environments which cannot be changed in any way, either because of physical constraints or organizational policy, but these are few when even minor changes are considered. The criterion is to try to adapt the training environment to its most effective within any constraints imposed.

BARRIERS TO TRAINING ENVIRONMENT EFFECTIVENESS

Factors which might work against effectiveness will include:

- too large and 'grand' a room
- too small a room for division of the group into sub-groups
- inaccessibility of the training location for all learners
- failure to inform security of visiting learners and guest speakers.

In addition you must ensure that requirements for physical comfort are satisfied:

- a suitable provision for note-taking facilities relevant to the particular training
- a visible clock
- administrative arrangements have been accommodated
- air conditioning
- arrangements for urgent messages to be relayed
- comfortable seating
- fan noise
- natural lighting
- nearby provision of telephones
- provision of paper and pens

- provision of refreshments and the times for these have been confirmed
- temperature control
- toilet availability
- visual aid equipment where necessary.

Also ensure other facilities are available and/or satisfactory.

- doors that open and shut and which, preferably, do not have glass panels through which outsiders can be seen (and see)
- location and suitability of electric points
- the shape of the room and its relevance to seating and training techniques
- windows which can be opened (or closed) and which can be shielded against glare.

Requirements will vary with different training locations, so ensure that you, and any support you may have, possess a complete and up-to-date checklist of items to be included in the preparation for the training event. An example of such a checklist can be found in *The Trainer Development Manual* (Rae, Kogan Page, 1994), but the construction of your own is a simple but worthwhile task. The first few possible entries are shown below.

TRAINING ENVIRONMENT CHECKLIST

This checklist is intended as a guide only; omit any items which are not relevant to your actions and add any others which have been omitted.

Environmental Check

Training room booked	....	
Syndicate rooms booked	....	
Access method	....	etc.

Equipment

Audio recorder and tapes	....	
Video recorder, monitor and tapes	....	
Video camera, camcorder, mixer, tapes	....	etc.

Materials

Nameplates	....	
Blotter pads	....	
Small felt tip pens or similar	....	
Large felt tip pens or similar	....	
Drymarker pens	....	etc.

Immediately Before Training Event

Check all seating, tables, extra seating available	....	
Check all other rooms available	....	
Check equipment available and working	....	
Check refreshments – water and other supplies available	....	etc.

STARTING A TRAINING EVENT

Before we look at some of the specific techniques and methods used in group course work, we have to start the event. Starting a training event is described by many trainers, inexperienced and experienced, as the part of the course which gives them the most concern and problems. This is common to the start-up of many different events – in training, giving a presentation can make the speaker very nervous.

But a training event starts long before the day of the actual course. All trainers must be fully aware of the need to plan their training event. Many hours will be devoted to preparing scripts and briefs, visual aids and handouts, to ensure that the training to be delivered is comprehensive, accurate and clear. Perhaps less time is spent in preparing for the activities, games and exercises which should also make up the course – 'I'll just run that activity. You never know how it's going to work out, so I'll take it as it comes!'

Even less time is usually afforded to physical planning. This can include the important, though often neglected question of how the group is to be seated. Too often the trainer appears in the training/conference room in a hotel or conference centre to find the seats laid out in a particular way – usually theatre style – and it is too late/he cannot be bothered/he does not think to do anything about it.

The trainer should be asking, during the planning stage, such questions as:

'Which type of seating arrangement is going to be the most effective for the type of event I am going to run?'
'Do I know what range of seating variations there are?'
'Do I know which types of seating variation are possible in my training environment?'

Many trainers have found that the wrong environment can at worst ruin what would otherwise be a good learning event, and at best reduce the learning capacity of the event. So further questions may include:

'Will the seating arrangements have any effect, positive or negative, on this training?'
'Can I change the seating to a more effective arrangement?'

A GUIDE TO TRAINING ROOM SEATING ARRANGEMENTS

Training rooms can be arranged in a variety of ways and the ideal arrangement will obviously depend on the circumstances – the type of room, the seating available, the number of participants, the style of training and so on. Some of the possible arrangements with their advantages and disadvantages are discussed in the following paragraphs.

THE LECTURE THEATRE OR CLASSROOM LAYOUT

In this layout the trainer is located at one end of the room with the training group/audience facing him in rows placed one behind the other. The width of the rows will depend on the width of the training room and the number of people to be accommodated, as will the number of the rows. The rows may be broken by aisles, mostly to make movement into and out of the rows easier, but also for safety reasons. In custom-built lecture theatres each successive row from the front rises above the level of the one in front of it. (See Figure 6.1.)

The main advantage of this type of layout is that a large number of people can be accommodated in the smallest possible space. Even this can be varied by the amount of space between the seats in a row and between the rows. When the rows are in stepped tiers, everybody is able to see the trainer/lecturer and the trainer can see all the members of the group. In the flat classroom format, this is not always possible.

Figure 6.1 Lecture theatre or classroom layout

Little interaction can take place between the members of the group not only because the group is too large, but individuals in each row can only see the back of the heads of the people in the rows in front. It is only easy for them to see the person on each side of them in their row. When questions are asked of the trainer, few can see the questioner and therefore do not associate with the question. The response to the question by the trainer can then lead to a dialogue between the trainer and the questioner alone. When the session is a lecture (in the narrowest sense) or information/knowledge giving only and there is no need for group interaction, this may be quite a satisfactory format.

THE BOARDROOM LAYOUT

This layout is normally encountered in the boardroom itself. Here the course members are placed round the long 'boardroom' table or series of tables placed together. (See Figure 6.2.)

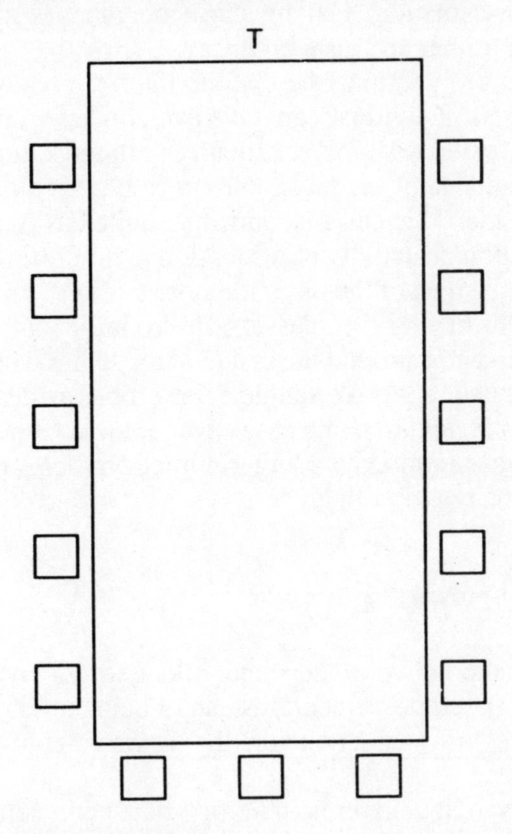

Figure 6.2 Boardroom layout

The trainer can be located anywhere around the table, but most often at the 'head' of the table so that all can see him (more or less) and similarly he can see (more or less) all the members.

The table(s) are useful to place papers on, for note taking and so on, but can act as a barrier – people face each other 'across the table', the usual form of conflict positioning. The trainer is prominently placed in the power position at the head of the table – this may be desirable for boardroom functions, but not necessarily for training.

In technical forms of training, this layout can work well, but because of the formality and constrained atmosphere of the boardroom it will be much less effective in interactive events.

In order to avoid putting the trainer into the prominent or power position, group members can be seated alongside him and thus remove his isolation. Having close neighbours may, however, disturb the trainer and his activities.

Again, a problem may be that the interface between members is limited. An individual can have eye contact with two or three people opposite, with more difficulty with those further away on the opposite side of the table, and no contact at all with those on the same side. This can be confirmed quite easily by asking the members after an activity or discussion to describe the non-verbal gestures and so on of the other members.

Instead of having this classic boardroom layout, the members can also be seated around the inside of the tables which are placed in a hollow square or rectangle. The problems described above apply equally, and in some cases even more so, but sometimes it is done to accommodate a larger number of delegates while still retaining the boardroom layout.

THE HERRINGBONE

This is an alternative to the standard classroom layout and it can produce some improvement. Instead of being arranged in parallel lines, the rows are offset diagonally in a herringbone pattern as in Figure 6.3.

The advantage here is that the occupants of a row have improved sighting of the others along their row and also along the row on the opposite side of the aisle.

THE U-SHAPE

This layout, with or without tables in front of the delegates, is the most common alternative to the classroom layout. It developed when training attitudes were involved in the rebellion against the very formal, passive, completely trainer-led, non-interactive form of training.

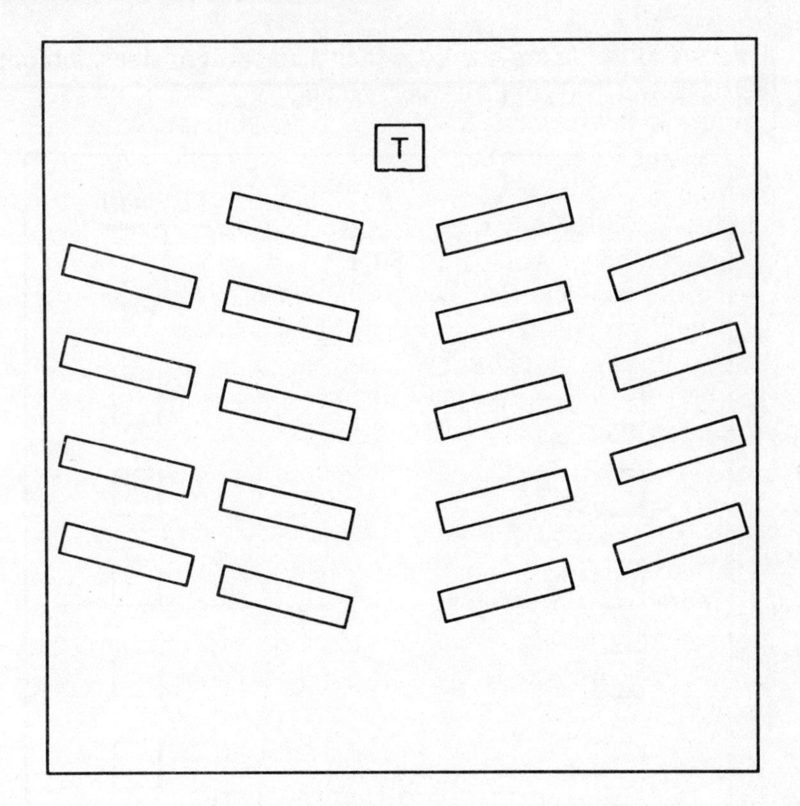

Figure 6.3 Herringbone pattern

Figure 6.4 shows the delegates seated in the shape of a U, the trainer being located at the open end of the U. When tables are used, the base of the U is usually squared off and either one or two standard table lengths across. If easy chairs are used, the base can be more rounded. Again, the normal configuration, particularly if tables are used, is with straight sides to the U, but without the constraints of tables the delegates' chairs can be placed in a more curved layout, almost like a circle with a segment removed. It has a less formal appearance and is more flexible in shape than the boardroom format which it resembles and from which it has developed. In the more flexible U, members on the opposite sides of the U (at a greater distance and therefore less threatening than at the boardroom table) can have easy eye contact with most of their colleagues, and also to a lesser extent with those at the base of the U. There is still the problem of continuous contact with those on the same arm of the U. However, this problem is eased if the arms of the U are curved rather than straight sides, although there is never 100 per cent easy contact.

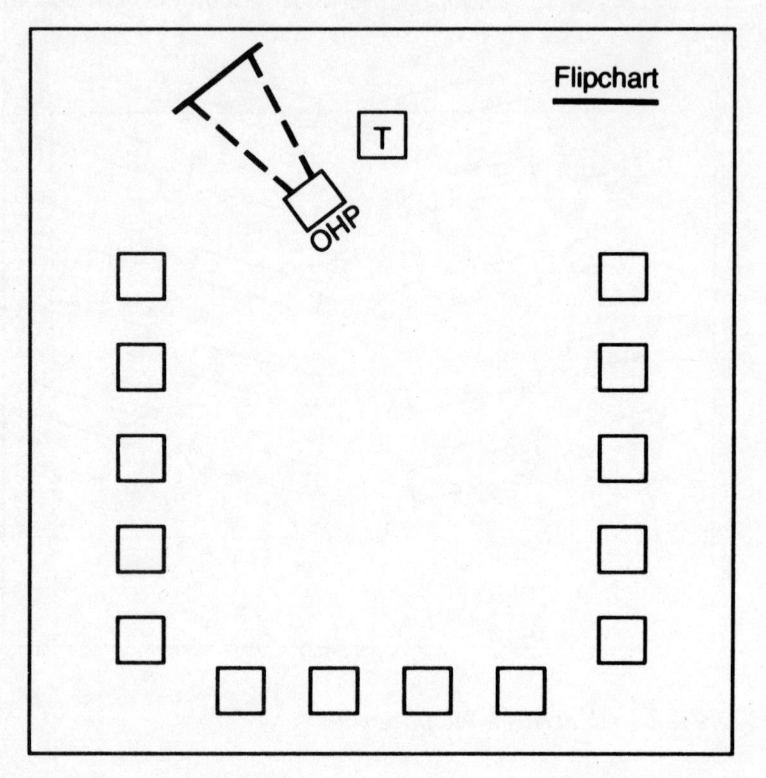

Figure 6.4 The U-shape

This layout is very effective in encouraging an informal approach and reaction between the trainer and members, and between the members themselves. If movement away from the layout is needed, this can be achieved easily, particularly if the U consists of easy chairs rather than chairs behind tables.

THE V-SHAPE

This is a development of the U-shape, intended to reduce even further any problems of restricted eye contact between members Because there is no arm at the closed end of the layout, the problems of no contact between people seated side by side there is removed. The sloping sides of the V give members on a side of the shape a better opportunity to have eye contact with the other members on the same side. Although this is yet a further improvement, 100 per cent visibility between members is still not achieved. (See Figure 6.5.)

Figure 6.5 The V-shape

CLUSTERS

This layout and its variants move away from the more traditional room layouts, with the delegates seated at tables spread out throughout the training room. (See Figure 6.6.)

The tables need not be placed symmetrically around the room, but can be scattered irregularly. This layout breaks up any appearance of formality and in courses which require considerable small-group working can be very effective. The numbers at the tables can reflect the predetermined size of any small working

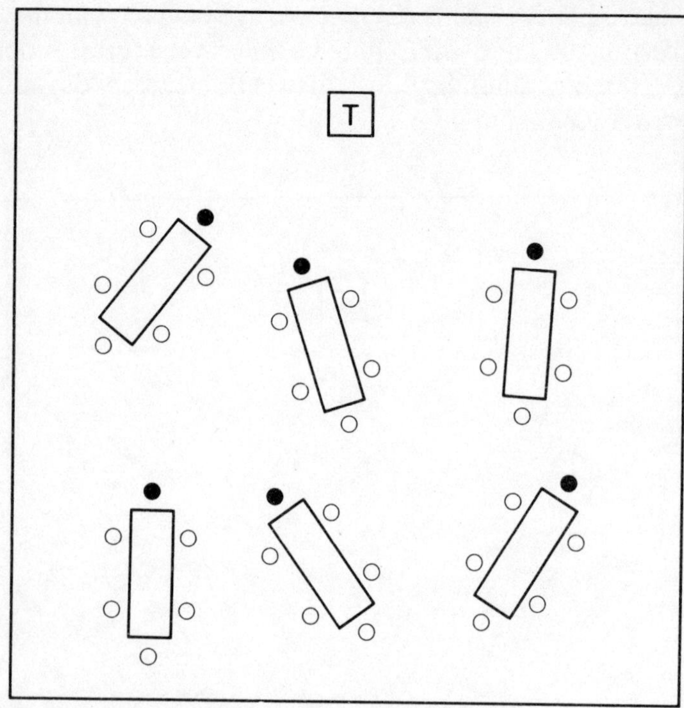

Figure 6.6 Clusters

groups, and mixing of groups can be achieved easily by moving members from one table to another. The trainer can move amongst the group whenever necessary. Some problems can occur when the whole group has to look in one direction, e.g. to the trainer at the front, to watch a video and so on, but I have never found this to be much of a problem.

A simple modification of the straightforward cluster arrangements is for each small-group table to have an additional empty chair. These chairs are used by the trainer who circulates around the room when the groups are performing tasks or having discussions. In this way the trainer can join a group unobtrusively to join in the discussions or observe the behaviour in activities or discussions.

The cluster arrangement works equally effectively with large and small groups and the largest group with which I have used it is a course of 72 delegates seated in 12 groups of six.

THE CIRCLE

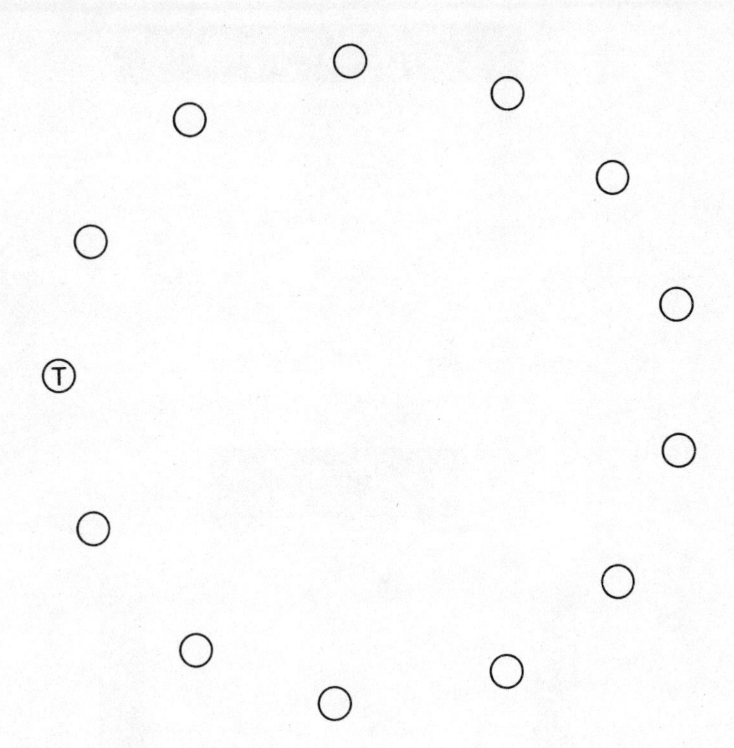

Figure 6.7 The circle

The circular layout (Figure 6.7) may be the ideal configuration when informal, complete interaction between participants is required. No one, including the trainer, is in a power position and everyone is in the potentially conflicting/supporting position of opposites. There are many similarities in this layout to the modified boardroom format, but intervisibility of both near and distant neighbours is improved, and usually tables are not used. However, the visibility is still limited in the case of nearer neighbours – this may not be too much of a problem except for the trainer who may wish to be in a position to see everyone. The layout also requires the trainer to modify his role from the traditional one as dominant leader, controller and presenter at the head of the group, to one of integrated facilitator, helping but not leading the group.

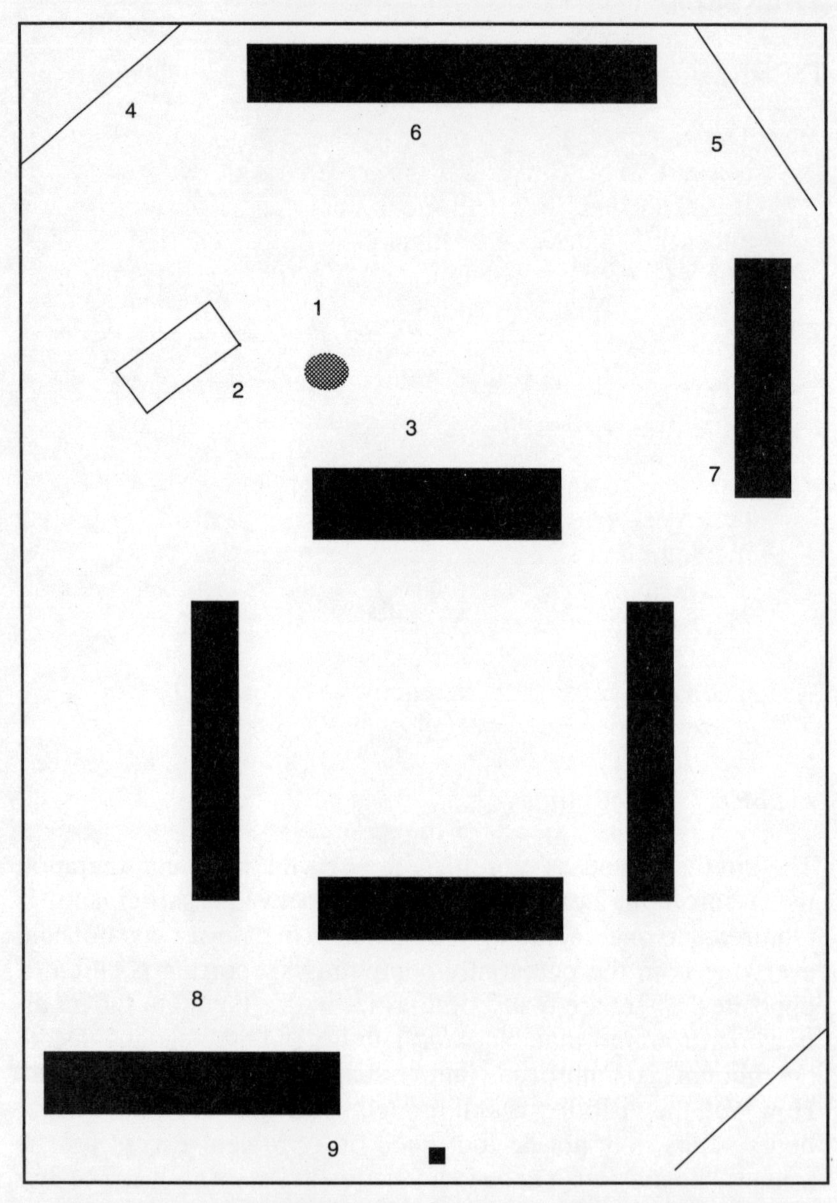

1 = TRAINER 2 = DESK FOR SCRIPT, HANDOUTS, VIDEO (WHEN IN USE)
3 = OHP 4 = SCREEN 5 = FLIPCHART
6 = WALLMOUNTED WHITEBOARD(S)
7 = TABLE FOR REFRESHMENTS, ETC.
8 = TABLES FOR MATERIALS, EXHIBITS, ETC. 9 = CLOCK

Figure 6.8 A suggested training room layout

A RECOMMENDED ROOM LAYOUT

The advantages of the layout shown in Figure 6.8 include:

- The trainer has full use of the front wall, particularly if there is a system of whiteboard and screen tracks.
- It is relatively simple to move from the trainer position to either the whiteboard or flipchart.
- The 'U'-shaped configuration of the learners' seating affords reasonable visibility.
- Tables can be placed in front of the seats which can be easy chairs or 'student-type' chairs with a flat arm to take a notepad.
- The trainer has good visibility of all the learners and can therefore maintain good eye contact, and is not behind a table/desk barrier although one is near at hand for briefs, handouts and as a video table when necessary.
- The seating configuration can be easily altered, for example, for buzz groups or paired discussions.
- The OHP is easily available.
- The video can be kept in readiness, but out of the way, to be placed on the trainer's table when required.
- The screen is more easily visible from most of the learner positions.
- The tables at the back of the room can be used for reference material, computer positions or as refreshment tables if these are to be taken into the training room.

Other environmental factors There will obviously be other factors than seating which can have an effect on the effectiveness of the training. The trainer must take into account as many of these as are relevant during the preparation period and over which he or she will have some measure of control.

REFERENCES AND RECOMMENDED READING

Facilitation: Providing opportunities for learning. Trevor Bentley. McGraw-Hill, 1994.

How to Conduct Training Seminars. Lawrence S Munson. McGraw-Hill, 1992.

How to Design and Introduce Trainer Development Programmes. Leslie Rae. Kogan Page, 1994.
How to Talk so People Listen. Sonya Hamlin. Thorsons, 1989.
How to Write a Training Manual. John Davis. Gower, 1992.
Ideas for Training Managers and Supervisors. Patrick Suessmuth. University Associates, 1978.
Practical Training. Jonathan Coates. Nimrod, 1984.
Running an Effective Training Session. Patrick Forsyth. Gower, 1992.
Teaching Hard Teaching Soft. Colin Corder. Gower, 1990.
The Instructor's Pocketbook. John Townsend. Management Pocketbooks, 1991.
The Skills of Interviewing. Leslie Rae. Gower, 1988.
The Trainer Development Programme. Leslie Rae. Kogan Page, 1994.
Writing Your Own Scripts and Speeches. Suzan St Maur. McGraw-Hill, 1991.

7 The use of training aids

There are few successful trainer input sessions that rely on the trainer's presentation alone. Most are supported by some form of training aid, usually a visual aid and this is the common term in use, whether or not the aid is visual alone. The range of the training aids now is wide, although most trainers are restricted to a few basic ones.

The training aids in common use today include the:

- audio cassette player
- combined audio and slide presenter
- computer
- episcope
- flipchart
- handouts
- interactive video
- object
- overhead projector
- slide projector
- trainers themselves
- video player
- video projector
- whiteboard.

From the list shown above, although all are in use, there are about five only that can be described as almost universal in use – the object itself, the trainer, the flipchart, the whiteboard and the overhead projector (OHP).

THE OBJECT ITSELF

If it is possible to have the object itself physically present, this is the most effective training aid, whether the training is in the classroom or at the site of the object on which the learners are to be trained.

In some cases it will not be possible to have the object itself in the training room – for example a large piece of equipment, a location and so on. In such instances an alternative can be a photograph of the object, passed round the learners or projected; an OHP diagram; a computer graphic; an audio recording (for an audio object), or a video recording, particularly where a sequence is involved (even home camcorders can be valuable for this purpose).

The object as a visual aid requires little verbal description – objects speak for themselves and so make effective training aids. The trainer can demonstrate this use, for example with an OHP, using the 'Tell, Show, Do' technique. The OHP can be described verbally as an instrument used to support the trainer during an input session; the OHP itself can then be revealed and described in detail. Finally, the learners can be given the opportunity to handle the OHP.

This approach can be used for many objects, although some will require careful handling both by the trainer and the learners.

THE TRAINER AS A VISUAL AID

Although many trainers may not appreciate the fact, they are themselves one of the most powerful and visible aids, which can have a considerable impact on the learners. The learners are seeking knowledge, advice, guidance and skills in an area in which they will soon be practising. The trainer is helping them along this path and the learners naturally assume that their mentor is a skilled, experienced and effective trainer.

Consequently there will be some role modelling – consciously or subconsciously. This is not to be encouraged as the learners should develop their own styles, but mimicry is natural, particularly if the trainer is especially effective (and popular).

In an attempt to try to avoid this role modelling, the introduction of a number of trainers into the programme, particularly if they have different styles, can be valuable. It can, of course, however have the reverse effect of helping the learners to compare (sometimes unfavourably rather than as different styles) training and trainer styles.

FLIPCHARTS, WHITEBOARDS AND OVERHEAD PROJECTORS

The other three aids from the five mentioned are artificial objects and all have their advantages and disadvantages. The flipchart, a pad of fairly substantial A1-size paper is the modern equivalent of the earlier 'newsprint', consisting of sheets of thin, brownish-tone paper. The whiteboard is a development from the flipchart and is the modern equivalent of the old chalkboard or blackboard, as it was more commonly called even though it was often green! The OHP is the electric, projecting version of the flipchart/whiteboard. All three have fairly similar uses, the variations being the result of different requirements and sometimes environment.

FLIPCHARTS

Advantages

- *Transportable* The flipchart can be easily rolled up and the easel can be collapsed so that both can be relatively easily carried.
- *No power required* Unlike the OHP, slide projector, video, etc., no power supply is required so it is not susceptible to power failure.
- *Adaptable* Can be used as a blank sheet on which items can be added or as a prepared sheet the contents of which can be disclosed in a variety of ways.
- *Any paper usable* The 'flipchart paper' itself need not be a commercial flipchart; any large sheet of paper can be used.
- *Easy to use* Few basic skills, other than clear writing, are required.
- *Retained for reference* Each sheet used can be torn from the flipchart pad and retained as a poster on the training room wall.
- *Simple, cheap, needs little training* A principle advantage, the training necessary perhaps including skills in large, clear writing and using various other techniques for impact and use.

- *Usable for immediate recording* No preparation is necessary if it is to be used as a large jotting pad during a training session.
- *Postable anywhere* Sheets of paper, even the A1 size of the normal flipchart, are relatively light and can be posted on walls, doors, cabinets, and even curtains, using a dry, reusable adhesive such as Blu Tack.

Disadvantages

- *If badly prepared, can look unprofessional* A poor appearance can be off-putting to the learners, and the trainer's credibility can be reduced.
- *Usually only of temporary measure value* The paper medium will have a limited life which can reduce the value of the aid if it is important enough to be retained and reused.
- *Easily torn, dirtied and dog-eared* Although easily portable, it is also easy to damage the sheets in transit or in storage.
- *Special techniques difficult* There are some special techniques relevant to the use of flipcharts and these can take a certain amount of skill and dexterity. For example, a disclosure approach using covering cards held by Blu Tack or paper clips can be used, or constant reference back and forward to various sheets can be helped with folds and clips; both these techniques can go wrong very easily.

THE OVERHEAD PROJECTOR

Advantages

- *High visual impact* Because the image is projected by a light source, the visual impact can be high compared with a rather dull flipchart.
- *Usable in light* Unlike slide and film projectors, the room does not need to be darkened and so the trainer has continuous eye contact with the learning group.
- *Large image* The projected image can be large, the actual size limited only by the size of the screen or projection area, the light intensity of the projector and the type of lens used.

- *OHPs widely available* This item of equipment is nowadays almost as freely available in many locations as the flipchart; if it is not available where required, it is easily transportable, particularly the models specifically designed to be portable.
- *Used sitting or standing* Some trainers prefer to sit while presenting, others prefer to stand and/or walk about; the OHP permits either method of use, although it was designed for the trainer to be seated beside it.
- *Professional production* OHP slides can have a very professional appearance, whether they are made skilfully by hand, by commercial photographic techniques, or, more commonly now, as a computer graphic.
- *Slides easily portable* The acetate slides used with the OHP, whether mounted in card frames or in transparent folders, can be carried easily in a folder, briefcase or slide carrying case.

Disadvantages

- *Power required* Unlike, for example, the flipchart, an electric power source is required. Under most conditions this will not be a problem, but power failures still occur when the OHP cannot be operated, or only unsuitable power sockets are available and the trainer does not have a converter plug.
- *Older versions noisy* Older (and modern but cheaper) OHP models are cooled by a fan which can be very noisy in operation.
- *Condition variable* Although as mentioned in the list of advantages, OHPs are found in many locations, many are older, well-used models which can be in a poor condition.
- *Head post can obscure* Part of an OHP is the angled mirror mounted at the top of a column; this head can obscure part of the screen image from some parts of the group unless particular care is taken in seating arrangements.
- *Keystoning* Keystoning occurs when the top of the projected image is wider horizontally than the base, usually the result of a too acute angle of projection. The effect is off-putting and can sometimes be difficult to rectify.
- *Crowded slide encouragement* An acetate sheet from which OHP slides are produced can tempt the trainer to

include too much material on one slide. A major advantage of the OHP is its possibility for impact; overcrowding reduces this possibility.

THE WHITEBOARD

The whiteboard is the modern equivalent of the chalkboard on which, with the appropriate dry-marker pen, writing or drawing can be made. It has many similarities also with the flipchart though it is less portable, being usually much larger (although whiteboards about 6 inches by 4 inches and increasing sizes can be obtained). Like the flipchart, whiteboards can be easel-mounted or wall-mounted. Entries can be erased – this is an advantage and a disadvantage: the board can be continuously used and re-used, but unless you have more than one board, entered material cannot be retained. Some advanced whiteboards have more than one 'board' which can be displayed electrically and others have a photocopying facility so that the entered data can be copied onto A4 paper, a useful facility as an immediate handout.

COMMON FLIPCHART, WHITEBOARD AND OVERHEAD PROJECTOR FACTORS

All three training aids have certain factors in common. The trainer can introduce these in a brief input, brief to avoid over-passivity by the learning group, particularly as they can be later asked to look more closely at these and other areas and present their findings. The aspects can be considered under the headings:

- *Legibility* Each aid has specific requirements for size regarding entries, each based on the distance of the furthest learner from the aid, the lighting conditions and so on.
- *Writing on the medium* Writing or drawing on all the training aids is different from making the same entries on, for example, an A4 sheet of paper. Trainers must practise these different skills to ensure a professional approach which links with the legibility issue. There are also physical requirements concerned with writing – keeping lines

horizontal, not talking to the flipchart, and even not writing on the projection screen (it does happen!).

- *Use of colour, etc.* There are many opportunities in the use of visual aids to ensure the impact of the message. This can be achieved by such means as a use of colour, underlining, upper and lower case, boxing entries and so on.
- *Material media used* All the aids being considered can be used in a variety of ways with a range of materials – writing, drawings, graphs, cards to hide or disclose and the use of variety can add further impact.

GOLDEN RULES FOR THE USE OF THE FLIPCHART, WHITEBOARD AND OHP

Flipchart

- It should be clear enough and the writing large enough to be read from anywhere in the training room
- When its use is complete, flip over to a blank sheet
- Do not turn away from your audience when writing on the flipchart.

Whiteboard

- All the flipchart rules apply, but remember to use the correct dry marker pen
- Remember that it is only too easy for whiteboard entries to be erased.

Overhead projector

- Point to the slide on the projector, not at the screen
- Switch off as soon as you have finished with a slide, but remember switching on/off, on/off, on/off in swift succession is distracting.

THE CONSTRUCTION OF VISUAL AIDS

The new trainers themselves must learn to produce visual aids in addition to using the equipment effectively. Some mention has been made earlier about some of the common aspects of the three aids under discussion: legibility, impact, the use of colour and so on. However, there are some special techniques that can be used to improve the effectiveness and the impact of the aids. Some of these are applicable to the flipchart, some to the whiteboard, some to the OHP and some to all.

These include:

- disclosure techniques – all the three media
- additive techniques – all the three media
- pencil guidelines for lines or words and other physical aids – flipchart.

Disclosure techniques One of the problems of showing a complete visual aid, whether flipchart, whiteboard or OHP slide, is that while you are talking about the entries the learners are ahead of you on the chart – they can read faster than you can talk and extend the limited chart entries. This means that they may not be listening effectively to what you are saying.

One technique for avoiding this is to disclose only part of the chart, the part to which you are referring. The chart or slide is prepared before the session and, apart from the chart heading, all the entries are covered up.

With the flipchart, the most effective method of covering in this way is to have rectangles of card fixed over the several chart entries. Fixing can easily be made by using a dry adhesive such as Blu Tack. The principal problem encountered with this method is that you are unable to see the entries under the covering cards, unless you are so familiar with the charts that you can remember all the entries. It is safer to have a prompt on each card – a pencil entry on the card describing the hidden material will be seen by the trainer but not the participants.

If a dry adhesive is used frequently with a whiteboard to disclose entries, the surface of the board will deteriorate. Many whiteboards can be magnetic, and the cards can in these circumstances be held by small magnets. It must be said that the disclosure method of pre-prepared material is not as successful with the whiteboard as with other media – the pens used to write on the board are intended to be erased; this erasure can be accidentally done by the disclosure cards.

Several variations are available for the OHP. The cards can be simply laid over the slide entries without any fixing agent, although there is always the risk of slippage and premature disclosure. A sheet of opaque A4 paper can cover the items, being pulled down as required. This latter method has several caveats. If the paper is placed over the slide, the entries beneath it cannot be seen and the sliding movement makes pencil entries unworkable. Also, as the sheet nears the bottom of the slide, because of the paper overhang plus air movement caused by the OHP fan, the paper can fall off the slide. These problems can be easily avoided by placing the paper sheet *under* the OHP acetate slide. The slide holds the paper sheet down and the entries of the slide can be seen. This method of disclosure, however, makes the disclosure inflexible as entries *must* be uncovered in the order of their positions progressively lower down the slide.

The card disclosure can be made more effective on the OHP slide by some means of anchoring. One end of each card can be anchored as a hinge by means of adhesive tape, the card being swung to the side when required.

Obviously the card covers need not be rectangles, regular or otherwise: if the chart or slide contains graphic entries rather than words, the cover can be roughly the shape of the graphic – the rough shape can make the covered graphic even more interesting!

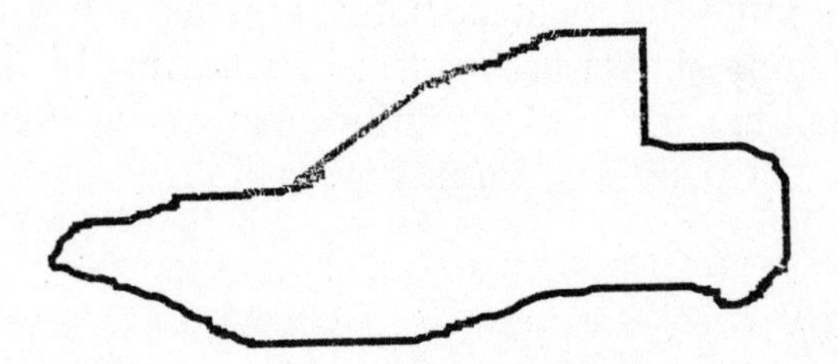

Additive techniques The additive technique, as its name suggests, is the opposite to the disclosure method and starts with a blank flipchart, whiteboard area or OHP slide. Obviously, little preparation can be made before the session and, in fact, the method is intended to be used as an immediate technique.

With the flipchart and the whiteboard, the straightforward addition during a session is to start with a blank area and as the result of asking the group questions or simply writing on the area, material is added. The card technique can be used in reverse – pre-prepared cards can be added to the area as required by fixing them with a dry adhesive or magnet. For example, the training group might be asked to suggest the ten advantages of using such-and-such. As the advantages are called out, the trainer can place the relevant card on the area, not necessarily in a neat logical table. Or in an input session, as the trainer starts to describe the ten advantages of using such-and-such he or she can place the card on the area as the advantage is introduced. The principal objection to the method of adding cards from the suggestions by the learners is that it is obvious that the trainer has the information cards and can be accused of wasting time by waiting for the information to be called out. Another 'problem' for the trainer is when the learners do not call out all the required information – the missing information cards have then to be produced and the trainer can again be accused of manipulation.

Similar methods can be used with the OHP slide with written additions being made to a clear acetate sheet or prepared acetate pieces placed on the OHP. A more permanent additive slide can be produced by using the hinged disclosure cards. In this instance the cards are folded away from the slide and folded onto it when the item is required.

An alternative additive method for the OHP can be to place progressively a series of slides on the OHP to build up a composite picture. Registration must be accurate – marks can be made on each slide – or the slides can be bound together at one edge so that they can be hinged over as required. The former method permits flexibility but has the non-registration danger, whereas the latter is inflexible but ensures accurate registration.

PREPARATION CRIBS

Some of the methods described above can produce problems for the trainer, but there are ways to avoid them; for example, the method of pencil entries on the disclosure cards was mentioned. There are other cribs and tips for use.

Invisible outline If you are unsure how much space will be used on a flipchart, not used to writing freehand on flipcharts, frightened that the writing will slide away from the horizontal, or are not sure about drawing a graphic in front of a group, an outline can be prepared before the session.

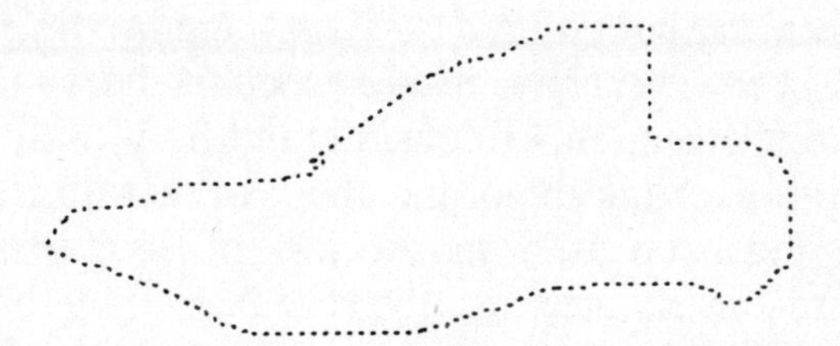

To help the writing along steady, horizontal lines, faint pencil lines can be drawn across the flipchart where required. Similarly, if key words are to be written on a flipchart during a session these can be pencilled on lightly before the session. If the pencil entries are made lightly, it is relatively easy for the trainer to see them, but it is unlikely the group, sitting some distance away, will see them at all.

Corner brief crib If you have to move away from your brief to the flipchart during the session and are concerned that you may forget what to enter on the flipchart, in the top corner of the sheet lightly pencil the key words so that you but not the learners will be able to see them. This avoids having to carry your brief with you every time you move to the flipchart.

Bookmarking There are times during a session when you are working with a flipchart sheet, whether pre-prepared or not, that you might wish to refer to a sheet which you have prepared and which is later in the pad. This sheet can be 'bookmarked' by placing a paper clip at the base of the sheet – this identifies the sheet and enables you to go to it immediately. If you have several sheets of this nature, two, three or more paper clips can be employed. Similarly, if you have just completed a sheet and you know you will have to refer to it later in the session, 'bookmark' it for easy reference.

Tearing sheets from the pad Some pads of flipcharts have the tops of each sheet perforated for easy removal, but many pads do not have this facility. Without a perforation, a certain 'law' will ensure that tearing the sheet off the pad will almost certainly result in an imperfect tear, at worst only half the sheet tearing off! One pre-preparation can be to score the top of the sheet lightly with a metal ruler or craft knife and actually cut the first inch – this will ensure a smooth tear and no embarrassment.

Finishing with an aid When you have finished with an aid, *get rid of it.* If you have used a flipchart sheet and you no longer need to refer to it, either detach it and fix it to the training room wall, flip it over the top of the chart, or tear it off. A whiteboard entry having been used and no longer required should be wiped off immediately after use (be sure that you will not want to return to it!) Failing to remove a used chart invites the learners to look at this rather than listen to your current input or other actions. When an OHP slide has been used, switch the projector off – you can always switch it back on again if you require the slide again, or a new slide. The light from an OHP is very invasive and attracts attention, even more so if there is no slide on it!

Colours, sizes and graphics Even if your favourite colours and shades tend towards the pastel or pale yellow, light red and light green, beware of these as they are not always clearly visible in the projected light. Instead use dark colours: the main image on the screen is produced by the marking interrupting the light beam from the projector bulb.

Write more clearly and bigger than you would normally do or think of doing. Small, rather unclear writing may be obvious to you at the flipchart, but 30 feet away at the rear of the group, it will possibly mean nothing. To ensure clarity, write more slowly than you normally do – it may seem very slow to you, but the learning group will probably not notice anything, especially if they can now read what you have written.

Use graphics – drawings, images, pictures, cartoons – as much

Figure 7.1 Supplementary graphics for visual display

as possible, either supplementing the words on your chart or slide, or taking their place. This approach is simple if you prepare your slide by means of a computer software package. The graphics in Figure 7.1 are typical of what is available in addition to the usual text symbols referred to earlier.

Post-its When you are asking the group for ideas, suggestions, items of information, or anything similar that you would normally write on a flipchart which would then be posted on the training room wall, use Post-its. Have the learners write their key words clearly on Post-its, then stick them all on a flipchart or flipcharts or whiteboard. A similar use can be made of pieces of acetate to be placed on the OHP – this would normally be a temporary activity.

OTHER TRAINING AIDS

Other training aids include:

- Audio cassette players and combined slide/audio projectors
- Episcopes
- Handouts
- Interactive video
- Slide projector
- The computer
- Video OHPs
- Video player.

Space does not permit a detailed description of these more advanced training aids, but the recommended reading list suggests some of the sources of further information which may be required when you are called upon to use them.

REFERENCES AND RECOMMENDED READING

Developing Training Skills. Tim Pickles, Bruce Britton and Howie Armstrong. Longman, 1991.
Faultless Facilitation. Lois B Hart. Kogan Page, 1992.
How to Develop and Introduce Trainer Development Programmes. Leslie Rae. Kogan Page, 1994.

How to Develop and Present Staff Training Courses. Peter Sheal. Kogan Page, 1989.

How to Write and Prepare Training Materials. Nancy Stimson. Kogan Page, 1991.

Practical Training. Jonathan Coates. Nimrod, 1984.

Presentation Skills. Mike Fenwick. Fenman Training, 1994.

Producing Teaching Materials: A Handbook for Teachers and Trainers. Henry Ellington and Phil Race. Kogan Page, 2nd edition, 1993.

Running an Effective Training Session. Patrick Forsyth. Gower, 1992.

Selecting and Using Training Aids. David Flegg and Josephine McHale. Kogan Page, 1991.

Teaching Hard. Teaching Soft. Colin Corder. Gower, 1990.

The Instructor's Handbook. John Townsend. Management Pocketbooks, 5th edition, 1991.

The Staff Development Handbook. Peter Sheal. Kogan Page, 1992.

The Theory and Practic of Training. Roger Buckley and Jim Caple. Kogan Page, 2nd edition, 1992.

The Trainer Development Programme, Leslie Rae. Kogan Page, 1994.

Using Video in Training and Education. Ashly Pinnington. McGraw-Hill, 1992.

8 One-to-one interaction training

The training in groups discussed in the last chapter involved individuals learning skills within a group. The activities included require a group of whatever size to interact within itself and allow a more individual learning, with the side benefit that others in the group will also learn. The learning of task skills can result from these approaches, but some form of human relations training is the more usual end result.

The more common training aim in this different group approach is one or more of the many types of interview or one-to-one interactions. This training can involve counselling approaches, interview techniques in discipline, grievance, conflict, negotiation and so on.

In any skills or knowledge training event, many approaches are available to the trainer, and the more successful courses often utilize a mix of the methods appropriate to the training needs or the group atmosphere. A similar variety of methods can also be introduced in one-to-one learning. Few trainers nowadays would design such a course on purely lecture lines, even the more enlightened lecture approaches. Naturally, where the techniques involved are new to the trainees, there will be a need for some input by the trainer, but the achievement of real learning will depend strongly on an experiential approach. This will be the case when the trainees are given the opportunity to practise the techniques in the 'safe' atmosphere of the training course. There is little doubt that these practical activities are integral to this form of training, both to reinforce learning the techniques and to rehearse them before returning to work and to real-life, critical interactions. There can be nothing more frightening for a would-be interviewer in, say, a job appraisal review than having to perform without ever having had a previous try without the pressures of real life.

The main problem encountered in providing opportunities for practice is the difficulty of making the interactive situation as near real life as possible. If the practice can be identified too readily as a training exercise, the trainee can rationalize his failure by saying that the artificiality of the situation prevented him from behaving as he would in real life.

ROLE PLAYING

The simplest way to provide a scenario for practice interviewing is to put the trainees into role-playing situations. In this approach, two roles have been constructed by the trainer, one for the interviewer and one for the interviewee. Both participants are given time to study the roles and in the practice interview are expected to put themselves as fully as possible into them. The main advantage of constructed role plays is that the trainer can include a number of attitudes and situations so that the required teaching points are brought out during the interview. On the other hand, however, the interview could fail completely if one or both participants do not for some reason carry out their roles, or feel that the situation is too unreal.

A variation of the requirement for both trainees to learn and enact roles is for the trainer to take on one of the roles, the particular role depending on the relevant training. This ensures that at least one of the roles is performed according to plan, but if the trainer is too involved in the event, he can be accused of making the situation too unreal. This is common when the trainee has not done as well as he had hoped and enters a defensive, rationalizing state. The first objection can be overcome by using the rest of the group as observers and appraisers, or by recording the interview on videotape. After the interview, the event is played back and the trainer and trainee can view the recording together, using a tape-stop method to review critical incidents. The defensive attitude of the trainee is more difficult to combat and reliance must be placed on the trainer's skills to avoid or reduce such a reaction.

One attempt to make the roles more realistic is to use cases from real life with which the trainees can identify. This approach can make the role situation more acceptable to many participants, in the same way that structured exercises for groups based on work events can be more 'live'.

REAL PROBLEM ROLE PLAYING

Even more realistic is the use of a real problem brought to the course by a course member. In this event, the owner of the real problem takes the part of either the interviewer or interviewee with another member taking the other part. Unfortunately, although the problem is one of real life, we have to rely on almost total role playing. The participant who is not the problem owner has to be briefed on the role he has to play. This briefing has to be very thorough and can be more difficult to assimilate than the carefully thought out, written role briefing produced by the trainer. The problem owner may similarly have to act out a role in most cases, if he takes the part of the person with whom he has the problem at work. In spite of the difficulties resulting from this approach, it has much to commend it as the problem owner is forced to see the other's point of view. The difficulties are reduced if the problem owner takes the role that he would in real life, namely that of the interviewer: the training event becomes very much a rehearsal for the real event, and the trainee gains insight into how he can approach it.

Whatever the degree of role playing, there is very little opportunity for learning from the situation if there is no appraisal of the interaction. This means that the event must be observed, which can introduce further problems.

ROLE-PLAYING OBSERVATION

Two standard methods of observation are commonly used, although there are numerous variations within each. The basic method is for the trainer to act as the observer and use his observations as a base for the subsequent appraisal. The advantages of this approach are that the trainee is skilled in noting both critical incidents and giving balanced feedback after the interview; problems can arise if the trainer is not sufficiently skilled. Even if he is, the criticism, however constructive it may be, may not be acceptable to the trainee, often because the trainer is viewed as the power figure and the rejection is a natural opposition to power.

There is less risk of rejection if the rest of the group takes the observational role and gives the subsequent appraisal. The interviewer under review is usually more ready to accept criticism from his peers. However, this requires the remainder of the group to be present during the interview – the fishbowl situation – and the actors in the interaction may feel constrained. The trainer, of course, has a much lesser role to play in this variation as the chairman of the appraisal and perhaps 'sweeper-up' of any important aspects that may have been omitted or avoided.

The risks of defensiveness on the part of the recipient are still present even when the criticism comes from peers. Perhaps the most effective approach is to involve the interview interactors themselves as the principal appraisers. In this approach, following the interview, the interviewer may be the first one to be asked about his own performance. An individual is likely to be more critical of himself than others would be, although there is the danger that he is so unaware of his own performance that he is unable to give a realistic appraisal. The self-appraisal of the interviewer is supported or it may be contradicted, particularly if the self-appraiser has low awareness, and the interviewee is then asked for his reactions. The interviewer is in a very difficult position to argue, as the interviewee was reacting directly to his behaviour. If anything else needs to be said, additional comments can then be made by the observers, with the trainer taking a very minor role as 'sweeper-up' or summarizer.

The problem has been raised earlier of disturbance of the interview by the presence of observers. But such a presence is essential, as has been pointed out when we considered observing group activities. As discussed, the remainder of the group can act as the observers, or, more usually and often more effectively, several role plays can be taking place at the same time, each with one or two observers. In order to help these observations of the face-to-face interaction, each observer can be provided with a guideline sheet or checklist to give some indication of what to look for and what to feed back. Such checklists can concentrate the observer's attention on the task or the process, or a combination of both. There will normally be a number of generic questions, whatever the type of role play task, and also questions specific to role play. A typical observation checklist is shown in Figure 8.1; this is intended to be used in observation of a negotiation role play, but it can easily be modified for other purposes. The checklist is taken from *50 Activities for Developing Management Skills, Volume 1* by Leslie Rae (Gower, 1988).

Checklists of this nature can be used generally as described

NEGOTIATION APPRAISAL SHEET

1. (Check on the Negotiation Techniques handout and identify which techniques were used by both negotiators.)

2. How satisfied were you with the outcome of the negotiations?

   Extremely dissatisfied — Extremely satisfied

   1 2 3 4 5 6

   Comment:

3. How satisfied were you with the performance of the negotiator?

   Extremely dissatisfied — Extremely satisfied

   1 2 3 4 5 6

   Comment:

Figure 8.1 Observation checklist

4. Mark an 'x' above the number best describing one negotiator on each dimension, and an 'o' above the number best describing the other.

Rigid					Flexible
1	2	3	4	5	6
Suspicious					**Trusting**
1	2	3	4	5	6
Inconsiderate					**Considerate**
1	2	3	4	5	6
Competitive					**Cooperative**
1	2	3	4	5	6

5. How willing would you be to negotiate with either party at some stage in the future?

Very willing					Very unwilling
1	2	3	4	5	6

6. Why do you feel that way?

7. Any other comments?

Figure 8.1 concluded

earlier for use with group activities. Perhaps the most effective feedback and appraisal is to follow this format.

Immediately following the interaction

1) Invite the interviewer or initiator of the interaction to appraise their own performance, either in terms of the learning which may have preceded the role play, or in any appraisal terms they choose.
2) Invite the recipient of the interview to comment on how they saw the interaction and the behavioural/task skills of the interviewer from their viewpoint.
3) The observer(s) then give(s) neutral feedback from the viewpoint of the outside observer, stressing only those points which have not already been made and perhaps giving examples of incidents which describe all the appraisal aspects.
4) Finally, the trainer, if he has been involved in watching the interview, can add any significant comments which have not already been made. Otherwise, the trainer's role is to relate the interview and the feedback to the process being considered (in this case negotiating skills), and of course to thank the participants for taking part.

A possible solution to observer problems was suggested in the case of appraisal by the trainer when he was involved himself in the interview. This introduced the use of video-recording, and the technique can be used in a much wider sense.

USE OF CLOSE-CIRCUIT TELEVISION IN OBSERVATION

The criticism of the interviewer and interviewee being surrounded by observers can be avoided by removing them to a viewing room at the end of a link provided by closed-circuit television (CCTV). In addition to removing a potentially distracting audience, placing the observers in front of a TV screen polarizes their awareness of the behaviour of the two participants without the distractions of the surroundings. At the end of the interaction the observers and participants can be brought together for the appraisal. If video-recording has also been employed, the recording can demonstrate aspects of good and weak performance to the participants, particularly if they were not aware of the incidents on which comments had been made.

There are naturally a number of schools of thought on how appraisals of this type of interaction should be conducted. If CCTV with video-recording is used, the simplest approach is to have the interviewer play back the recording and draw his own conclusions about his performance. This requires diagnostic skills on the part of the self-observer. The next step from this solo stage would include the trainer with the interviewer in the appraisal process, with the trainer identifying critical incidents. The progressive stage from this would be as described earlier, with a group of observers also making appraising comments.

Effective appraisal can still be attained without the use of CCTV and video-recordings and some trainers believe that they can be too great a distraction.

My own approach to appraisal when I am not using CCTV is based on the philosophy that most people will be more critical of their own behaviour and activities than external observers, and provided there is a conducive atmosphere, will express their views openly. In fact, one of the main problems is that they can be over-critical, but this can work in favour of the other appraisers who can concentrate on the good points and show the interviewer that he wasn't as bad as he thought.

Even if real-life problems are used for the interaction, there is still a problem that at least one of the participants has to act a role. An even more effective approach is to give the problem owner the opportunity of acting out the problem without recourse to role playing. The opportunities for this approach are found commonly in counselling training, where the interviewer is practising the counselling interview techniques with no requirement to act a role other than as counsellor. There is a very practical difficulty in attempting this approach unless the training climate is open and supportive; if it is not, real involvement and interest in the expression of the problem are difficult or impossible and artificiality returns.

Once the atmosphere is right and the participants are willing to talk openly about their problems in front of others, variations on the straightforward interaction can be attempted.

REVERSE ROLE PLAYING

One of these variations is known as 'reverse' role playing and is a useful introduction when, although the problem is being openly discussed, the learner is doing little more than exposing the problem and his feelings. It may be necessary to go further than this so that the problem owner can become aware of the deeper implications of the problem, how the problem is viewed by the other person and also to show how one is perceived by others. At a critical stage in the interaction, the facilitator causes the two participants to switch roles and places. The problem owner then becomes the person against whom the grievance is aimed and begins to see the problem from the other point of view. New insights may be gained from this role switch into how others feel when problems are directed against them. As a result of this new insight, the problem owner can look anew at the problem or how he is interacting with the other person.

Reverse role playing requires very sensitive control by the facilitator, who must be able to assess when the switching should take place. He must also have a deep awareness of human behaviour and the implications of enabling complete openness about feelings. The event could be dangerous to the mental state of the individual, and the trainer must be capable of handling this.

DOUBLING ROLE PLAYS

A less traumatic variation is 'doubling' or 'ghost' role playing. This approach can be helpful to an interviewer who is having difficulty in progressing the interview. Several variations exist within the general description. In one, the trainer takes an active part by moving behind the interviewer and taking over the role temporarily, leaving the original participant to continue after the intervention.

Another variation is for a member of the group, rather than the trainer, to step forward and act as the 'ghost' for a temporary period. At different times during an interaction, several members of the group might intervene.

There are a number of reasons why another person might wish to take an active part in the interaction. The principal participant may have reached a point in the interaction when he is unable to proceed, having perhaps lost confidence or ideas; the external observer may be in a better position to assess the next move. It may be that the observer has seen that the interviewer has missed an opportunity to progress the interview in an effective manner. For example, the interviewee may have made a significant comment which is missed by the interviewer and if it had been seized would have given a real insight into the problem. Again, it may be that the observer sees more than the people directly involved, or there may be simpler reasons. The observers may see that there are other, perhaps better, solutions than the one being used.

A very specific use of doubling is when all members of the group are encouraged to double for longer periods, rather than temporarily. In this way, a number of members of the group are given the opportunity of exploring alternative ways of handling a problem. Laird refers to this as a form of brainstorming.

Doubling has dangers in practice, particularly in the version where the trainer, without prior notice, steps in. His decision to do this may be wrong, with the interviewer resenting the intervention. It may be better training practice to allow the trainee to work out his own salvation. The situation may have been misread and the trainee may have been about to follow an effective line of action. However, these are risks that a trainer or facilitator must face if he is to move from the relatively safe 'chalk and talk' approaches.

The trainer can exercise some control in doubling in the variation in which other group members become involved as the interviewer, either for a short period or for a longer part of the interaction. Members in turn can be quietly designated to intervene rather than make a spontaneous entry. The risks described can still remain, however, unless everybody is aware of the intention of this approach.

THE EMPTY CHAIR ROLE PLAY

A more extreme variation of the real-problem approach is based on a gestalt technique and is known as the 'empty chair' or monodrama. This method can only be attempted at a stage in a training event when feelings are completely open and the participants have no inhibitions about exposing their deep feelings to the group. Only one individual is needed for the event and he must have strong feelings about problems, so strong that perhaps the individual will want to try this approach when others may have failed.

The scene is set with two chairs facing each other. The person with the problem sits in one chair; the other remains empty. When the participant feels ready, he starts to describe the problem to the 'person' in the empty chair and develops this monologue by talking through the problem as far as possible. This development can reach the stage when possible solutions may be discussed or even conclusions reached. At the very least, the technique offers the participant the opportunity to verbalize his problem without fear of interruption by the 'other person'. The benefit may even be based on the concept that a problem expressed is a problem at least eased. A variation of this approach, which demands the complete involvement of the participant, is for him at critical points, to change chairs and ask the 'speaker' questions about the problem or make comments. These comments may come easier in this way rather than being spoken directly by the 'real' individual.

NEGOTIATING SKILLS TRAINING

One of the many problems encountered in one-to-one interaction training using a group with similar training needs, especially when new techniques are introduced, can be the limited opportunity available for practice. A course in which I have been actively involved is concerned with negotiation skills, particularly in the one-to-one situation. Most of the course participants had little experience of actual negotiating and even less of the specific techniques that can be applied. To gain the skills and knowledge required inputs of information on techniques in addition to practice of them. The course had to take place within three days and consequently it was difficult to ensure that all members had some opportunity to practise the techniques. A further constraint was that CCTV was not available, so reliance had to be placed on 'live' appraisal methods. Obviously a compromise had to be reached and the programme was planned to include three complete negotiations in which all members had the opportunity to participate.

For each of the three negotiations, sets of two people were

chosen to negotiate with each other, and, as the course membership was limited to eight, four sets of negotiations were run simultaneously on each occasion. No observers were used – none was available – and as I was assisted by another trainer, we were able to observe approximately half of two sets of negotiations each. Our observations had to be supplemented in some way, so rather than ask the negotiators to appraise their own performances immediately following their negotiations, an intermediate stage was introduced. The participants were asked to complete a diagnostic questionnaire which related to aspects of negotiating and using this as a base, to discuss their own performances and reactions to each other for a period of time. After these dyadic discussions, all course members were brought together in plenary session to assess the success or otherwise of the negotiations and to share any significant and common problems of the process that had emerged. At this stage, the trainers were also able to add any observations. My experience of this approach to appraisal has been that as much, if not more, useful feedback emerges in the dyadic discussion as in most other appraisal events. However, it can fail if the pairs are not given some guidelines as to what aspects they should try to recall and discuss. In the event cited, the questionnaire served this purpose by asking specific questions about the behaviours and techniques used and observed.

1992 AND ALL THAT

It was expected that the 1992 revolution in European business would demand, alongside the basic negotiation techniques, an even greater variation in negotiation skills. This has indeed happened. Business negotiations have taken place throughout the world for a long time now, but each year international and national demands have increased. In the days of the British Empire and trade supremacy, British businessmen found no necessity to negotiate, but cultures and demands have changed and brought with them a widespread need for negotiation.

There is no longer one simple approach to negotiating, particularly as different cultures are involved. Consequently the approach to training must now take in a variety of approaches to suit an international market. For many years English has been one of the main languages of international business, so much so that non-English-speaking countries without a common language have used it as such. Some observers comment that two non-English-speaking negotiators can make themselves mutually understood better than can a British negotiator speaking English!

Changes are, however, now being observed in different cultures and relate mainly to attitudes and behaviours, although the negotiating structure can change too. Even within Europe these differences are significant. The Germans, who are well known for their efficiency, demand a guarantee of consistent standards and deliveries, for example. Hard bargains are the order of the day and because of the wide range of their own markets, such bargains may be difficult to fulfil apart from very specialist products. Formality is prominent in the negotiation, in comparison with the Americans who in general from the start want to be on first-name terms. Many negotiations with German businesspeople have been spoiled or at best retarded by too early a use of 'Hans' rather than an extended use of 'Herr Schmidt'!

The French negotiators use different ploys, one of which is likely to be an insistence on the use of their own language, even if they speak English well. If they do speak English, this is often a signal that they *do* need your services. Whereas the Germans are very formal, the French tend to be distant, apart from the physical movement of shaking hands with everybody on every occasion. Time is a peculiar aspect in negotiations with the French – they can tend to pay little regard to it, but you are expected to be punctual. Experiences have been recounted by negotiators and salespeople that late arrival has meant non-reception and consequently a lost sale. Good relationships need a long time to develop.

The Italians and even more so the Greeks, are less exacting in punctuality, so it is always useful to check beforehand whether the meeting is still on. Negotiating in these countries has been traditionally a way of life and its more informal nature must be recognized. Above all, the British negotiator must learn to slow down and not be concerned with the passage of time, even towards a deadline.

In contrast with the Europeans, even their own varieties, the American negotiators take a much more informal approach, although even they can become very impatient and aggressive. Within the constraints of general business requirements, they are much more open than their European counterparts. Usually the

Americans are after the best deal, rather than a well-negotiated, fair deal which is so often the British aim.

In even more contrast is negotiation with the Japanese, whose behaviour is the traditional, oriental one of patience, formality and a search for large concessions. One benefit in negotiations is a strong personal relationship, but even here 'yes' must not immediately be taken to mean exactly this.

Negotiating with the Arab race is different again. Many of the differences stem from the Arab devotion to the 'family' and consequently foreigners are foreigners in every sense of the word – they are not part of the 'family'. Negotiations may be interrupted by what might appear to a foreigner to be trivial reasons. But it would be disastrous to let this impatience show – time has little place in the Arab culture.

We must also look at ourselves. In general, the British are seen as arrogant and haughty in negotiation, ignorant of the language and culture of the other party, and are considered amateurs at negotiation – unprepared, inflexible at times and often not giving an impression of commitment. Obviously, this does not relate to every British negotiator, and many companies who have had to extend their markets have improved considerably. But there may still be a long way to go.

So the negotiation trainers in the 1990s must:

- research and plan the background and international needs more thoroughly
- know the cultures with which the potential negotiators are likely to be in contact
- know the negotiating vagaries of the various cultures
- look to a wider form of training than hitherto to produce more flexible and knowledgeable negotiators
- talk to members of the various cultures to assess current attitudes, because national attitudes and approaches can change with time.

TRIADS

In one-to-one interactions effective communication is recognized as an essential skill. What is not always realized is that a component of this communication is the ability to listen. Breakdowns in communication are probably more often caused by a failure to listen to what the other person is saying, than by the inability of one person to express himself. An exercise known as triad communication is designed not only to exercise precise expression, but to stimulate careful listening.

The members involved in the training are formed into triads – groups of three. One member of each group is nominated as the observer and judge, while the other two discuss a topic for a determined period of time. The topic is chosen so that both sides have strong, opposing views in order to promote active discussion. One of the participating members starts the discussion, but before a reply can be given, the receiving member must summarize accurately what the speaker has said. The speaker must agree that the summary is acceptable to him and the discussion cannot proceed further until this has been done. The observer takes no part in the actual discussion but acts as referee and timekeeper. He adjudicates on points of disagreement between the two speakers over the content of summaries.

At the end of the allotted time, the observer changes places with one of the original participants and a further discussion takes place. The roles are changed again when the second discussion is completed and the third member acts as the observer. In this way, each member of the triad acts as observer once and participant in two discussions.

Common elements of learning in triad activities include:

- feedback to the speaker on inaccurate expression
- discovery that the two speakers are not talking about the same thing.
- failure to listen to all that is said – selective listening
- saying too much in one contribution.

There are a number of drawbacks and quite often the participants complain that the summaries impede the discussion and make it too artificial to be realistic.

SOLVING PEOPLE PROBLEMS

Most one-to-one interaction training is concerned with techniques to solve problems of some nature and there is usually concentration on the solution of task problems. There are few systematic approaches to the problems of dealing with people and even fewer to solving one's own problems. Peter Honey has recently attempted to fill this gap with what he refers to as 'BMod' and 'FMod' approaches to solving people problems.

BMod is the abbreviation for Behaviour Modification and FMod for Feelings Modification. These are the bases of his approach to people problems. Honey freely admits that his approach has a long lineage, dating back to Sechenev's considerations in 1860 of people's behaviour and its relationship to reflex actions and internally planned activities. Also involved in the development of the approach was Pavlov at the turn of the last century, with his experiments on salivating dogs and their reaction to stimuli.

Honey suggests that where problems exist with people, some traditional methods of approaching solutions can be difficult, uncertain or even dangerous. Perhaps the most dangerous is the approach that starts with a manager wondering '*Why* did Fred do that?' In other words the problem is approached by attempting to consider the covert aspects related to the problem person – motives, attitudes and feelings. We can rarely be certain of the assumptions we have to make about others' internal events, but we can be certain about the overt behaviours we observe and the reactions to these behaviours of ourselves and others. The BMod approach concentrates on the overt behaviours and applies a sequence of events that can be considered as a logical approach.

If behaviour occurs, it must have a cue or trigger, and the individual behaving in this way must be gaining something from the behaviour – consequences or payoffs. In order to produce the new, desired behaviour, new cues or actions must be introduced and the new behaviour must give rise to new payoffs to attract the individual to the behaviour modification – BMod.

The application of BMod can be summarized in the model:

Cues → Undesirable behaviour → Payoffs
New cues → Desired behaviour → New payoffs

BMod can be applied to the problems one has with others – peers, subordinates, bosses, and even wives or husbands, when

- the problem results from someone else's actions or behaviour
- the problem is significant to you

- you have regular and frequent contact with the problem performer
- the problem is persistent.

FMod is the extension to BMod and is applied when the problem is caused by your own undesirable feelings. Your behaviour may need to be modified because of these undesirable feelings and you are not functioning at the level you feel you should.

These hindered feelings may result from

- vulnerability or embarrassment in talking to others
- feelings of inadequacy
- feelings of guilt
- fears of rebuttal
- irritation or anger
- uncontrollable thoughts – often when you want to sleep
- nervousness.

The approach to the identification of the problem and provision of a solution follows essentially the same lines as BMod, except that, naturally, covert aspects become involved. The model requires the individual to identify the unproductive feeling that is hindering effective behaviour and the cues that have triggered a mental reaction producing these feelings. A difficult stage follows in self-identification of the payoffs that are obtained as a result of the unproductive feelings. The question of modifying the unproductive feelings is now raised. This requires an internal discussion of the previously determined cues – can they be changed or modified? Can the mental reaction produced by these cues be modified to a more productive output? Can the payoffs remain but in a changed form? Linked with these, it may be necessary to release the unproductive feelings in some way or perhaps suppress them, although the latter approach is not recommended.

The FMod model produced follows the paths:

```
External cue       Hindered behaviour  →  External payoffs
     ↓                    ↑                      ↓
Mental reaction    Unproductive feelings  Internal payoffs
      ↓ replace     release ↓                    ↓ change
New cues    →   Productive feelings   →   New payoffs
```

Training in one-to-one interactions can be extremely satisfying to both trainer and student, but it is very demanding on the skills of the trainer, not only in providing as realistic situations as possible, but also in his ability to give or control feedback on performance. In group situations the individual can hide to some extent within the group and receive protection from direct comment. In one-to-one interaction training the individual is exposed in a singular situation and can feel very vulnerable. One way in which the trainer can come to terms with the probable feelings of his student is to draw a parallel with his own vulnerability and feelings at the front of a class, particularly in his early days as a not very experienced trainer. Training of this nature must also be highly effective, as many of us in our working lives spend much of our time in one-to-one, face-to-face interactions with very rarely any opportunities for feedback or guidance on the job. The manager, for example, can be a very concerned and lonely man when he has had a difficult interview with a member of his staff: the individual has left the room and the manager is left to wonder whether his approach was appropriate, and whether they were able to communicate effectively. Good training will at least have ensured that he has planned for the interaction as fully as possible, has used a structure appropriate to the situation in an intelligent manner, and his behaviour was in step with both his objectives and the demands of the interaction.

Most appraisals at work must be necessarily self-imposed and subjective, but an attempt to replicate the training environment appraisal can be valuable. Immediately after the interview, the interviewer can ask himself a set of questions designed to assess the effectiveness of the interaction. The answers inevitably have a subjective bias, but even this is better than no questions and answers at all. A typical self-assessment list of questions is shown below as an example. If this technique is given to the manager as part of the training course, the trainer has contributed in a positive way to the manager's continuing self-development and has tried to ensure that the training is transferred realistically.

PRACTICAL GUIDE AND CHECKLIST FOR EVALUATING PERFORMANCE AS AN INTERVIEWER

		YES	*NO*
1	'Did I have a firm idea in mind as to what the objective of the interview was?'		
2	'Did I make the purpose of the interview clear to the interviewee?'		
3	'Did I indicate to the interviewee where I wanted him to sit?'		
4	'Were we physically comfortable in the interview situation?'		
5	'Were we free from needless interruptions?'		
6	'Did I avoid doing other things while I conducted the interview?'		
7	'Did I have well-prepared introductory remarks?'		
8	'Did I try to develop a good atmosphere for the interview?'		
9	'Did I establish rapport with the interviewee?'		
10	'Did I make an effort to overcome any defensive attitude on the part of the interviewee?'		
11	'Did I talk to him on his level and in terms with which he is familiar?'		
12	'Did I instil confidence in him?'		
13	'Did I listen carefully to him?'		
14	'Did I make an effort to understand him?'		
15	'Did I avoid interrupting him?'		
16	'Did I avoid making snap judgements?'		
17	'Was I primarily non-judgemental in my attitude to the interviewee?'		
18	'Did I work from general to specific subjects?'		
19	'Did I look for hidden meanings in what he was saying?'		
20	'Did I give him the opportunity to express his feelings and emotions?'		
21	'Was I objective?'		
22	'Was I interested in what he was telling me?'		

		YES	*NO*
23	'Was I encouraging to the interviewee?'		
24	'Did I use the technique of asking encouraging questions?'		
25	'Did I utilize the technique of reflecting his views and feelings?'		
26	'Did I avoid asking closed and dead-end questions?'		
27	'Did I summarize what had been said and decided?'		
28	'Did I give him the opportunity to ask me questions?'		
29	'Did I avoid too much repetition?'		
30	'Did I give him the opportunity to formulate his own plans?'		
31	'Did I give unwarranted assurances?'		
32	'Did I try to get him to recognize his own problems?'		
33	'Did I avoid persuasion to get him to accept things?'		
34	'Did I handle adequately the discussion of sore subjects?'		
35	'Did I close the interview firmly, reviewing an action plan to which we had both agreed?'		

REFERENCES AND RECOMMENDED READING

The Effective Negotiator. Gerald M. Atkinson. Quest, 1975.

Counselling People at Work. Robert de Board. Gower, 1983.

The Interview at Work. John Fletcher. Gerald Duckworth, 1973.

Solving People Problems. Peter Honey. McGraw-Hill, 1980.

Approaches to Training and Development. D. Laird. Addison-Wesley, 1978.

Effective Performance Appraisals. Robert B. Maddox. Kogan Page, 1988.

The Role Play Technique. Maier, Solem and Maier. University Associates, 1975.

The Skills of Interviewing. Leslie Rae. Gower, 1988.

Role Playing: a Practical Manual for Group Facilitators. Shaw, Corsini, Blake and Mouton. University Associates, 1980.

The Skills of Appraisal. John Slater and Peter Packard. Gower, 1988. (A training package).

Practical Performance Appraisal. Valerie and Andrew Stewart. Gower, 1978.

How to Negotiate Worldwide. Donald Hendon and Rebecca Hendon. Gower, 1989.

The Effective Use of Role Play. Morry van Ments. Kogan Page, 1994.

Tidman's Media Interview Techniques. Peter Tidman and Lloyd Slater. McGraw-Hill, 1992.

9 Human relations training – I

Up to a dozen or so years ago, most training – with some notable exceptions – was concentrated on the acquisition of skills and knowledge. The skills and knowledge taught were directly related to technical or practical expertise. It was felt that skills related to human relationships were the province of the pyschologist and psychiatrist only. However, skilled and experienced trainers realized that they were able to enter the fields of behaviour, feelings and attitudes when they were relating well-validated human relations models to the practical problems of work, fields in which they had considerable practical experience. The borderline between human relations training and group therapy is indeed uncertain, and the trainer without psychological skills and experience must himself have a sensitive awareness of his limitations and dangers of playing games with the emotions and feelings of people. This principle is clearly outlined in my view by Valerie and Andrew Stewart who, when discussing T-Groups say

- they should never be run by amateurs. The professional trainer who has himself attended one or two T-Groups remains an amateur for this purpose
- they should be run by people with industrial experience who are anxious to help industry work better.

The same sentiments can be applied to any form of human relations training, not just the extreme example of the T-Group.

This chapter and the following one are both concerned with a variety of methods and approaches to human relations training and development. I make no apology for devoting two chapters to this particular aspect, as human relations training has developed to such an extent that to perform it effectively a greater range of training skills is needed than in any other field of training.

Practical human relations training, having translated psychological models to the working environment, has also introduced to the training world a plethora of jargon terms. Many new terms have been introduced that have only a quasi-psychological base, and psychological terms are bandied around often without real understanding of their meaning. After all we are all amateur psychologists! Perhaps there is more jargon in human relations training than in any other sector of the training and development field. In defence of jargon, many of the terms have a technical purpose with the intention of substituting a single word or phrase for a long explanation. The jargon of the trainer then becomes his language, perhaps in shorthand form, but unfortunately he can forget that others are not always *au fait* with the language.

My broad definition of human relations training is that which has specifically behavioural objectives. These objectives relate to such aspects as operating or managing style; awareness of behaviour in its many forms; modification, shaping or planning of behaviour; improvement of relationships, whether applied to an individual, group or inter-group. The overriding factor is that these objectives must be related to the individual's role in the organization in which he is employed. As a side-effect there may be an improvement in his total life structure, but this must not be allowed to subsume the work-related objectives. If someone has problems in his marital relationships, his approach to these should be through a marriage guidance counsellor, not, say, an interpersonal skills course arranged for his employing organization. Of course, if he learns during this course to relate more appropriately to his colleagues, there may be an application of this modified behaviour to a wider range of interactions.

Three broad approaches to human relations training and development can be identified. The structured approach involves the learners in events that are planned to progress them logically from an unaware state to one of increased awareness. The final level may be a predetermined aim of the trainer or of the learners themselves.

A modification of this approach can be described as semi-structured, in which, although a certain amount of the learning is structured by the trainer, a greater degree of direction is transferred to the learner at assessed stages.

The other end of the spectrum from the structured approach is the completely unstructured, unguided or unplanned event in which the learning is completely controlled, both content and degree, by the learners.

THE STRUCTURED APPROACH

Structured human relations training is very similar to the more technically biased courses, but as already described, the objectives are directly related to human relationships and behavioural skills, rather than work-related tasks, and practical and technical skills or knowledge. Such courses will normally include theory inputs, films, structured exercises, games, activities and discussions, all following a predetermined planned approach based on a particular behavioural model or models. It will be recognized that there is little room for variation within this approach. This restriction has advantages in addition to some disadvantages. The learners know where they are going, can recognize the progress and can anticipate what is to come. Other than the unavoidable threat when people's behaviour is being examined, threats to the security of an individual's feelings and emotions are held to a controlled level. Obviously this may be a constraining factor to the extent that the learners become committed to any proposed modification of behaviour. Commitment, however, is very difficult to define in any human relations approach, and whatever the type of approach, translation is completely in the hands of the learner. This will be even more so than in technical training.

One important advantage of a structured approach is that the trainer avoids the difficulties of unexpected events, and knows to some extent the demands and risks that will be required of him. As the activities themselves are largely structured, the trainer is able to cope with these using his professional experience and his own skills in and knowledge of the organizational needs. There will be little opportunity for trainers with a tendency to manipulate people for their own selfish reasons and less skilled trainers will have some confidence in approaching a difficult training area. After all, most training needs that can be approached by activities can be dealt with by a relevant structured activity rather than an unstructured approach, which is riskier for both the trainer and the learner.

THE MANAGERIAL GRID

Several specific techniques and methods can be employed in the structured approach. One of these is the managerial grid of Blake and Mouton. The management style of an individual can be identified, analysed and demonstrated on a two-dimensional grid. One dimension of the grid is related to the concern of a manager for the completion of a task. The other dimension is the concern of the manager for the people involved. This can result in polarized descriptions of various styles, obviously with intermediate shades.

Consequently, a managerial style of 1,1 is completely unconcerned with either the people or the task and demonstrates an impoverished management style in which there is minimum effort to get the work done. In many ways the manager has abdicated his responsibilities. On the other hand, 9,9 style is the team approach manager who has both high concern for people as well as production. This manager gets things done with high commitment from his workers. Other styles include the 1,9 style where there is high concern for people, but low concern for production – the manager is so involved in keeping his people happy that he ignores the principal task of a manager, that of getting the job done efficiently. The 9,1 style has low concern for people, but high concern for production. Here we have the dedicated autocrat who is determined to get the job done with minimum human interference. The organization man is shown by the 5,5 style where there is medium concern for both people and production. This manager achieves his production to an adequate level while maintaining morale to a satisfactory degree.

During a grid course, structured activities and questionnaires are used to identify, analyse and define the styles of the course participants. Linked with these activities, tutorials give the learners the opportunity to consider the style differences and their significance. Once the existing position has been clarified and, as far as possible, accepted by the learners, opportunities are afforded, mainly in the form of structured activities, to the learners to modify to a more appropriate style, or at least experiment with different approaches.

THE UNSTRUCTURED APPROACH –T-GROUPS

Let us jump to the other end of the spectrum and consider the unstructured approach to human relations awareness training. This was initially described as T-Group (T for training) or laboratory training and appears in varied forms as sensitivity training or encounter groups. Whatever the name, the aims and methods are broadly similar, namely to increase the personal awareness of the individuals and to give virtually complete control of the learning to them. Structured exercises rarely appear, and if they do they are related to the event rather than to the work of the participants. Such an activity could be an invitation from the facilator for the group to consider the barriers to the development of a group.

The trainer or facilitator in a T-Group takes a minimal role other than encouraging the group in the early stages to develop its own identity and purpose. He will then become even more passive when this is under way and the group will become totally responsible for its own development and progress. The facilitator will always make himself available as a resource to the group and even formal sessions and structured activities can be included and arranged by the facilitator, but only at the request of the group. It will be recognized that any T-Group can and will be quite different from any other T-Group, since its eventual format will depend on the needs of differing individuals in different groups. In fact it is common for a single T-Group to divide for the duration of the event into two or more groups because the participants feel they can progress more effectively in this way. Because of the infinite and unexpected ways a T-Group can develop and the variety of demands on the facilitator, he must have a high degree of skill in assessment, consulting, counselling and intervention techniques. He must also have a wide range of techniques and methods upon which to draw on demand by the group. Above all he must have a high degree of sensitivity to behaviour and emotions, and, from this, know when he should intervene, whether he should, and how he should, if events are becoming out of hand. If this occurs, the sensitivity training purists will maintain that whatever the degree of catastrophe, the group should have no external interference and should be left to solve all its own problems.

In the same way there can be variation between the development and end result of different T-Groups, so the initial stages of the event can vary. This is completely in the hands of the facilitator, although as seen earlier the control passes quickly over to the group. One strategy is for the facilitator to open the course in the usual way and then inform the group that what it learns is completely in its hands. He then sits back and refuses to take any further active part until the later stages, when the group may invite him to join it as a resource. Some events inform the participants of the date, time and location of the start of the course, but when they have congregated no facilitator appears. Consequently they are forced into group action and decisions right from the start.

There is little doubt that the principle behind the T-Group approach is a potentially powerful and educative one, but serious doubts have been expressed about the usefulness of the approach in real learning terms and the atmosphere of the event can in fact damage rather than remedy.

The approach is certainly one concerned with an individual's personal life constructs, and participants may have difficulty in relating these to the principles and philosophy of their organization. Most frequently the participants form a 'stranger' group, that is a group composed of individuals who do not know each other and come from different organizations. At best it can be a 'cousin' group – people who belong to one organization but do not know each other, or who perhaps may have met somewhere else. It is rare to have a group which consists of people who are well acquainted with one another, perhaps from the same unit of an organization or even a single section or department. It usually happens when a consultant is brought into an organization or the event is organized in-house by the company trainers. If the T-Group has been a stranger or cousin group, participants have reported that on their return from the event, which to them had been fully effective and meaningful, they were distressed to meet apathy or even resentment from their colleagues who were not as aware as they. The result of this was that the learning and new behaviours were stifled.

Even greater problems have arisen with individuals during the event because of the personal learning levels that are attained. The basic intention of the event is to encourage the participants to expose their feelings and emotions to others, whether these become friendly or antagonistic. One danger is that the participants can attempt approaches at which even a professional psychologist would blanch. If the facilitator is absent, the event could become extremely traumatic with dangerous effects on the participants; if he is present, but is not highly skilled in intervention, he could make the situation worse.

As a result of misadventures such as those cited people have left a group in a highly distressed condition. Some participants have completed the course only to return to a working atmosphere that they found completely alien and antagonistic to the attitudes they had been led to believe they should pursue, with a variety of disastrous results. It is, of course, difficult to determine the extent of these particular cases, as it is to identify those who have obtained benefit from the experience. The Training Services Agency of the Manpower Services Commission (as it then was) funded a survey of T-Groups run by reputable training organizations and concluded that 5 per cent of the participants were hurt by the experience and 30 per cent had been helped. This survey was restricted in scope and hardly conclusive, but it did point to dangers, particularly for certain individuals to whom damage was more likely to occur. It must also be recalled that not every T-Group is arranged and run by a reputable organization.

THE SEMI-STRUCTURED APPROACH

It was mentioned earlier that a halfway house exists in the semi-structured approach to human relations or interactive skills training. In this approach the intention is for the participants to increase their awareness of their own and others' behaviour and how to handle this in as non-threatening a way as possible. It also tries to relate the event and the learning achieved directly to the individual's working environment and relationships. My own philosophy of interpersonal skills training follows this approach and differs significantly from the T-Group particularly in the early stages of the event. I fully support the axiom of Skinner in that to acquire behaviour, the student must engage in behaviour, but I also feel that in the early stages of an event some help and guidance is necessary, if only to put the learners on the road to self- or mutual discovery. I do not believe that the activities in which they engage must necessarily be job-related, but they should be able to be related to the participants' work or be translatable to that environment. In any post-activity discussion, the group is encouraged to relate the emerging lessons or learning points to their own situations.

It may be useful to describe the training in interpersonal skills that I run, not putting this forward as an ideal event, but as one from which in my experience success is achieved, both from my point of view as facilitator and the expressed views of large numbers of participants.

The objectives of the course are

- to increase the participant's awareness of his own behaviour
- to increase the participant's awareness of the effects of his behaviour on others
- to increase the participant's awareness of the behaviour of others and the effects of these behaviours on self and others
- to give the opportunity to participants to consider and apply, where necessary, behaviour shaping, behaviour modification and behaviour planning.

The course begins at a Monday lunchtime and ends at the Friday lunchtime, and has a normal complement of twelve members. With this full course membership two facilitators are employed, although if the initial number decreases to between six and nine, I act as the sole facilitator.

Immediately after lunch on the first day, the full course meets in one group to have a normal course welcome. There are differences, and at this stage the differences between the event and a traditional training course are stressed and every attempt is made to describe the event in open terms and to respond to any questions in a similarly open way. The comments about the philosophy of the course include reference to:

- the emphasis on behaviour rather than personality
- the existence of a structure to the event as far as the facilitators are concerned at this initial stage, but
- the complete acceptance by the facilitators, at any time, of requirements and needs of the participants and particularly those which will involve any change of learning direction
- the transfer of control from the facilitators to the learners at any time on demand by the learners, but with some reservation of the rights of the facilitators to propose activities that they feel are relevant.

The full group is quickly divided into two groups, each with a facilitator, with the aim that both groups will work independently for most of the time unless they decide on other approaches. The selection of the groups has been made in a variety of ways: an arbitrary mix based on location/sex/age of members; a mix of high contributors only in one group and low contributors only in the other group; a mix of both high and low contributors in each group, and various mixes of activists, theorists, reflectors and pragmatists. None of these mixes has shown any significant influence on the learning.

The first small-group activity attempts to ease the stranger atmosphere having the members decide how to and perform introductions of themselves to each other in terms of 'What sort of person are you?' The facilitator demonstrates his role intention by taking a passive, non-directive part in this activity. Following the introductions activity, an attempt is made to encourage further opening by suggesting a discussion on personal objectives, sometimes encouraged by the use of learning style questionnaires or personal objectives identification instruments. The day is usually brought to a conclusion with a final activity aimed at bringing the group together. A list of short discussion topics is posted on newsprint and the group is invited to use these topics for mini-discussions of each. The topics normally include 'A weakness I would like to improve is . . .', 'When I enter a new group I feel . . .'. 'I came on this course because . . .', and 'My first impressions of this group are . . .'.

The second day starts with the small groups being asked to consider the activities performed during the previous day, in buzz groups first, then as a group, to determine the helping and hindering actions and attitudes they observed. They are then recommended to discuss and formulate guidelines by which the group can operate during the remainder of the course.

From this point in the course, the movement of events can depend on the attitude of the group and can result in an almost complete take-over of control by the group or continued reliance for a time on activities provided by the facilitator.

A recent event was typical in many ways. During the guidelines discussion a problem arose about the specific role of the chairman or group leader, the appointment of whom on a rotating basis had been decided during the discussion. This led to the group's decision that it would take time to consider the role of a leader and the qualities necessary, as an unstructured activity. This led in turn to two self-determined unstructured activities concerning first the role and position of the facilitator in or with the group, and then a consideration of what makes a team effective. In the latter activity, views started being expressed that were concerned more with the relationships and attitudes within the group than with the task alone. The end of the second day had been reached by now and it was apparent that the group was settling down into a working relationship rather than as the initial stranger group.

The next morning, the group decided that as it seemed to be in a formative stage as a working group and was developing apparently effective ways of operating, it required a vehicle to test these attitudes. An activity that would satisfy this objective was requested and provided. Afterwards, a full, reasonably open, and personalized discussion of the event took place, and although the various conflicts that had arisen were looked at, they tended to be smoothed over.

To this stage I had been taking a relatively passive role intervening for the most part in a questioning and issue-raising manner when significant incidents occurred – a contract made when the group had discussed my role. Sometimes I was told by the group to keep out of it, and at other times the task was interrupted to take up the points raised. But more importantly I was performing two other tasks. First, I was making my own assessments of the individual behaviours and the group relationships to give personal feedback later in the course – another part of my contract made with the group. Second, I was using Behaviour Analysis as an objective means of collecting behavioural data which would also be used as an eventual feedback to the group. I shall return later to this particular subject in more detail.

It was at this stage of the course that I assessed that the group might welcome and find of value guidance on behaviour awareness and methods of improving this skill. The group agreed and we spent some time discussing various approaches to this skill, concentrating especially on Behaviour Analysis as a form of interaction analysis. This period included information giving on my part, discussion and practice in the skills of Behaviour Analysis.

The learning event continued to develop and progress with structured and unstructured activities, feedback on observed behaviour, analyses of the group and individual progress to what all participants considered to be the climax of the course. This developed into a very full and open consideration of 'Where are we now, and where do we go?' This was reached during the afternoon of the penultimate day. By this time, conflicts were being brought out naturally into the open, discussed and resolved; comments on each others' behaviours and reactions to these were being made, usually in a constructive way and not threatening to the recipient; and honest doubts of various natures were freely expressed and discussed. I was asked to become a full member of the group at this stage and we looked closely at behaviour shaping, planning and modification.

During the final morning of the course, the group discussed the translation of the overall learning to their working environments, made personal action plans for putting what they had learned into practice, and discussed these plans with each other.

Incidentally, on this occasion no thought was given by either group to joining with the other group, which had reached a roughly similar stage of development by quite different means. This is quite common during a course of this nature and depends on the emerging needs of either or both the groups.

The foregoing has been a description of a typical, as far as 'typical' is relevant, interpersonal skills course of a semi-structured nature. Descriptions of the same course with different groups could be completely different and a course utilizing these methods is obviously not the only approach.

TRANSACTIONAL ANALYSIS

Another approach to human relations training is offered by Transactional Analysis. This is a method that attempts to give people insight not only into how they behave, but also why they behave in that way. As a training approach it has developed from a method of psychotherapy introduced by Eric Berne in the United States. In his observation of patients he noted that behavioural changes occurred in response to different stimuli as if the person were being controlled by different inner beings. He also noted that those behaviours controlled by the 'inner selves' produced transactions or interactions with others in different ways, and these transactions could be analysed. Other observations made by Berne were that there were hidden motives beneath many of the apparent transactions and people used these to manipulate others, particularly in 'game' playing.

The structural analysis part of Transactional Analysis (TA) identifies the aspects of individual personality and TA analyses what people say and do to each other. The basis of the approach is that each person has three ego states which are separate and distinct sources of behaviour originating from the person's experience throughout life from babyhood. One can consider these states as three internal tape recorders which record experiences and play them back throughout our lives.

The three ego states are referred to as the Parent, Adult and Child states. The Parent state contains all the feelings and emotions learned by an individual as an infant from birth to about the age of five, primarily from parents, but also from other parent-type figures in a child's life. The stances, attitudes and behaviours of our parents are indelibly stamped on us and are played back as part of our own behaviour when we ourselves are grown up. This playback is evidenced as the prejudiced, critical or nurturing behaviours to others. When one acts, thinks, feels, behaves as one's parents used to do, one is acting in the Parent ego state – the Parent tape recording is being played. This often becomes very evident when we are ourselves parents, seeing in our actions and comments to our children the reflection of our parents. But it can also be seen in the working environment when prejudiced, critical or nurturing reactions occur with our colleagues or staff.

The Child ego state contains all the feelings and emotions engaged in as an infant, again up to about the age of five or so, the free and uninhibited expressions of joy, sorrow, distress, distaste and so on. The playback behaviour as a grown-up is expressed in almost exactly these terms, and when one is feeling, expressing and behaving as a child, one is acting in the Child ego state.

The Adult ego state can operate at any age and is concerned with the collection of information and its logical application. When one is examining current facts, gathering information and tackling problems in a rational and logical way, the Adult ego state is operating.

The important application of this analysis is the development of awareness of which ego state one is behaving in and in which one should be behaving. Additionally, there should also be awareness of the ego state of the other person with whom the interaction is taking place. If this awareness exists and the ego states are matched, the transaction, whatever its level, should be satisfactory. If the ego states do not match, particularly when the interactors are unaware of this, the interaction breaks down and both people walk away wondering what went wrong.

A human relations training event using TA as its basis starts with an exposition of the model, followed by activities designed to demonstrate to the participants the different states in which they can operate and their effects. Having identified the states and improved their awareness, the participants can then take part in activities which will help to improve their transactional skills.

The awareness of ego states and their appropriate use is not the only aspect of TA that can be discussed and considered in a behavioural manner. TA has its own collection of jargon terms, which includes strokes, rituals, pastimes and activities, scripts, games and trading stamps.

GAME PLAYING

A very popular pastime for some people is identified in *game playing.* A game is a series of transactions indulged in by two or more people and follows a predictable pattern resulting in an outcome of 'bad' feelings on both sides. Many varieties of games exist, typical of which is the game of 'Yes, but'. The originator of the game is someone who purports to have a problem to solve and who approaches a group of colleagues to describe the problem to them and to ask for help. The unwitting victims of the game offer possible solutions, but the response to all the suggestions is 'Yes, but (that won't work because)'. When the game originator has had enough of the game, he goes away implying or even saying 'Well I didn't expect you to come up with anything'. This leaves the victims feeling annoyed about the way their contributions have been received and the time that has been wasted. The originator, or persecutor in TA terms, has an internal 'good' feeling that he has scored over his colleagues. This game can lead to a further game of NIGYSOB (Now I'll get you, you son of a bitch) on the part of the victims who, having been put down, will try to do the same to the persecutor in some way, and so the games continue.

STROKES

A basic concept in TA is that people require *strokes* which give them recognition, affection, attention in a variety of ways. Strokes can be of a positive nature, praise for something well done, or recognition for achievement. They can also be negative in their application, in the form of a rebuke or reprimand, since some people feel that to receive negative strokes is better than to receive none at all. One of the problems that can occur when strokes are not given is that there is a greater likelihood of games being played so that the players can obtain at least negatives strokes, e.g. the game of 'Kick me'.

TRADING STAMPS

Trading stamps describes the concept in TA of an individual collecting and storing feelings which are later discharged. Gold stamps relate to good feelings that are collected by praise and can be cashed in by the collector giving himself some time off. Brown stamps are the collector's items of bad feelings. Normally these are collected when reprimands are given that the recipient feels are unjustified, but are accepted; when things go wrong but nothing is said at the time and so on. The cashing-in time occurs when a further incident occurs that produces a brown stamp to fill up the book. The brown stamp collector at this point explodes and vents all his pent-up anger in one go. Unfortunately, the final trigger can be a minor event which leaves the victim of the explosion bewildered and hurt.

RITUALS

Rituals are the games we play that are not harmful in themselves and can be satisfying to the participants as the responses and counter-responses are those expected. Bill meets Fred and says 'Good morning Fred, how are things going with you?' expecting the ritualistic response 'Good morning Bill. I'm fine thanks. How are you?' Normally, the expected response results and as the two interactors have determined they are in step, the interaction can continue to real business or to a more complex ritual. Rituals of this nature can be observed in many situations, including training courses, parties, meetings and so on. Problems arise if a traditional ritual is broken unexpectedly. Fred, instead of responding ritualistically, might launch into a description of his problems, problems in which Bill has no interest in spite of the question asked. Bill will then try to terminate as quickly as possible an uncomfortable situation.

PASTIMES

Pastimes are similar events to rituals which are most noticeable at parties or refreshment breaks at work where groups talk about cars or football or recipes, or other non-threatening subjects. Pastimes such as these can provide links with other groups with one member leaving a group to enter another group, saying ‘We have just been talking about X. What do you think?’ In this way, the superficial approach of the pastime can be used to take the interaction to a deeper and closer level.

LIFE SCRIPTS

Perhaps the most powerful concept of TA is that of the *life script*, which is the personal plan determined by an individual. Berne suggested that the life script is formulated in one’s early years – up to the age of seven or so – and is conditioned by reactions to external influences. These influences can be parental or other authority figures, and the script produced can be so strong that our adult lives may be dominated by it, even if progress and relationships are disrupted by it. Awareness of the existence and nature of the script can mean that we are able to modify it when it appears not to be appropriate.

GESTALT

A rather different training approach developed from psychological and psychiatric methods is the technique known as *gestalt*. Gestalt therapy was developed by Dr Frederick Perls, a Freudian analyst from the longer established gestalt psychology, and like TA, has been introduced into human relations training. The term ‘gestalt’ is difficult to define, but is concerned with the organized whole rather than parts.

Many of the methods used in gestalt therapy or training involve personal experience, often initiated by role play usually of the 'hot' variety. One of these has already been discussed – the 'empty chair' technique, or psychodrama. Another which can be more or less traumatic, is the identification of an individual with an object in order to draw out the inner feelings and attitudes of that person. A willing volunteer is requested to select an object in the training room or perhaps outside the window. He is then asked to imagine himself as that object and to start to describe it. Usually, the description starts quite superficially with a factual description of the object. With or without support from the trainer, the individual is encouraged to express his feelings, still as the object.

For example, a picture on the wall might be chosen and after a simple description, the speaker might continue, saying 'I sit up here on the wall. Sometimes people look at me, others ignore me and I don't like it when this happens . . .'. It soon becomes obvious that the speaker is no longer describing the object, but it is the inner feelings of the person that are emerging. This awareness is usually evident in the observers first, who realize quickly what is happening, but the individual realizes too. By this stage, the speaker is in full flood and, even with the realization of what he is saying, he rarely stops and is more likely to continue to develop his feelings and emotions.

GESTALT IN TRAINING

A number of the activities used in gestalt therapy and training associated with this technique can be used (with care) by the more experienced trainer, sometimes for apparently different reasons on a 'non-gestalt' training event. One activity which I have described elsewhere as useful for starting a training course or other event (see the activity 'Trust Me' in *50 Activities for Developing Management Skills, Volume 1*) is developed from a 'gestalt' experience. In this activity the delegates are paired off, usually by inviting them to choose somebody they do not know. One of the pair is blindfolded and taken for a walk by the other through the grounds of the training centre. However, a number of constraints and ground rules are imposed:

- no verbal directional information can be given at all by the guide
- directional statements can be given only by a non-verbal code which the pair must work out themselves non-verbally
- conversation can take place during the walk, in the form of cross-communication about each other; or questions by the guide about how the guided person feels, what images are being produced and so on
- during the walk the guide should have the guided person smell, touch, sense objects and describe their feelings.

This walk takes place for about seven or eight minutes, after which the roles are reversed and the end of the second journey is back in the training room. Return of all the pairs is followed first by discussion, within the pairs, about their fears, concerns, joys, feelings, thoughts during the walks and an overall impression of what they gained from the activity. The principal aspects which emerge can then be shared if desired in the full group.

This experience not only starts a training relationship with one other person in the group by finding out about them in different ways, many of them unusual perhaps, but helps to concentrate each delegate's mind to a greater or lesser extent on a number of feelings about themselves which may not have surfaced previously. On the other hand, some delegates may view the activity only superficially, but may consider it more deeply when the feelings of others are shared.

This type of activity can be seen as a starting point for the gestalt philosophy of combining in the whole a number of parts. If we look at the configuration of the dots in Figure 9.1, we describe it as a circle, more often than we describe it as a number of dots in a configuration to produce the effect of a circle. In other words we are using the whole image rather than the individual parts in isolation. This is the aim of gestalt in training, to encourage delegates to think in terms of a combination of learning skills and concepts, rather than look on them as isolated, independent skills and so on. It also aims to bring together a variety of behavioural skills and attitudes to enable effective relationships to be constructed and maintained. The basic assumption of gestalt in training is that people have considerable potential for growth in relationships, generally much more than they realize. There is also the secondary aim of helping the individual to recognize the limits of his/her competence.

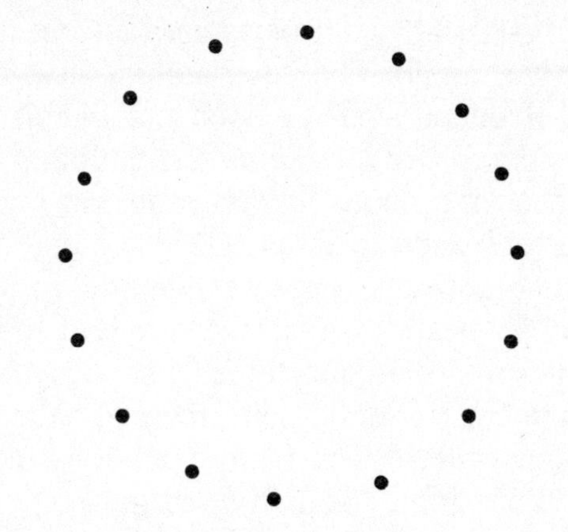

Figure 9.1 Configuration of dots as a circle

Some trainees react against one of the basic elements of gestalt training, even in the early stages, because it attacks one of the social behaviours which, certainly in Britain, was taught strongly to us from an early age. This step involves a contract within the training group not to use such words as 'we, one, they and so on' – for example 'we think that', 'one tends to do such and such'. Rather, individuals are encouraged, and contract to try to take on a greater degree of personal responsibility, and if they mean 'I' when they say 'we' to use the personal pronoun 'I'. This works against the upbringing which declared that using 'I' signified egoism. Certainly, an excessive use of 'I' can be for egoistic reasons, but it is inappropriate not to use it if individuals are just trying to avoid responsibility. Similarly, the use of 'can't' often avoids the real use of 'won't', again an avoidance of personal responsibility for what is said. Within the group contract, authority is given to all the individuals to challenge others if they feel that personal responsibility is being avoided – incidentally, this contract usually includes the trainer-facilitator.

Another behavioural intervention in a gestalt group, whether by the trainer or one of the delegates, is the use of probing questions. In general when someone in response to the question 'Why do you always smile when someone is having a go at you?' says 'I always smile when that happens', the verbal interaction frequently stops. Gestalt training requires the questioner to ask 'Why?' to that response, and to keep on asking 'Why?' or similar probing questions. This continues until the questioner is satisfied with the answer and/or feels that nothing else will emerge. The respondent, if encouraged to open out in this way, frequently obtains considerable relief and understanding by being helped to talk through an internally hidden problem, one perhaps which they have never been forced to talk about previously.

The use of questions is also challenged in terms of whether they are really questions, and not simply disguised statements. This identifies for the 'questioner' the real reason behind the behaviour and consequently helps them to understand more fully their own. For example, on many occasions the question 'Why did you do that to Fred?' is really a disguised personal statement, 'I didn't like what you did to Fred'. Acknowledgement of this brings the individual closer to the experience and enhances a feeling of comfort with themselves and the success of their actions as a result.

In the same way, imagery plays a large part in gestalt as described earlier – the 'picture on the wall'. A development of this is that if during the event a delegate makes a statement like 'I feel as hot as if a fire is raging in me', he is encouraged to 'be that fire' and describe himself from that position.

In summary, gestalt with its concentration on the inner feelings and their real meaning, perhaps as opposed to the outward manifestation, helps individuals not only to a deeper understanding of themselves, but why they feel that way. This helps them understand others too. From the viewpoint of the individual the learning is achieved through the experience and the relating of the here and now to the what and why, without intellectualizing, theorizing and considering abstractions. Creativity and pro-activity increase from knowledge such as this rather than the defensive attitude of waiting for something to happen.

Gestalt application is very much on the borderline between therapy and sensitivity training and as such should be approached with extreme caution and only by skilled and experienced executors.

REFERENCES AND RECOMMENDED READING

A Trainer's Guide to Group Instruction. Richard Ayres. BACIE, 1977.

Games People Play. Eric Berne. Penguin Books, 1968.

Developments in Interpersonal Skills Training. Don Binstead. Gower, 1986.

The New Managerial Grid. R. R. Blake and J. S. Mouton. Gulf Publishing, 1978.

Unfinished Business. Neil Clark, Keri Phillips and Dave Barker. Gower, 1984.

Winning Ways to Succeed with People. Helen H. Clinard. Gulf, 1985.

Improving Interpersonal Relations. Cary L. Cooper. Gower, 1981.

I'm OK, You're OK. Thomas A. Harris. Pan, 1973.

Face to Face. Peter Honey. Gower, 2nd edition, 1988.

Born to Win. James and Jongeward. Addison-Wesley, 1971.

Manual of Management Development. John E. Jones and Mike Woodcock. Gower, 1985.

Approaches to Training and Development. Dugan Laird. Addison-Wesley, 1978.

Activities for Trainers – 50 Useful Designs. Cyril Mill. University Associates, 1981.

TA for Management. Theodore B. Novey. MCB, 1976.

Handbooks of Structured Experiences for Human Relations Training. Volumes 1–8. Pfeiffer and Jones. University Associates, 1974–1981.

Annual Handbooks for Group Facilitators. Pfeiffer and Jones. University Associates, annually from 1972.

Developing Interactive Skills. Neil Rackham, Peter Honey *et al.* Wellens, 1971.

Behaviour Analysis in Training. Neil Rackham and Terry Morgan. McGraw-Hill, 1977.

The Management of Interpersonal Skills Training. Keri Phillips and Tony Fraser. Gower, 1982.

The Skills of Human Relations Training. Leslie Rae. Gower, 1985.

Information Paper No. 4. *Improving Skills in Working with People: The T Group.* P.B. Smith. HMSO, 1969.

Managing the Manager's Growth. V. and A. Stewart. Gower, 1978.

Ideas for Training Managers and Supervisors. Patrick Suessmith. University Associates, 1978.

About Behaviourism. B. F. Skinner. Alfred A. Knopf, 1974.

A Handbook of Management Training Exercises. Volumes 1 and 2. BACIE, 1982.

ACTIVITIES. A number of publishers produce an extensive collection of activities covering a wide range of subjects. These include BACIE (now part of the Institute of Personnel and Development), Connaught Training, Fenman, Gower, Kogan Page, Longman, McGraw-Hill and Pfeiffer; trainers interested in these should write to the publishers concerned for a current list. See also the article 'Activities for Trainers – bane or boon', *Training Officer,* December 1993, vol. 29, no. 19, by Leslie Rae.

10 Human relations training – II

Human relations training can involve more than pure interactive skills, whether in a structured event or an unstructured event such as a T-Group.

TEAM DEVELOPMENT

The most effective form of human relations training takes place where training really belongs – at the workplace, when it is necessary either to build or to develop a team of individuals working together to common objectives. Often a group works together yet remains simply that – a group – as opposed to a strongly welded team where the people retain their individuality yet act as a corporate entity. The process that aids the formation of such a team is referred to as team building or team development. The principal advantage of team building *in situ* is that the problems encountered with the translation of the learning when the individual returns to his organization are avoided. Any process that aids the development of the team occurs in the team's working environment using the continuing work of the team itself.

The approaches to team building can vary according to the specific needs of the team and the organization. When some aspect of team building is identified as a need, a decision must be made on whether an external consultant should be introduced as a catalyst, or whether the facilitation of the development can be contained within existing resources. The event will need specific skills, and if the team leader has these, the best approach will be for him to arrange the development in which he himself will be involved. However, team building can be a sensitive business and if there are any doubts about the availability of existing skills, it may be more appropriate to introduce an outsider. Of course, the team leader can attend a special course to develop skills before returning to the team to practise the techniques.

The method of team building can vary according to the agreed 'best' approach, the team itself being fully involved in any agreement reached. An internal course can be mounted at work in which the team participates, and the form of this course can follow any of the human relations approaches – structured, semi-structured or unstructured interactive skills courses, grid approaches, specially tailored team building courses – or less formal approaches.

It may be useful to describe one approach to team development in which I was involved directly as team leader. The team consisted of myself and four other trainers, two of whom had worked with me for some time, and two relative newcomers to the team. During one of our team discussions which were held whenever possible, the subject of team identity and effectiveness arose. It was eventually agreed that we should attempt some form of team development to build on the effectiveness that existed. We also decided that we should, as relatively experienced trainers, be able to facilitate our own development.

Once this decision was made, a further meeting was fixed, with each team member agreeing to research during the intervening period possible methods of progressing. These approaches were discussed fully at the meeting and agreement was reached on a composite technique. A further agreement was that each member would be responsible for certain parts of the programme rather than the team leader only directing the operation. A programme of events with specific dates was agreed and all members offered their commitment to the programme. Even at this stage, as we realized later, team development had already started.

The first structured event was to state the present position and to identify any barriers that might have to be overcome. A questionnaire completed by each member initiated this stage, the responses being collated by a member of another team. This was a natural step forward in producing an open team identity, by allowing an 'outsider' to see that the team had weaknesses. The results were surprising, as we all considered that the team was working well with few problems; the questionnaire results showed that a number of problems existed that had not been previously recognized.

The questionnaire looked at the nine areas that Woodcock considered to be the building blocks of effective teamwork:

- clear objectives and agreed goals
- openness and confrontation of disagreements
- support and trust
- cooperation and resolved conflict
- sound working and decision-making procedures
- appropriate leadership
- regular review
- individual development
- sound inter-group relations.

When the responses to the questions are totalled, barriers are apparent from any lower scores.

The team considered the collated results individually and used the results to form conclusions. At the next meeting it was agreed that some problems did exist and that the team wanted to try to overcome them. Priorities were agreed and objectives determined, the latter stemming from the team's ideas of what might be achieved in a year. Before the next meeting the team gave itself the interim task of considering how the barriers might be raised and the objectives attained. The formulation of a plan occupied this next meeting.

It is beyond the scope of this book to detail all the activities agreed and operated during the ensuing months, but the end result was a team identity and effectiveness that surpassed even the aims set. The approach to team development and the end results will obviously vary from team to team, and the process can be relatively easy or traumatic and threatening. But if the commitment to succeed is there, a considerable amount of success and enjoyment will ensue. It is also important for the team to consider before it starts whether or not a third party or consultant should be invited to guide the team in its development. The need for this facilitation will vary a great deal, depending on the initial openness of the team, its knowledge of the ways that could be utilized and its skills in appraising its own performance.

ROLE NEGOTIATION

One common team-building technique that was employed in the

occasion just described was role negotiation. Once the development was well under way there was real openness, and one meeting was devoted to this approach.

Typically each member of the team has a number of sheets of paper containing the headings:

- It would help me if you were to do less . . .
- It would help me if you were to do more . . .
- It would help me if you were to continue . . .

Each individual identifies aspects under one or more of these headings with relation to any other member or members of the team. For example, John feels that Jim keeps interrupting him on too many occasions, but also puts forward proposals that help the group, and in particular, John himself. John completes a sheet to this effect, asking Jim not to interrupt him so much, but to continue putting forward useful proposals on which he can build. The other members do the same with each other until all requests have been exchanged. It is helpful to wait until all requests have been handed over, as there may be some contradictory requests from different people. For example, Fred may ask Jim to continue to interrupt John as he (Fred) feels that John is otherwise allowed to get away with too much.

At this stage requests are either accepted or rejected and the person making the request is informed in writing. To produce an effective contract, the individual accepting the request must ask the originator also to accede to a request. It is at this point in the exchange of contracts that discussion can take place to determine what is meant by a request, the reasons for rejection and so on. In this horse-trading way, an open agreement about mutual needs takes place and the development of the team progresses.

The quid pro quo contract agreement is an essential part of the process as if this does not occur it must be assumed that there is a greater possibility of the agreements not being carried out since there could be reduced commitment.

The final part of the role negotiation, once all contracts have been discussed openly and agreed, is to ensure that the contracts are written down as a statement of the team's agreement. In the case of the team development described, the summary of contracts was posted on the wall of the team room so that they were always evident and progress could be monitored.

TEAM ROLE AND NEED ANALYSIS

In recent years a number of models have been promoted with the intention of helping trainers work with team leaders/managers and teams themselves to develop the teams and to:

- identify the preferred roles of the members
- analyse these roles to define the needs of the team
- use the model to help the team develop effectively.

Many of these models are based on the work of C.G. Jung and they generally offer a questionnaire which leads to the identification of the individual and team role strengths and preferences.

It should be the specific intention of the trainer in team building and development to assist in the early stages of starting the team on its path and, in particular, training the leader in the various ways of developing the team. Hence team development training passes to where it rightly belongs – with the team leader or manager – and it is one of the responsibilities of the trainer to ensure that the leader has the skills needed.

One of the more realistic of the models – mainly because it is one of the few directly related to the task operation in addition to defining the team and individual roles of the people involved – is the Team Management Resource (TMR) model developed by Tony Margerison and Dick McCann.

TEAM MANAGEMENT RESOURCE

The Team Management Resource is an analytical instrument to measure and utilize work preferences. Thus TMR aims to identify the team roles that the individuals or team members would prefer to fill.

The model proposes nine major team roles which are shown to be directly related to the key work functions of a team:

- *Advising*, in which information is obtained and disseminated
- *Innovating*, the creation of and experimentation with new ideas
- *Promoting*, the search for and persuasion of others of new opportunities

- *Developing*, where the applicability of new approaches is tested and developed
- *Organizing*, the functional establishment and implementation of ways and means of getting things done
- *Producing*, by which systems and practices are established and operated on a regular basis
- *Inspecting*, the essential checking and auditing to establish that the installed systems are working effectively
- *Maintaining*, ensuring that standards and processes within and without the system are maintained.

In addition to these key work functions which are related to team roles, 'linking' is a non-specific function arising within any of the other functions and bridging people and tasks.

Many tasks require the balance of all these functions and consequently a team required to perform the cyclic operation needs members who will be able to, and want to, satisfy all the team and functional needs. Fulfilment of these functions is a sign of a high performance team which succeeds with minimum effort and maximum efficiency, effectiveness and team satisfaction.

Not every task or work function requires all the roles and aspects and not every team possesses members with preferences shared out amongst all the functions. If one task demands one set of operations, the next may require a different set – the balanced team is capable of utilizing the relevant skills of all its members. If all the preferences are not available, the awareness and flexibility of the high performance team allows its members to adjust to the demands of the situation.

In all these cases, the linker is a key role member and function, ensuring that the different approaches are used and facilitating their enactment, whilst maintaining a spirit of human resource satisfaction and development. This role may be, but is not necessarily, that of the team leader, other members can assume the responsibility.

THE BASIS OF THE INDEX

The Index is based on the personality types of Jung and the role developments are measured in a work context, within the Team Management Resource. The constructs are measured and compared using a 60-item self-assessment questionnaire. They relate to the *Extrovert/Introvert* aspects of *relationships*; the *Practical/Creative* way in which people collect *information*; the logically *Analytic* or inbuilt *Beliefs* preferences for making *decisions*; and the *Flexible/Structured* ways of *organizing* the work of themselves or others.

These construct comparisons are built into the 60-item questionnaire in which respondents are asked to choose between the two polarized alternatives. They are asked to relate their agreement or disagreement as far as the statement relates to themselves (self-identified), using a particular scoring method, OUTPUT.

The scores are analysed by means of a computer program and the information supplied is a numerical statement of the respondent's extent of polarization in each pair EXTROVERT-INTROVERT and so on. The maximum score on either side of the polarized pair is 30, signifying a very strong preference to that pole, e.g. E(xtrovert) 30 or I(ntrovert) 30, to 0 where the preference is a balanced one or non-existent. The combination of these scores identifies primarily the main role preference of the respondent as applied in the descriptions of the Team Management Wheel. This wheel relates the key work functions mentioned earlier to the eight functional team roles. The team roles which are easily identified with the key function aspects are:

- Creator Innovator
- Explorer Promoter
- Assessor Developer
- Thruster Organizer
- Concluder Producer
- Controller Inspector
- Upholder Maintainer
- Reporter Adviser.

The 'Wheel' representation is shown in Figure 10.1.

Within the program the eight main roles are separated into two categories of preference. One is the standard preference (the 'norm') and the other is the dominant form of that role. For example, an individual who scores E20 C5 B10 F11 would be classified as ECBF which fits them into the 'dominant' sector of the Creator-Innovator role. If the scoring had produced, say I20 C5 A10 F11, that is ICAF instead of ECBF, the preferred role would still be that of creator innovator but at the standard level. Note that

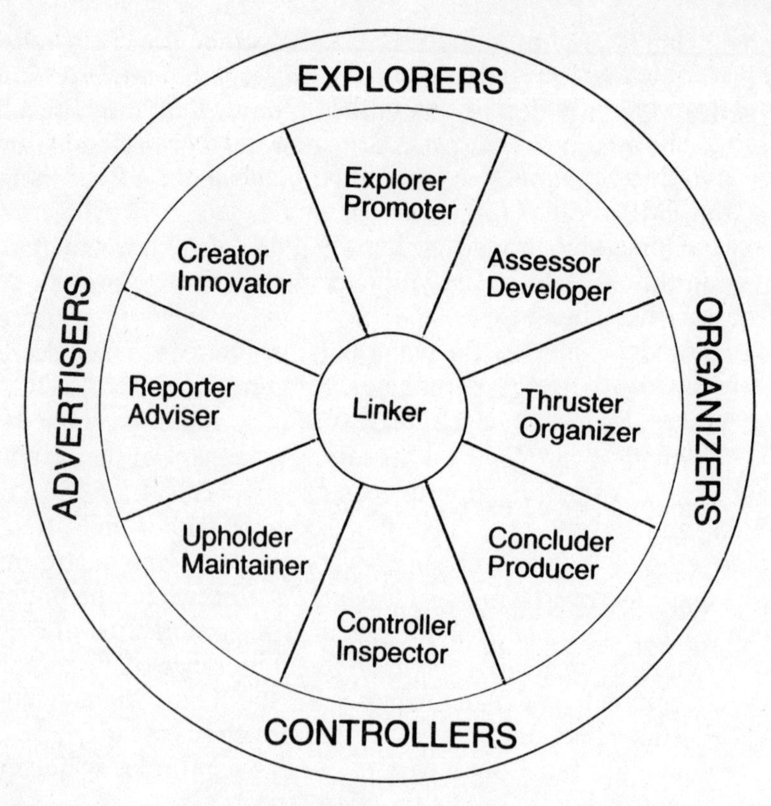

Figure 10.1 Team management wheel

the two types both have creative and flexible influences, but the ECBF creator innovator is extrovert in relationships and relies more on beliefs than logical analysis. The ICAF on the other hand is more inclined to introvert behaviour and to prefer the analytical approach although still relying on creativity and flexibility. The instrument also identifies supporting or secondary roles, those which, although not the main preference, still have some influence in the preferred overall stance of the individual. The final analysis of the program produces a printout of which there can be 128 variations depending on the association of the primary and secondary preferences. The printout is a descriptive profile, usually about 3000 words in length, based on the role preferences.

USES OF THE TMR

The main uses of the TMR are obviously directly related to teamwork. They identify the individual's preference for one or more sectors of team requirements, and thus if used with a group which is a team or a developing team, the style identifications can be used to show where the team is strongest and weakest and where it has to do something to ensure improved balance. If, for example, the TMR profiles for a team show that there is an over-provision of Concluder-Producers, but the work of the team requires more in the way of creativity, the team has failed to provide the necessary balance of skills.

It may appear to be an overwhelming problem if the TMR shows an imbalance of preferences, but once this has been identified at least the problem is known. Then, to produce a better balance three options are available to the team leader:

- the unbalanced team can be left as it is, hoping that at least something is achieved
- some members can be replaced by other individuals who have the missing preferences
- training is used to instil some of the skills necessary – for example, new approaches to creativity can help where this aspect is missing; problem-solving and decision-making skills can be learned; members can learn appropriate methods of planning and organizing if the TMR shows that these skills or preferences are low or missing, and so on.

At the very least, the identification of the team role preferences of the individuals and the effect of these on the team can be shared in discussion. This increased enlightenment sets the scene for one or more of the developments possible as mentioned above.

SWOT ANALYSIS

Another technique for helping in the team-building and development role is the increasing use of the SWOT analysis. The title of this type of analysis is derived from the acronym

S(trengths)
W(eaknesses)
O(pportunities)
T(hreats).

The existing or developing team or group is divided into a number of smaller groups. These may be arbitrarily defined or, as is often the case, divided into the natural sub-groups within the group. The groups are asked to consider their working group, as they see it in reality, and analyse as specifically as possible that group in the light of SWOT. For example, the groups might consider a number of strengths held within the group in terms of skills, specialist knowledge, attitudinal abilities and so on. The weaknesses might include those of communication within the group, with the main group and with other groups or teams outside (this is a common weakness). The opportunities might be the imminence of a new range of work which is to be given to the team and which could have many benefits to all the members. The threats might relate to this new work in that other groups are jealous of the 'honour' and as many other groups will have a peripheral interest, they may not be as helpful and cooperative as the main group would require.

If the work and requirements of the group are SWOTted in this way, and the views of each sub-group brought together to produce a composite picture, the main problems can be identified and plans made to overcome them.

For example, in the SWOT summarized above, the communication skills of two of the members can be concentrated to ensure that communications of all types are enhanced by them within the group – the full group can propose their own ideas on what can be done (particularly the Creator-Innovators!). The opportunity can be taken with this 'new' team spirit with everybody completely motivated and informed. Ways of strengthening relations with other supporting groups can be planned.

The result is a plan of operation, not only to perform more effectively the task of the team, but also to cement the relationships of the team members so that they feel part of the team and give it its due trust and support.

The SWOT analysis will certainly help this process in a much more logical and realistic way than merely hoping that the problems and their solutions will emerge. But, because it is intended to be a deep analysis, in which not only the 'team' but also the individuals are scrutinized, a facilitator has to keep a careful watch, particularly in the early stages, for hurtful aspects. Not that these have to be ignored or avoided; if they are the team has little chance of real development. But they must be faced, discussed and solved with appropriate behaviour and empathy for the other team members. In approaching people problems in this way, the team is developing naturally. The team leader or manager is very sensitive to criticism, because the threats and problems are often due to him or his actions. He must be aware that conclusions of this nature may be reached and brought into the open, and he must be ready to accept they may hold back the development of the team. Similarly, the rest of the team members must be prepared to criticize the 'boss' if he appears to block team development. But care must be taken that the feedback stage does not degenerate into a 'moan' session, with no intention to change to a positive attitude. It is in this area that the trainer, or other facilitator, even the trained leader himself, can be of immense value. In the early stages of team development, there are strong arguments that an external agent should act as development facilitator – a role for which trainers should be admirably suited. But this role must not be retained longer than necessary; the team/team leader should be encouraged to take over the practical progression of the team from inside.

Whichever type of approach to team building and development is taken, it must not be forgotten that it is a real activity, not an artificial training game. All the analyses and discussions must lead to real planning and decision making about operational and strategic planning, budgeting and budget forecasting, the realistic use of resources and so on. A fully working and related team will be able to tackle and accept these problems and tasks much more easily than a group, which although working together does not have the extra relationship evident in a high performance team.

THE JOHARI WINDOW

Whatever the approach to human relations, the basic aim is to improve awareness of behaviour and create an atmosphere of behaviour modification. An understanding of a model such as the Johari Window will aid the process of behaviour awareness.

This model was originated by Joseph Luft, a psychologist, and Harry Ingram, a psychiatrist (Joe and Harry, hence, the JOHARI Window). The model (see Figure 10.2) depicts a window which reflects the aspects of our behaviour, with communication flowing out from us to others through the window, and flowing in to us from others.

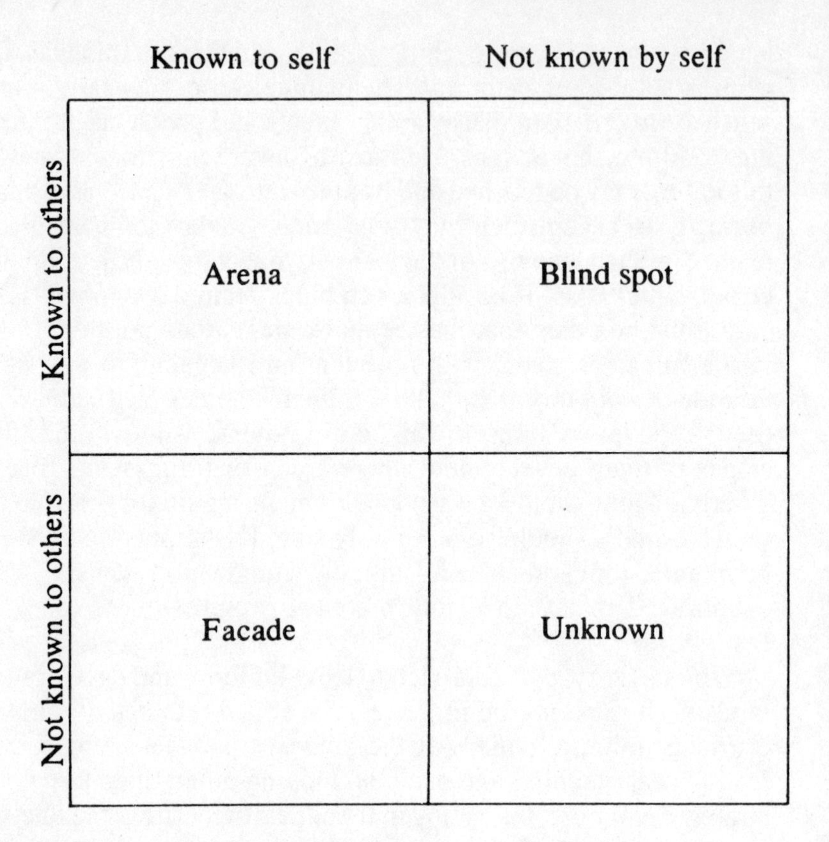

Figure 10.2 The JOHARI window

The window has four 'panes' each representing an area of ourselves, the panes varying in size from one individual to another, and capable of being modified, usually with a change of trust level in a group and as the result of feedback from the rest of the group.

The first pane is known as the Arena. This pane contains aspects of self that are known to self and are evident to others: the open face of an individual that he has no objection to others knowing.

Another pane is the Facade. This covers the aspects that are known to self but are hidden from others – the false facade that is presented to the world, the false role that is played for a variety of reasons. Often this facade is maintained because the individual is afraid to reveal his true self to others as he feels that if he does so, he will be attacked emotionally.

The third pane contains the Blind Spot which represents the aspects that are known by others, but not by oneself. These blind spots in our behaviour can take a variety of forms, and without feedback from others we remain unaware of them. They can appear as words or phrases we use constantly, but of which we are unaware, and which with repetition may become distasteful to others. We may have annoying mannerisms, verbal or non-verbal, such as an extreme use of 'er' and 'um', an incorrect use or pronunciation of a common word, of facial movements or other gestures. Such aspects of our behaviour can be permanent or variable, and most can be modified or terminated once the owner has been made aware of them and has the will to change.

The final pane, the Unknown, contains those aspects of which neither we nor others are aware. Few people have no lurking mysteries to their characters, either just below the surface or deep down within the unconscious self. These aspects, whatever feedback may be given and whatever self-disclosures made, may or may not surface, but where openness exists within the group the likelihood of disclosure must increase.

Within a training event, or as the basis of a training course, the Johari Window can be used to symbolize the development of a group in terms of their behaviour. At the start of a group event, the Arena pane of the group as a whole is small as few members are willing to disclose or seek information. Consequently the group Facade is large with individual roles being enacted or false images projected. The Blind Spot and Unknown pane sizes will depend on the individuals' and group's awareness of the behaviour exhibited. As the event progresses the Arena will normally increase in size as further aspects of real behaviour are revealed, with a consequent reduction in the Facade. This initial increase of openness encourages feedback of reactions to the behaviour within the group and as a result some shrinkage of the Blind Spots will occur. By the end of the event, if the learning has been effective, enlargement of the Arena and shrinkage of the Facade and Blind Spots will have continued and, in some cases, Unknown area aspects may have come to light.

A similar development of individuals can be observed, and the Window can usefully identify individual styles. The member with a large Arena displays openness in feedback, in both the giving to others and receiving and accepting it from others. The ones with extensive Blind Spots can be insensitive to the feelings of others, showering feedback in all directions whether it is justified or not, and unaware of what the reactions may be. The owner of a large Facade is the one who neither gives real feedback nor receives it, his behaviour being evident from his constant questions to others about what they are doing and how *they* feel. After a while, this type of individual is challenged by the group to disclose his own feelings rather than appear to be concerned about others. The facilitator may be in danger of falling into this style and lose an opportunity for empathy with the group.

The individual with an obtrusive Unknown pane is typified by the silent member, silent because he knows little about himself and is not sufficiently interested to learn about others. A common example of this behaviour is the silent type who says that although he is saying nothing, listening is his best way of learning. This may be relevant to some extent in the learning of technical skills, but the effect in human relations events is that others cannot assess silence and tend to be suspicious. Consequently others do not give any helpful feedback. Even in technical training, when a member of the course is silent and gives no feedback to the tutor, although he states he is learning there is no active confirmation of this, unless the course includes practical tests.

There are a number of approaches to introducing the Johari Window concept and practice to a training event with the objective of facilitating the feedback process. A common method is to introduce the members to the concepts of the Window and then ask them to complete self-rating questionnaires which will identify their positions as far as the Window is concerned. Various schools of thought question whether these self-rating instruments should be completed before or after the information input, as the results may be contaminated if completion follows the description. Whatever the approach, the responses are discussed as fully as possible, first by self-analysis and then by wider discussion to encourage interactive feedback and to compare an individual's perception of his role with that observed by others. Once attitudes have been identified and confirmed, activities can be performed to experiment with role modification and movement of the barriers shown by the Window.

Techniques like the Johari Window can be useful to the trainer in mixing groups or sub-groups to achieve various objectives. If, for example, the full group of 12 has to be divided into two groups of six and included are two or three individuals with low Arena panes or large Blind Spots and Unknown areas, the groups could be selected to help solve these problems. Two of the Blind Spot people could be included in the group with several high Arena attitude people. The intention would be that the Arena members would encourage the other two and assist movement across the Window. Or perhaps, more traumatically, all the Blind Spot, Facade or Unknown members could form a group and would need to modify their behaviours in order to progress.

Mixing can be produced by other interactive processes. Behaviour Analysis identifies the high and low contributors and reactors and this information can be used in several ways. The high contributors can be placed in one group, the low contributors in another. In order to progress their interactive skills, the high contributors must control their contributions and the low contributors must increase their rate of contribution. If neither group modifies as necessary, little progress will be made. It may appear divisive to take this approach, but left in a completely heterogeneous grouping the quieter members run the risk of dominance by the remainder. As the event progresses there will normally be a natural modification, but appropriate mixing can speed the process, particularly in a course of restricted duration.

INTERVENTION TECHNIQUES

Anyone concerned with training will encounter the term 'intervention' and may find this technique the most difficult one to achieve, particularly in human relations training. Some trainers never achieve full skill, and appreciate the difficulties this produces. Others never achieve it, yet wonder why things go wrong with their relationships with the group and the consequential effect on the training. When the trainer is involved in discussion, appraisal, report back and feedback events with the group, intervention skills can be defined as knowing when the trainer should make a contribution, what type of contribution it should be, how it should be made, and, perhaps more importantly, why it is being made. The trainer always runs the risk of intervening at the wrong point; the group members may not be prepared for an intervention; they may view it as an interruption and reject it, or the action that the trainer may want to occur may have happened at a slightly later stage without the intervention. The 'right' occasion has to be chosen for the intervention and the trainer must try to let it be a natural occurrence rather than an interruption.

Skill is needed in the phrasing of the intervention and the way it is expressed, particularly if it involves giving feedback of a personal nature. Finally, the motive of the trainer in making the intervention must always be for the benefit of the group or individual, not to satisfy the trainer's personal desires. This temptation becomes strong when the trainer is taking a verbally passive role; the need to be part of the group and the discussion can become overwhelming, and he may either simply say something to relieve his internal tension, or to 'put the group right'.

Many of the skills of intervention can come only through experience and learning the lessons of error, hard though this may be on both the trainer and trainee. One approach intended to give the trainer some help in deciding the type of intervention to make has been provided by Heron with the Six-Category Intervention Analysis. In this approach, interventions can be classified into six categories, three directive and three facilitative.

1) *Prescriptive intervention.* This seeks explicitly to influence and direct the behaviour of the group. A typical prescription might be 'I think that it would be useful to follow up that new idea of John's.' However, in order to be effective, the intervention must be acceptable to the group and made in such a way that it is at least not unacceptable. Degenerative modes of this intervention are likely to occur when a moralistic approach becomes evident from the use of such words as 'must', 'should' and 'ought'; the intervener then proceeds to take over from the group. The intervention in the prescriptive manner might be inappropriate, e.g. it should have been a different type of intervention with a particular group.
2) *Informative intervention.* This is less directive than prescriptive intervention, in that the trainer gives information to the group that will enable it to fulfil its aims. The intervener must be careful not to make this into an over-teach by launching into a lecture and effectively taking over the group.
3) *Confronting intervention.* This is a direct challenge by the trainer of the restrictive attitudes, beliefs and behaviour of the group or individual. It must be made in a challenging

mode rather than suggesting an attack. Degeneration of this intervention can occur when the trainer comes in too early and the group or individual is not ready to be challenged. Or there is an over-kill in the intervention in which, although the challenge is made, the intervener himself follows on with, for example, an exposition of a theory explaining the reasons for the event being challenged.

The authoritative interventions are, on the whole, the easier ones to make from the trainer's point of view, but must be handled carefully to avoid negative reactions from the group or degeneration on the part of the trainer's motives. More difficult are the facilitative interventions, and the trainer must have considerable skills in handling their possible effects.

4) *Cathartic intervention* has the intention of encouraging the group or individual to release emotions, whether these be rage, sorrow, anger or pleasure, but at a level the facilitator, the group and the individual can handle without feeling threatened. The individual can be encouraged to talk through an event that has aroused his emotions; can repeat emotive words or phrases that are producing problems; be persuaded to verbalize a slip of the tongue or a non-verbally demonstrated thought; or to self-role play by saying what was left unsaid at the time of the event. The empty-chair technique can often be usefully introduced in these situations.

The more the emotions of people are introduced by an intervention, the greater the dangers for the facilitator and the individual. The intervention may be made too soon and require too deep a release of emotions when the individual is not ready to make this release, or the group is not ready to accept it even if the individual is. The facilitator may prematurely close the interaction either because he is unaware of its real progress or he may feel he is getting out of his own depth. The third danger is that the intervention centres on what could be volatile emotions which could produce dramatization or over-dramatization on the part of the individual, rather than a realistic release of suppressed feelings.

5) *Catalytic intervention.* This can generally be less traumatic and encourages learning and development through a

self-centring method. The group or individual can be encouraged to reflect on what has happened or is happening and be moved towards this by the facilitator who reflects back to the group statements or events that have occurred, or tests his and the group's understanding of the event. The group can be moved into a problem-solving or self-discovery mode by the intervention, or led to an analysis of the options open to it. Dangers exist here, however, and may be based on an incorrect interpretation of what is happening by the facilitator who thus leads the group down the wrong road. Or, if self-disclosure is the aim, the individual may over-disclose and subsequently feel remorse or worse.

6) *Supportive intervention*. This is relatively easy for the facilitator in that he approves, confirms and validates the worth and value of the group and what it is doing. But it can be difficult for the group to realize that this is support. The intervention may take the form of simply giving full attention to what is occurring, expressing positive support for what is being done, or validating the activity of the group within the event. If the group is having a good experience, the facilitator may join in to share the good feelings and experience, or disclose facts, feelings, emotions of his own. Unfortunately, these approaches may be seen in a different light by the group who may view them as patronizing and insincere.

Interventions are an essential part of the trainer's or facilitator's approach to help the group in its progress through the learning process. Yes, there are dangers, but abdication of responsibility for the role may lead to failure for the group, reflecting the failure of the trainer. The skill must lie in knowing which type of intervention to use, at which stage and in which manner.

ASSERTIVENESS TRAINING

A recent innovation in human relations training is known as Assertiveness training, which is based on the practice of the human rights that every individual possesses. These rights include the right to:

- express one's own views and feelings
- make mistakes
- have one's own needs accepted as important
- refuse to do something when requested
- behave according to one's own wishes, but taking responsibility for these actions, always with the rider that the rights of others are not violated.

The model of behaviour described under these rights is, in one school of thought, the AR model, in others simply the Assertiveness model. Within the model five modes of behaviour can be identified as

- aggressive behaviour in which one presses one's own rights, but denies the rights of others (abbreviated to AGG)
- non-assertive behaviour in which one denies one's own rights (NA)
- assertive behaviour in which one acknowledges one's own rights and accepts the rights of others (A/r)
- responsive behaviour which acknowledges, encourages and actively seeks the rights of others (a/R)
- assertive-responsive behaviour which combines A/r and a/R behaviour by acknowledging equally one's own rights and those of others (AR).

Examples of these behaviour modes can be demonstrated by the initial contribution in a negotiation about the provision of a training course.

- 'My research shows that a course of four days' duration is necessary. That's what I would agree to.' (AGG)
- 'Well, I think the course should last four days, but you seem to be insisting on two days, so I'll go along.' (NA)
- 'I consider that the course requires four days to make it effective. Extensive research has brought me to that conclusion, so you will need to take this into account when considering my proposals.' (A/r)
- 'I would be interested in learning how you come to the conclusion that two days would be sufficient. Could you tell me how this came about?' (a/R)
- 'My research shows that four days are required for the training. How do you react to this proposal?' (AR)

Assertiveness training follows a similar pattern to that found in the description of Managerial Grid training. The programme will typically start with a discussion and description of the theory and philosophy of the assertiveness model. The participants are then guided to self- or mutual identification of their behaviour modes and practice is given in behaving in different modes. Opportunities are given for rehearsal of role modification as necessary and consideration of how the appropriate modes of behaviour can be translated 'back home'. The training can be adapted to one-to-one interactions, social skills, interpersonal interactions, negotiating skills and so on, the changing emphasis being mainly in the types of behaviour practice and role rehearsal.

ACTION LEARNING

Most of the human relations training discussed has involved the learners attending a training event. Human relations training is no different from other forms of training in that an equal or often more effective approach can take place nearer the working environment than completely off the job. The best known of this type of approach is known as Action Learning. A group of people, sometimes from the same company, sometimes from stranger companies, is brought together to form what is known as a set. Normally a facilitator assists in the operation of the set, but, as with most facilitative roles, a relatively passive approach is taken. No specific objectives are produced prior to the set's meeting; usually the first few meetings will be spent in the members setting objectives for themselves. Often the objectives can involve the solving of a real work problem, and although the onus is on the problem owner to provide the final solution, he is helped in this process by the set in which unconstrained possible solutions can be generated. However, in addition to the positive movements towards the final solution, a variety of other forms of learning can arise within the set through exposure to the group – interactive skills, decision-making skills, consulting skills and so on. In fact some sets look to these other forms of learning as the main objectives of the set.

The facilitator can be used as a catalyst to generate activity in the set and/or as an expert resource or provider of other experts as required by the set. To achieve its aims the set meets regularly at frequent intervals over a period until all the objectives and the emerging needs have been satisfied. Following this the set breaks up, although long-lasting relationships can result.

A variation of the Action Learning set can occur when members join the set from stranger companies. Instead of each member moving towards solutions to their own problems, each member takes on the problem of another member and spends time in the stranger company to work towards a solution. Obviously the set and the support of set members is essential in this approach, and frequent reports-back are discussed at the set meetings.

QUALITY CIRCLES

Similar in a number of ways to Action Learning is the relatively new concept of Quality Circles. These were initiated as practical events in Japan in the 1960s and are now rapidly spreading through the rest of the world. There are, however, significant differences between Action Learning and Quality Circles.

The basis of a Quality Circle is the voluntary meeting on a regular basis, say one hour weekly, of a group of people – usually no more than ten – who work for the same manager, foreman or supervisor. During these meetings, job-related problems are identified, analysed and solutions proposed. The group then has the task of presenting and selling the proposed solution to their seniors and, if accepted, implementing and monitoring its progress. The benefits are those of a group already working closely together, looking at problems that affect them directly and using the synergy of an effective working group to provide realistic, self-imposed solutions.

The Quality Circle should be backed up by an active, committed and supportive senior member of the organization, and a facilitator who can enter the circle to assist with process problems and give any training necessary. The training needs can vary considerably, depending on the existing skills of the Circle members, but commonly include meeting skills, action planning techniques, and Circle administration skills. The Circle is very much a full-scale problem-solving group and may require skills or techniques in analytical or free-thinking problem-solving techniques, in addition to information and analysis instruments and presentational skills. But the emphasis must be on the self-generative process of the Circle itself and its demonstration to the outside world that products of sufficient quality and quantity can emerge.

In an authoritative book on the subject, Robson gives various examples of problems tackled by Quality Circles in the UK, ranging from a group of cleaners in the shipbuilding industry who saved the organization £25 000 per annum by solving a problem of waste disposal; through a group in a supermarket devising a more efficient warehouse layout; to a group of automobile paint sprayers who saved £3000 a year by suggesting changes in the system of marketing vehicles.

In this and the previous chapter, as many as possible of the approaches used in human relations training at the present time have been described. Many more variations on themes exist and 'new' approaches are constantly being proposed. Trainers beware! The field of human relations training is particularly prone to new fashions, some of which stand the test of time, others fade away to oblivion. The main danger for the trainer is that he is dealing with the emotions and feelings of real people and the temptation can exist to play games with them. This must be resisted at all costs and the trainer must be absolutely certain of his objectives and the needs of the group: in particular, is the training for life or for work styles; can any learning be transferred back to real life; what is the social norm of the participant's organization and so on? The dedicated and skilled trainer will feel exhausted and drained at the end of each course, even though to the casual observer he may not appear to have done very much in the traditional training sense. Experienced human relations trainers know that they have lived on a knife-edge of observation, analysis and, most of all, effective intervention for the duration of the course and have needed to be prepared for any eventuality that might, and usually does, arise.

REFERENCES AND RECOMMENDED READING

The Superteam Solution. Colin Hastings, Peter Bixby and Rani Chaudry-Lawton. Gower, 1986.

Six-Category Intervention Analysis. John Heron. University of Surrey, 1975.

Assertion Training. Colleen Kelly. University Associates, 1979.

'The Margerison-McCann *Team Management Resource – Theory and Applications*'. C.J. Margerison, D.J. McCann and R.V. Davies. *International Journal of Manpower*, vol. 7, no. 2, 1986.

Management Teams: Why They Succeed or Fail. R. Meredith Belbin. Heinemann, 1981.

Quality Circles: A Practical Guide. Mike Robson. Gower, 2nd edition 1988.

Assertive-Responsive Management. Malcolm Shaw. Addison-Wesley, 1979.

How to Use Assertiveness at Work. David R. Stubbs. Gower, 1985.

Team Development Manual. Mike Woodcock. Gower, 2nd edition 1989.

The Unblocked Manager. Mike Woodcock and Dave Francis. Gower, 1982.

A Practical Guide to Facilitation Skills. Terry Spinks and Phil Clements. Kogan Page, 1993.

Team Building. Neil Clark. McGraw-Hill, 1994.

Successful Team Building. John David *et al*. Kogan Page, 1993.

The Staff Development Handbook. Peter Sheal. Kogan Page, 1992.

11 Feedback

One of the most important aspects of any form of training and development is a system that gives information to the trainer on how his training is being received and understood, and to the learner on whether he is performing effectively. This is so whether the learning event relates to the acquisition of technical skills or progress in human relations. The movement of such information is called feedback or appraisal and can be either a one-, two-, or multi-directional process, demanding skill in operation. It is probably easier to give feedback in technical training, since in many instances there is a right or wrong answer. Greater difficulties abound in appraising the learning of less specific skills, such as management techniques, where there are various uncertain areas. It is in the field of human relations training that the greatest difficulties occur and here feedback is of paramount importance. The importance lies in the situation itself where the emphasis is on personal development, awareness and openness of the disclosure of reactions. The difficulties are mainly to do with a natural tendency of people to reject without consideration any criticism, implied or direct, of themselves, unless the atmosphere is right. People can reject personal feedback in many ways and for a number of reasons. They can simply ignore the feedback or react against it in a defensive mode, or, dangerously, can appear to accept it overtly whereas internally there is still rejection. Rejection can occur either because they are unwilling to accept comments on their behaviour or because they are so unaware themselves that they are unable to see what others have seen.

Some methods of feedback and appraisal have already been discussed and the various methods can cover a spectrum of trainer involvement. This spectrum does not necessarily consider the method in value terms, but there are some indications within it. At one end of the feedback spectrum where the learner has a minimal involvement, the trainer gives all the performance feedback. Progressive movement through the spectrum involves feedback by the learner's peers as well as the trainer; feedback involvement of the participants themselves; to viewing a video recording of the event in which the participant appraises his own performance.

Human relations training demands a special form of feedback with considerable sensitivity. In one way, human relations training is really feedback with intervening activities. A powerful form of behavioural feedback is one of the many variations of interactive analysis.

SIMPLE CONTRIBUTION SCORING

The simplest form of analysis of a group's behaviour and performance is known as Simple Contribution Scoring. The observer has a sheet of paper on which the names of all the members of the group are written. As the meeting progresses and any member speaks, or makes a contribution, a stroke is placed against the name of the member making the contribution. The end result is a set of strokes against each member's name indicating how many contributions each made during the meeting, as shown below.

Fred	~~1111~~ ~~1111~~ ~~1111~~ ~~1111~~ ~~1111~~ ~~1111~~ ~~1111~~ ~~1111~~ ~~1111~~ 1111	49
Joe	~~1111~~ ~~1111~~ ~~1111~~ ~~1111~~ 1	21
Jean	~~1111~~ 11	7
Harry	111	3
Mary	~~1111~~ ~~1111~~ ~~1111~~ ~~1111~~ ~~1111~~ ~~1111~~ ~~1111~~ ~~1111~~ ~~1111~~	45
Rita	1	1

The analysis shows the level of contribution of each member, high, medium or low. Often chairmen of meetings feel at the end of the event that some people have been quiet or talkative, but do not know exactly *how* quiet, or active. The chairman indeed may not even be aware that someone has been quiet. The scoring analysis gives this type of information in quantitative terms.

However, Simple Contribution Scoring does little more than quantify the contributions in stark numerical terms. It should raise questions in the mind of the leader: if Rita was as quiet as recorded, did she try to come in more often but was not allowed to by Fred and Mary, and was the leader not aware of this? The analysis does not show the value of content of the contributions, nor the length of time each contribution lasted. To obtain this additional information a variation or a different form of analysis is required. One variation of the simple analysis is to place a stroke for each 10 seconds of a contribution rather than a single stroke per contribution. Or instead of strokes, the sequence of contributions can be shown: the first contribution is scored as 1, the second as 2 and so on. The exact method or methods will be determined by the reasons for performing the analysis. The simplest approach can be most useful for a new leader who needs to obtain some information about the group as quickly as possible.

DIRECTIONAL SOCIOGRAMS

A more ambitious analytical approach, for different objectives, is the directional sociogram. In this form of analysis the group is shown symbolically as individual circles in the positions in which they are seated. Lines join each circle and there are additional lines leading outwards from each circle. Whenever a member makes a contribution, an identification is made as to whether the contribution is made to another member or to the group as a whole. If the contribution is made to another member, a mark, for example an arrow, is placed on the line joining the two members; if to the group, the mark is made on the line pointing outwards. An additional identification can be made by the entry of a different mark, for example a short stroke across the line, denoting the interruption of a member by another.

A typical sociogram might appear as shown in Figure 11.1. The sociogram demonstrates that the particular activity analysed contained four sub-groups. Member D was in almost complete isolation, being interrupted by C and E, the only members to whom D was able to speak, but with little success. Finally D was reduced to making contributions to the group – but nobody replied. B and C were forming a sub-group of two, directing their contributions in the main to each other. On the other side of the group, E, F and G formed a triad sub-group, again ignoring the remainder of the group most of the time. The leader A was ignored most of the time, completely by D, E and G, interrupted by B and C, and consequently, like D, was forced to address most of his contributions to the group as a whole, but these were ignored.

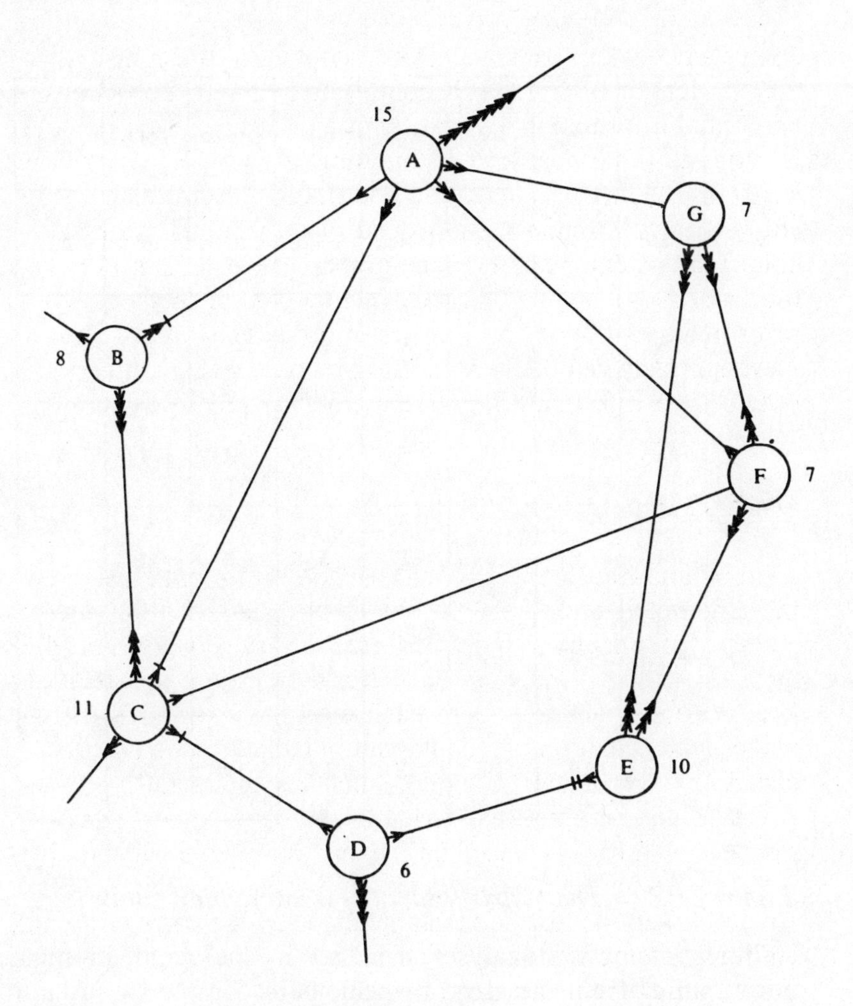

Figure 11.1 *A directional sociogram*

The flow of interactions shown in a sociogram can also be demonstrated in a matrix form (see Figure 11.2). In the matrix, the members of the group are shown on both vertical and horizontal indices, the record of contributions being placed at the intersections.

The contributions by each member made to the group as a whole are entered in the vertical column headed 'Group' against the name of the member making the contribution.

In the example, Fred spoke to Joe on eight occasions, Joe to Mary on six occasions, Bill to the group twice, Mary to the group not at all.

To

From		Fred	Joe	Mary	Bill	Group	Total	% from
	Fred		8	10	2	6	26	40
	Joe	4		6	6	4	20	31
	Mary	2	0		2	0	4	6
	Bill	6	5	2		2	15	23
	Total	12	13	18	10	12	65 / 65	100
	% to	19	20	28	15	19	100	

Figure 11.2 The matrix form of flow interaction analysis

Flow interaction analyses, whether in sociogram or matrix form, suffer from the same limitations as Simple Contribution Scoring in that the content, value, duration and so on of the contributions are not analysed, although the behavioural pattern of the group is demonstrated.

If it is necessary to analyse group or one-to-one interactions to a much more detailed extent, some form of complex interaction analysis must be used. However, no form of analysis can show every interaction aspect. One could be designed, but it would be too complex and difficult for any observer to use.

INTERACTION PROCESS ANALYSIS

One of the earlier forms of content interaction analysis was introduced by Bales in 1950 and was called Interaction Process Analysis. This analysis sought to relate behaviour categories to identifiable problem areas in the task and socio-emotional aspects.

Bales described one dimension of a group activity related to the task. He described the behaviours in this task-related dimension as a number of categories in three stages of the task performance – orientation, evaluation and control.

The categories in the orientation stage, when the group is collecting information for problem-solving purposes, relate to

- *Asking for information* by the use of behaviours seeking information, clarification, confirmation or repetition
- *Giving orientation* by informing, repeating, clarifying or confirming.

The evaluation stage, when the group is considering the information obtained, is distinguished by

- *Asking for opinion* by using the behaviours of seeking evaluation, analysis or expression of feelings
- *Giving opinion* with the use of expression of evaluation, analysis, wishes, views and feelings.

The final stage is described as 'control', and the categories and behaviours found during this stage are

- *Asking for suggestions* by seeking proposals, direction, solutions
- *Giving suggestions* by proposing, suggesting, directing, giving solutions.

However, Bales also defined another aspect of group behaviour in the socio-emotional dimension. In this dimension the problem areas are integration, tension management and decisions. Both positive and negative behaviours are identified in each area.

Behaviours in the integration area are categorized as

- Positive: *showing solidarity* by raising others' status, helping and rewarding
- Negative: *showing antagonism* by deflating the status of others, or defending or asserting self.

Tension management is exhibited by

- Positive: *showing tension release* by joking, laughing and showing satisfaction
- Negative: *showing tension* in withdrawal or the seeking of help.

The decisions area is identified by

- Positive: *agreeing* with behaviours demonstrating agreement, passive acceptance, understanding.
- Negative: *disagreeing* by disagreement, showing passive rejection and withholding help.

It will be seen that the process is complicated and identification of behaviours difficult and susceptible to subjective interpretation. Rackham and Honey, when considering interaction analyses to evaluate training programmes, certainly found these difficulties. When the Bales analysis is used in training it is usually modified to varying extents.

INTERACTION SCHEDULE

Klein in 1963 found that the categories used by Bales appeared tidier than they were in fact, with difficulties encountered in trying to differentiate between opinions and suggestions. As a result Klein produced her Interaction Schedule which borrowed strongly from Bales.

The basis of the Klein Schedule is that

- facts are impersonal and cannot be altered by discussion
- values are not verifiable, being personal experience of value judgements or preferences. Views are treated as contributions in which facts and values are combined.

The categories of behaviour fall into three dimensions: task-related factual; task-related combining facts and values; and task-irrelevant, expressive. The categories are given the following notations for ease of analysis recording.

Asks for information	inf –
Gives information	inf +
Asks for views	vi –
Gives views	vi +
Makes explicit proposal	pro

Disagrees	agr –
Agrees	agr +
Expresses hostility	expr – h
Expresses withdrawal	expr – w
Expresses friendliness	expr + f

In practice, the Klein categories are easier to identify and score than those of Bales, but still suffer from dangers of subjective interpretation and the differences between the dimensions may be more apparent than real.

BEHAVIOUR ANALYSIS

These practical difficulties were certainly found by Rackham, Honey and their associates when they tried to identify and measure behaviour change in their training group research for the air transport industry. Consequently, following a considerable amount of research, observation and experimentation, they evolved a simple but effective method of recording behaviour and analysing the correlations of categories of behaviour. The approach was also found to be an effective, non-threatening form of behaviour feedback to those observed, whatever the occasion, be it training or 'real life'. They called this new interaction observation method Behaviour Analysis and it has proved one of the major steps forward in interaction skills training of recent years. Many organizations use Behaviour Analysis (BA) as the basis of their human relations training and I have referred to it earlier in describing my own interpersonal skills training (p. 163).

One of the problems encountered in using BA is the decision about which behaviours should be observed in a group, as the list of possible behaviours is too extensive to permit recording them all. Rackham and Honey formulated five criteria to determine which behaviour categories should be included:

- the category must be meaningful to both the observer and those observed, and thus be readily identifiable
- the category must describe a behaviour which can be changed
- the categories must permit a high inter-observer reliability when used by several analysts

- the categories must be distinct from each other
- the categories must have a relationship to the outcome.

Rackham and Honey, using these criteria, evolved a set of categories for observing and analysing the behaviour of the training groups in which they were interested. These categories became the basis of BA, but the category grouping can be easily modified to suit the situation as long as the criteria are fulfilled. The set of categories developed initially were: proposing, building, supporting, disagreeing, defending/attacking, blocking/difficulty stating, open, testing understanding, summarizing, seeking information, giving information, bringing in and shutting out.

The categories used in my interpersonal skills courses have varied over the years, but there is a basic list that has been found helpful for general group observation. It is of paramount importance to be completely clear about the definitions of the categories used, in order to satisfy the criteria demanded. The categories I use in normal group situations are:

- *Proposing* A behaviour which puts forward as a statement a proposal or idea for a new course of action.
- *Suggesting* Where the proposal is put forward more in the form of a question than a statement. Recent research by Honey has shown that suggestions have a higher incidence of acceptance than direct statement proposals.
- *Building* A supportive proposal that extends or develops a proposal made by another person and which enhances the initial proposal.
- *Seeking information* Questioning behaviour that seeks facts, opinions, views, ideas, feelings or information from others.
- *Giving information* A stating behaviour that offers facts, opinions, views, feelings or information without extending into a proposal.
- *Disagreeing with reasons* A statement of view that involves a conscious or direct declaration of difference of opinion with another's views, stating the reasons for disagreement.
- *Disagreeing* A bald, blunt statement of disagreement without the reasons being offered.
- *Supporting* A conscious or direct declaration of support for another person or his views.

- *Testing understanding* A behaviour that attempts to check whether a contribution made by another has been understood.
- *Summarizing* A statement in compact form that collects the content of discussions and decisions made to that stage of the event or of a previous event.
- *Open* A behaviour in which the speaker accepts or admits an error or omission, or apologizes for his actions.
- *Blocking* A contribution that does nothing to progress the discussion and offers no alternative proposal for action.
- *Attacking* A behaviour which makes a statement of opinion against another with overt value judgements on the other and containing emotive overtones.
- *Bringing in* A direct and positive attempt to involve another person, usually linking with a question.
- *Shutting out* A behaviour which excludes, or attempts to exclude, another by interrupting, contributing when another has been brought in but hasn't had the chance to speak, or when two or more participants engage in side discussions outside the main discussion.

Behaviour Analysis is carried out by the analyst observing the group in action, identifying the contribution made by each member, categorizing these contributions and recording them by means of a stroke or other mark on the BA sheet. The BA sheet, as shown in Figure 11.3, includes vertical columns for each participant and horizontal rows for each category.

From this analysis, feedback can be given to the group and individuals on their contribution rates and the value of their contributions within the constraints of the categories. The feedback can be given in a non-threatening way by showing the individual the analysis and allowing him to draw his own conclusions. Preferably, a behaviour pattern is demonstrated with analyses of a number of events rather than a single event which may be unrepresentative of the individual's behaviour.

The flexibility of BA permits its use with events other than the normal group situation. The format of the BA categories must be modified depending on the reason for which the analysis is to be used. If the analyst wishes to examine the proposing behaviour within a group, rather than the general group behaviour, different categories can be used. These could include

BA 1 **NAME** W.L. RAE

ACTIVITY DISCUSSION 1600 – 1640 h.

	John	Michael	Brian	Joan	Mary	Ralph	Totals
Proposing	6	15		1	12	4	38
Building	3			1	3		7
Seeking ideas information	21	6	1	6	16	19	69
Giving ideas, information	12	22	12	14	14	25	99
Summarizing	7				1		8
Supporting	5	1	8	5	4	6	29
Open		1		1		2	4
Disagreeing		6		2	2	1	11
Attacking block, diff'y stating	1	8		2	6	6	23
Bringing in	10			1	2	1	14
Shutting out	6	15	1	6	8	14	50
Totals	71	74	22	39	68	78	352

Figure 11.3 The BA sheet

- procedure proposing
- content proposing
- suggesting
- caught proposals
- lost proposals
- rejected proposals
- repeat proposals.

BA observation can be used for events other than group events. A similar approach, using relevant categories, can be introduced for one-to-one interactions including appraisal, selection, discipline, and grievance interviews and negotiations.

Specific techniques are possible with the use of BA, whether the intention of the training is to teach analysis itself or to use BA and its philosophy in more general training events.

CONTROLLED PACE ACTIVITY

A well-known training method using BA techniques is Controlled Pace Activity. This approach was introduced by Rackham and has as its objectives the demonstration of the interactive problems that can occur between groups, in addition to consolidating any previous learning of behaviour categories. Typically the group is divided into two sub-groups which are located in separate rooms. Both groups are given a common problem-solving/decision-making task which is intended to introduce an element of potential conflict. Such a task could be the joint decision on the provision of cups of tea at the next tea break. With a course of twelve members, the information is given that there will be only seven cups of tea available. The task is for the groups to agree by negotiation who will have the tea, and also to agree any suitable recompense for those who will not receive tea. A constraint is placed on the event in that the groups cannot meet face to face, and all communications between the groups must be in writing.

The groups are also required to consider in depth, and in BA terms, the messages that are produced. When a message is sent, the originators make a note of the behaviour category to which they consider their message belongs. The recipient group on receiving the message, before reacting to the message, allocate it to the behaviour category that they consider is appropriate. The next stage is to consider and react to the message, making a note of its category before sending it. This process is repeated when the message is received and so the activity continues until the groups have reached agreement on the problem posed. The activity takes its name from the slowing down of the interactions by the requirement to categorize the messages received and sent.

The chief value of the activity lies in the appraisal of the process following the event. Considerable disagreement is usual over the reactions to the messages, demonstrated by variations in the categorizations. A message may be categorized by the sending group as a proposal, but seen by the recipients as an attack; they then respond in like manner. It is because of misunderstandings such as this that it can take twelve adults three hours to decide on the allocation of seven cups of tea!

BEHAVIOURAL GAMES

There are a number of behavioural games intended to consolidate learning in the effective use of behaviours. One such game is known as Prefixing. In this game the members of a group state, before making their contributions, to which category the contribution belongs. Part of the group can act as controlling observers, challenging an individual when they do not agree with a categorization when the contribution is actually made. Feedback of the process is self-generating as both the participating and observing members become aware of the behaviours being used.

A similar game is Suffixing, in which, instead of announcing the behaviour category prior to the contribution, this statement is made immediately after the contribution. Similar activities with the observing group can also take place as with the prefixing game.

An even more powerful variation of the prefixing behaviour game is known as Exclusion or Restriction, in which the group, or different individuals in the group, are constrained from using certain categories of behaviour, or are restricted to the use of certain categories such as Proposing, Building, Seeking Information, Supporting and Summarizing, for example. This is a particularly useful game when a human relations course has moved to the stage of considering modification of behaviour, the constraints helping an individual to avoid or concentrate on behaviours which he has decided to modify. An interesting variation on this approach is to have a set of playing cards on which behaviour categories are shown instead of the normal symbols. A game can be devised so that cards are taken by the players who have to use the behaviour shown on the card when they next make a contribution.

FISHBOWL OBSERVATION

Feedback on behaviour can be enhanced by behaviour games and some of the techniques discussed can be utilized. A structured activity can also be used linked with the Fishbowl techniques. Half the group can take an active part in the structured activity while each individual of the observing half observes and analyses, using BA, one individual of the participating group. At the end of the activity, each observer gives BA feedback to the individual that he has been observing. Then the roles are reversed so that the original participants become the observers, and the original observers, the participants. In this way, each individual receives feedback on his observed behaviour in addition to practising BA and giving feedback.

NON-VERBAL BEHAVIOURS

All the different analyses cited relate to the verbal behaviour of a group or one-to-one interaction in order that feedback of this behaviour can be given to the participants. But behaviour can be exhibited and observed in a non-verbal mode. There are probably as many categories of non-verbal communication as in verbal communication, with additional variations according to the culture from which the participant comes.

Argyle has suggested that the main non-verbal aspects involved in communication can be described in general groups:

1) *Body contact* can communicate a number of messages. These contacts are less common in Britain than in many parts of the world as a result of our cultural developments. Even in Britain itself there are variations, with certain parts of the country looking on almost any form of body contact as undesirable. However, frequently a touch on the arm can signify support for the person touched or can be a non-verbal warning signal not to proceed with either actions or verbal approaches.

2) *Physical proximity* can signal an overall aim of the level of intimacy or formality that is desired, and changes in proximity can suggest that the interaction has moved in some way. It is quite common at the start of a course for the members to remain in their places, quite well separated from each other. As the group becomes more open in its interactions, the members usually pull their chairs closer together when moving into an activity.
3) *Orientation* of the interactors to each other can signal attitudes, and often the 'across the table' position will suggest formality or even conflict. A diagonal orientation will suggest a less formal and more friendly approach, and side by side a very cooperative, friendly attitude. However, other aspects must be taken into account. These will include: the norm that people are accustomed to when, for example, they go to see their boss in his office; cultural conventions of the hierarchy in an organization; norms of friendliness and so on.
4) *Body posture* may suggest attitudes of interest, boredom, aggression, impatience and so on, and may be consolidated by verbal expressions that support the apparent non-verbal attitude.
5) *Gestures* of hands, feet, arms and head may give clues. For example, when emotions are aroused there is usually more gesturing – the clenching of fists, tapping of fingers – than when one is at ease.
6) *Head nodding* can be a particularly effective non-verbal way of expressing interest in what is being said, showing agreement or disagreement, and encouraging the speaker to continue. Head nodding is often usefully accompanied by non-verbal noises such as the 'mms', 'yeahs' and grunts that are intended as continuity and encouragement signals.
7) *Facial expressions* occur in movements of the eyes, eyebrows, mouth and the face as a whole, and can express disbelief, surprise, puzzlement, anger, neutrality, disgust and so on.
8) *Eye movement or gaze* can signal a variety of messages, ranging from shiftiness, through indications to the other to speak, to concentration or the lack of it.

It has been suggested that non-verbal communication plays a

greater role in our interactions than we are aware and deserves more attention. This may be so and interaction analyses can be constructed to measure its extent in interactions. However, analysis of the records will be very difficult in view of the many possible variations.

Let us consider the group member who is flopped in his chair with a bored or pained expression on his face; his eyes shut frequently; his feet are tapping regularly; his legs are crossing at intervals. These aspects may disturb other members of the group, each of whom may have a different reaction to his signals. But when challenged, he replies with surprise at the reactions of others, perhaps defensively, saying that these are his normal habits and mean nothing like the interpretations that have been put upon them. It is accepted that whether the behavioural signals are true or false, others react to them, but interpretation is both difficult and dangerous.

The more research there is into the effects of non-verbal communication or body language, the more the evidence seems to be mounting of its importance compared with other forms of communication. Estimates still vary, but most studies suggest that about 70 to 80 per cent of the messages we send or receive are concerned with body language. Some of the time we are reading these subconsciously and consequently, if we are not 'body' aware, we may be missing many important messages which do not record on the subconscious. So if we can make ourselves more aware of what we and others are doing in this respect, our communications should become clearer and less prone to misinterpretation. However, as suggested earlier, interpretation of body language is not easy and all sorts of problems can and do arise.

Two concepts will help us considerably in our awareness of the effective use of body language – clustering and congruence.

CLUSTERING

A number of body gestures and their possible interpretations have already been discussed, but many, if taken in isolation can not only be open to misinterpretation, but can also be dangerous. Imagine the case of a trainer looking round at the group in front of him and noting the general facial gestures are smiles or at least pleasant expressions. The interpretation made is that all is going well in terms of the interaction between them, the group is 'with him', and he should continue in the same vein. This may in fact be so, but these expressions could be hiding

- isn't this boring!
- how much longer have I to put up with this?
- can this guy not see that he is not in touch with us? and so on

but

- I don't want to hurt his feelings so I won't let these feelings show.

The real meanings behind the smiles may be clearer if the other body signals which are almost certainly being sent are noted:

- feet and hands tapping (they want to run away)
- legs crossing and uncrossing (nerves are building up)
- sitting back and forwards (they want to say what they really think, but decide not to)
- the smile is at the mouth only (look at the eyes)
- frequent movement of the hand to the mouth (stifling a yawn and stopping themselves from making the comment they want to make) and so on.

These various gestures, or a number of them, taken together as a cluster of body signals will give a better indication of what is really going on in the minds of the trainees.

CONGRUENCE

The clusters of body language compared with the initial, singular body gesture – the smile – also show in incongruence in the body talk alone. A more common occurrence is where there is an absence of congruence between the spoken and the 'unspoken' word – what we or they say or do contradicts what the body is saying. If you meet someone who says that they feel you are going to get on well together, but these words are said with the hand partly covering the mouth and/or with the other person not looking at you as it is said, the words and the body language are not congruent. The words appear to be of a positive, interactive nature, but the gestures are those not normally used in such positive situations. The hand over the mouth dates from childhood when we don't want to be found out in a lie and believe that if our mouth is not seen, the lie will be believed, or perhaps we really don't want to say the lie and the hand over the mouth will help to stop it. The not looking is typically reflective of the feeling we often express about people: 'He couldn't even look me in the eye when he was talking to me.' Congruence or its absence is not always as obvious as this, but if we use positive verbal and non-verbal communication in our dealings with others we are more likely to be successful, because the other person, consciously or subconsciously, will recognize the congruence and respond accordingly. But if the approach is otherwise, at the least suspicion can be raised and the interaction become more difficult.

Trainers must become expert at reading the body signals of trainees so that they can quickly and correctly pick up the messages and feedback which is being sent to them most of the time. Equally they must be masters at sending positive and congruent body signals so that the trainees are not confused by the trainer in addition to the training. Yet another skill of training!

NEURO-LINGUISTIC PROGRAMMING

Neuro-Linguistic Programming (NLP) is a technique designed to bring together the various aspects of our thinking patterns, our spoken language and our non-verbal language. The concepts relate our neurology (the way we think and produce action) and both the inherited or inborn and the learned patterns which produce our language. The model is described simply as the way we use our mental mechanism in relation to our sensory perceptions. Thought produces mental images, receiving and interpreting sounds both 'heard' and constructed, constructing feelings, and internalizing smell and taste to some extent. The research shows that people tend to concentrate or specialize on only one or two of the senses. Some people may find it easier to remember something if they associate the incident or object which they can reproduce in their 'mind's eye'; some will remember a distinctive aroma to retrieve a memory; others a feeling and so on. These aids to memory may be isolated or may be in combinations or sequences. For example, a memory of a pleasant place may be triggered by a vague mental/visual image which becomes clearer when the particular sounds are added and even clearer when certain smells are recalled – 'Ah, yes. That beautiful valley where we spent that afternoon, beside the field where they were cutting the hay and there was a very large herd of cows in the next field.' NLP uses what are described as 'accessing cues' to obtain indications of what people are thinking at a particular moment by looking for the behaviours of clues which give these indications.

NLP EYE MOVEMENT

Many of the clues to what may be happening in the neuro-processes are reflected in the eyes, and NLP suggests these as strong accessing cue instruments. Specific eye movements indicate the following. If the eyes are turning upwards, visual recall mechanisms are being used; if the eyes are turned to the sides, sounds are being used in the memory pattern; and if the eyes are turned down, this is a clue that an internal conversation is occurring. In the complete model, even the direction (left or right) of the up, down or side movement has a meaning which can help in the identification of what is happening in the person's mind.

SPEAKING

The eyes are not the only indicators of NLP activity. NLP is a combination of verbal and non-verbal communication, and it looks at what is said in the context of what is said. For example, saying frequently 'I see what you mean' or 'I hear what you're trying to tell me', are indications of the mechanisms at work in the interaction. These clues then suggest that perhaps in the former case the next step will be to offer a visual trigger to help this 'visually inclined' person to understand completely.

A TOTAL NLP MODEL

NLP thus tries to bring all the aspects of our thinking, communication and body language together to enable us to identify more clearly what is happening in our interactions with others. In training and other human interactions NLP attempts to help interactors to:

- build a rapport with the people with whom they are trying to interact
- understand how people are thinking
- express themselves in ways that are clear to the recipients and not just the sender, based on the observations of the apparently preferred 'thinking' mode of the other
- read the responses so that they can appreciate whether their messages have been correctly received, and
- modify their communication to fit the recipient if it is apparent that understanding is not complete.

With information of this nature about the recipients, the ways in which the training is given or learning opportunities provided can be tailored as far as possible to suit the learners and their preferred reception modes. The trainer can support the learner by ensuring that he uses congruent verbal and body language, or gives clear verbal and non-verbal signals so that the message cannot be understood. Or the learner can be encouraged by the trainer mirroring his body language so that the recipient is helped to feel more comfortable. The NLP approach attempts to bring all these aspects together, rather than emphasize one aspect alone.

REFERENCES AND RECOMMENDED READING

The Psychology of Interpersonal Behaviour, Michael Argyle. Penguin Books, 1967.

Interaction Process Analysis. R.F. Bales. Addison-Wesley, 1950.

Developing Interactive Skills. Neil Rackham *et al*. Wellens, 1971.

Working with Groups. J. Klein. Hutchinson University Library, 1963.

'Shaping Behaviour; Updating the DIS Techniques'. P. Honey. *Industrial and Commercial Training*, vol. 13, no. 9, September 1981.

How to Read a Person Like a Book. G.I. Nierenberg and H.H. Colero. Thorsons, 1980.

Behaviour Analysis in Training. Neil Rackham and Terry Morgan. McGraw-Hill, 1977.

Face to Face. Peter Honey. Gower, 2nd edition, 1988.

Effective Feedback Skills. Tim Russell. Kogan Page, 1994.

12 Evaluation and validation

No discussion of training can continue for long without these two subjects arising, often starting with an argument about which is which and what the differences may be, if any.

Specific definitions are given in a Department of Employment publication 'Glossary of Training Terms' as follows:

> *Evaluation*
> The assessment of the total value of a training system, training course or programme in social as well as financial terms. The term is also used in the general judgmental sense of the continuous monitoring of a programme or of the training function as a whole.
> *Validation*
> 1. Internal validation. A series of tests and assessments designed to ascertain whether a training programme has achieved the behavioural objectives specified.
> 2. External validation. A series of tests and assessments designed to ascertain whether the behavioural objectives of an internally valid training programme were realistically based on the accurate initial identification of training needs in relation to the criteria of effectiveness adopted by the organization.
> Evaluation differs from validation in that it attempts to measure the overall cost benefit of the course or programme, and not just the achievement of its laid down objectives.

Even these definitions do not appear to satisfy those who require precise statements of difference and it may be that it is not important. I would hesitate to add a further jargon word to the plethora already existing in the training world, but a constructed, compromise term might be 'evalidation'. What we are trying to achieve is some assessment of the success of our training under criteria which can include:

- does the course fully satisfy its stated objectives?
- does the course fully satisfy the personal objectives of the participants?

- is the course cost-effective for the organization it serves?
- do the participants put the learning into effective action on return to work?

The satisfaction of these and other criteria can vary considerably from one level of training to another. Technical/procedural training is often the easiest to assess – the learning is straightforward although it may be complex – and direct testing of skill and knowledge will show whether learning has been achieved. This is particularly so if the level of skill and knowledge is determined at the start of the course. Assessment of the translation to the working situation is similarly direct by posing the question 'Is he now doing the job correctly?' Less specific forms of training such as human relations and general management training can be very difficult to assess and some people suggest that it is impossible.

The difficulties of assessment should not deter the trainer from attempting at least some measure of evaluation or validation; perhaps even minimal assessment is better than no assessment.

Various levels of assessment can be identified as follows:

- Immediate: progressive validation through testing or other assessment during the training event.
- Immediate outcome: an end-of-course validation of the course by the participants in terms of how individual sessions and activities were rated.
- Intermediate outcome: an assessment of the retention and application of the learning at a stage some time following the end of the course, say three to six months.
- Ultimate outcome: a longer-term assessment after say a year's interval of retained learning and application, and the long-term benefits to the organization.

These levels of assessment were used to determine an evaluation system for management training in a large, national organization. This evaluation programme required the following action.

1) Formulation of the overall objectives of the course.
2) Formulation of objectives and learning points for each session and activity of the course.
3) The identification and assessment of the existing skill levels of the participating group before the training event.
4) The identification of existing skill levels of a control group that would not be involved in the training until a much later stage.

5) An assessment of the participant's levels of skill and training needs by the participant's bosses.
6) A pre-course briefing meeting of the participant and his boss to prepare the individual for the training and agree his personal objectives.
7) An assessment, at appropriate stages during the course, of the learning, by means of tests or tutor observation as relevant.
8) An assessment at the end of each training day by the participants of the learning achieved and their reaction to the training.
9) At the end of the course, a verbal review of the learning achieved during the course. This would be achieved by dividing the complete course of say twelve members into two groups of six. Each group would be asked to consider and list the main points of learning achieved during the course and also the problems of application envisaged. This would provide an immediate indication of how successful the training had been and would give a final opportunity to clarify any problems identified.
10) The course members would be asked to provide a written end-of-course review giving their immediate reactions to the individual sessions and activities in terms of tutor presentation, relevance of the material, learning achieved and use of time, with additional comments on the course as a whole. Other questions posed could include those relating to the role of the tutors and their helpfulness and any other general remarks. In order to provide a means of summary and comparison between individual responses, the reactions would be recorded on a semantic differential scale with space for specific comments, e.g.

Session: Desk-training techniques

Presentation by tutor	Clear	I	I√	I	I	I	I	I	Confusing
Presentation by tutor	Interesting	I	I√	I	I	I	I	I	Boring
Session material	Relevant	I√	I	I	I	I	I	I	Irrelevant
Session material	Taught or confirmed a lot	I	I√	I	I	I	I	I	Taught nothing
	Too much time	I	I	I	√ I	I	I	I	Too little time

Comments

11) Time would be given at the end of the course for the participants to consider which aspects of learning they intended to put into practice on their return to work – Action Plans. These would be constructed individually, but the opportunity would be given for the members to discuss their Action Plans with fellow course members and the tutors.
12) A post-course debriefing meeting between the individual and his boss soon after the end of the course, during which emphasis would be placed on the Action Plan and the demonstration by the boss of his intention of interesting and involving himself in the process.
13) At a period of between three and six months following the course, three evaluation activities would occur:

    (a) both the individual and his boss asked to comment on the progress of the Action Plan
    (b) the boss asked to comment on any increase in and use of skills or modifications of behaviour
    (c) the individual asked to make his assessment of any increase in and use of skills or behaviour modification.

14) At the same time that the participating group is being assessed for intermediate outcome success or otherwise, a similar assessment would be made of the control group. This would be an attempt to determine whether or not any improvements noted have resulted from the training rather than as a consequence of natural processes.
15) Longer-term outcome evaluation would be attempted after a period of about a year by repeating the approaches made at the intermediate stage, with the individual, his boss and the control group.

There are many difficulties in the path of carrying out successfully an extensive evaluation programme such as that described. The sector of the organization's management training selected for this approach was responsible for training some 600 managers each year in a variety of management topics. This would have involved an excessive amount of paper data collection which would have to be collated, analysed and interpreted, in addition to the use of human resources in direct contact with both the participant and control groups. In view of this amount of resource use, more time would have been spent on evaluation than on the training itself. This was considered to be unrealistic and not cost-effective, particularly as many of the aspects of the evaluation would be, by necessity, largely subjective. Consequently, although the approach was considered to have a chance of success in providing a reasonable level of evaluation, it was decided not to introduce all the aspects of the scheme. The aspects retained were considered to be the minimum necessary and included

- encouragement for the pre-course and post-course meetings
- the Learning Review
- Action Planning
- end-of-course reviews (sometimes referred to as 'happiness' sheets)
- the three-month follow-up of the individual's progress with his Action Plans.

It was left to the tutors to conduct immediate reaction tests and end-of-day reviews if they thought these were relevant to the particular event.

END-OF-COURSE VALIDATION

Perhaps the most common approaches to validation of training events are the end-of-course, immediate validation questionnaires, the so-called 'happiness sheets' referred to above. I feel that such a description is unfair, or more correctly, should be unfair. The title has arisen mainly because of the way that trainers in the past have planned, introduced and used them. An appropriate questionnaire, used in an effective way and valued, can give the trainer and the organization a great deal of realistic feedback on the effectiveness, and hence the cost-effectiveness, of the training.

There are naturally effective questionnaires, very effective ones, ineffective ones, and all shades in between. The science of producing them and using them is the subject of a separate book, but a basic knowledge of the various types is invaluable to any trainer, at whatever their stage of development.

STRAIGHTFORWARD SCORING SHEETS

The traditional approach to an end-of-course validation sheet has been to produce a questionnaire which asks the trainees to score a variety of items – sessions, activities, the environment and so on – on a rating scale, by ticking or ringing what they see as the relevant 'score'. One advantage of this type of questionnaire is the ease of analysis, the simple production of a numerical account of the scores given. If the score is above or below a certain score, the course/package is deemed to have been good. If the reverse scoring is shown, then the training has obviously been seen by the trainees as inappropriate or bad.

If the trainees have been completely honest in their scoring assessments, this type of questionnaire should present no problems. However, it is only too easy for a trainee, in the last few minutes of a course, to annotate scores without much thought. If the atmosphere of the course has been excellent, the trainees may be leaving in a state of euphoria – hence the likelihood of the production of 'happiness' sheets. Or if the course has been too hard-hitting for the trainees, or the group did not interrelate, for example, the scoring might be the reverse of the 'happiness' sheet.

VALIDATION QUESTIONNAIRE REQUIREMENTS

To ensure that there is at least some validity in the validation instrument itself, certain precautions and practices must be observed by the trainer.

First, there is little value in the trainer handing out the questionnaire in the dying minutes of a course and asking the delegates to complete them. Apart from the euphoria or its opposite, as described above, the minds of the delegates are probably firmly on getting away to catch their trains and so on. Consequently the questionnaire is seen as having little importance, because it has been given little importance (apparently) by the trainer. If the questionnaire is to be completed before the end of the course, a substantial amount of time must be built into the programme for this purpose, perhaps more than the activity would seem to warrant – this will stress its importance and encourage the delegates to think before they respond. There are some arguments against asking delegates to complete questionnaires before leaving the course. The euphoria syndrome is part of one argument; the other is that perhaps they have not had time to assimilate the learning and consider its importance to them and its significance to their work. The counter-argument is that, if the euphoria syndrome can be avoided, and the time action will help in this, immediate, 'gut' reactions are often better than considered ones where there is always the danger that delegates will ask themselves 'what *should* I put?' rather than 'what do I *really* think?'

An alternative approach is to issue the validation questionnaire and ask trainees to take it away with them, consider the learning, and answer the questionnaire honestly, then return it to the trainer. The danger of 'dishonest' completion mentioned above will always be there, but in addition there is always the problem of a low response rate. The delegates, if managers, are probably returning to desks groaning with work awaiting them, meetings to attend and all sorts of other activities which *must* be attended to. By the time the manager has settled down into a less hectic state (which should be soon if the training has been on delegation!) the questionnaire may have been forgotten or misplaced. Consequently it is not returned. Research gives various answers about response rate, but commonly quoted response percentages are between 30 and 50 per cent. If this is so, then perhaps it was a waste of time even issuing the questionnaire. Some organizations have administrative mechanisms which ensure a 100 per cent or near response rate, through directive follow-up or because of cooperation between the training organization and line management. Without this I prefer to use the end-of-course approach. To counter the immediate completion (which ensures 100 per cent return!), two questionnaires can be used. One can obtain the 'gut' feeling immediately at the end of the course; the other can be taken away for return within, say, two weeks, after post-course action and consideration.

A third option is to send a questionnaire one or two weeks after the end of the course, requesting return. If this approach is used, it is again useful if there is a mechanism to ensure response.

TYPES OF END-OF-COURSE QUESTIONNAIRES

The semantic differential scoring sheet As mentioned earlier, the most common validation questionnaire requires the delegates to give a 'score' to the elements of the training event determined by the trainer. These might relate to the sessions of the courses, blocks of sessions, activities, and also to the accommodation, the conference facilities, the administration, the handouts, the visual aids, the skills of the trainers, and so on. Usually, far too many questions are asked to obtain scores for aspects which are either irrelevant or require too many answers for the delegates to be bothered to be accurate/honest.

The scoring lines often have semantic differentials polarizing the ends of the scoring lines. For example, to one question 'How much have you learned?', there may be a scoring line with numbers to ring ranging from 1 to 7. At the '1' end of the line the words 'A lot' might appear and at the other end, the differential words 'A little". The delegate ticks or rings the number which he or she feels to be the level reflecting how much they have learned, or learned about that specific subject. An example of this type of sheet is shown in Figure 12.1.

The advantages of this type of questionnaire are that it is easy to complete – all that is asked for is a tick to indicate the delegates' views – and that analysis is easy – add up the various scores in whichever way is required.

One point of discussion is whether the scoring line should have an odd or even range of numbers e.g. 1 to 7 or 1 to 6 and so on. In the odd-number line, the danger is that the middle number might be used too frequently as an avoidance scoring, apparently signifying 'average'. It can, however, also mean that the training was so difficult to understand that the delegate was unable to allocate either a 'good' or a 'bad' score. Research tends to suggest this latter approach is more prevalent than the 'average' use. The argument *for* the even-numbered scoring system is that it puts pressure on the delegate to choose a side 'good' or 'bad'.

In my view this form of validation questionnaire can be dangerous because it is too sensitive to being treated in the 'happiness' sheet way, without much thought being given to the scoring. The delegates certainly are not required to justify their scoring.

Justified semantic differential scoring sheet This version is in my opinion considerably more effective than the previous example, in that not only does it ask for a scoring, thus enabling the trainer to analyse the scoring easily, but it also requires the

ELLRAY ASSOCIATES

V and E (SD)

'OPTIONS FOR TRAINERS' SEMINAR

A. OPTIONS: SEATING

Please enter a tick under the score which you feel is most relevant

		7	6	5	4	3	2	1	
Enjoyment	A lot								Little
Usefulness	A lot								Little
Content of session	Good								Poor
Extent of Learning	A lot								Little

(This type of approach is repeated for each session and for other elements such as 'Accommodation', 'Administration' as required.)

'Enjoyment' and so on can be extended with other questions depending on what information is needed. The scoring numbers can be used or omitted.

The scoring sections can have an even or odd range e.g. 6 or 7 sections.

Figure 12.1 Semantic differential scoring sheet

delegates to justify their scoring in a way which helps to avoid a random or unconsidered rating. This is managed quite simply by asking for their comments related to how they score.

The principal interest in validation is the determination of whether the learner has learned and the training has enabled this to occur. Consequently the predominating questions to be asked in any *validation* approach must relate directly to the learning aspect and also what will be done with the learning. Part of this can be achieved in a simple numerical approach by asking the learners to score a question such as:

AMOUNT OF LEARNING

Learned a lot	6	5	4	3	2	1	Learned nothing

But to avoid random scoring and reduction of the feedback to merely a numerical, pseudo-analytical statement, this scoring table must be followed by a requirement on the learner to justify the scoring and to state what has been learned and what is going to be done with it, or why learning has been minimal. The former requirement is requested if the learner has scored 6, 5 or 4, and the latter if the scoring is 3, 2 or 1. Other, subsidiary questions can be added requesting specific information about the learning event. An example of this type of questionnaire is given in Figures 12.2 and 12.3.

This type of questionnaire can be used at different intervals during a training event depending on the circumstances, complexity of the content and the length of the event. Too frequent a use can reduce the value of the questionnaires with the learners becoming annoyed with their use.

In a short event of two or three days, the questionnaire might be used most effectively as an end-of-course validation, the learning question relating to either the course as a whole (see Figure 12.2) or, if required, to specific sessions or blocks of training (see Figure 12.3).

When the event has a duration of more than three days, the questionnaire would certainly be used as an end-of-event validation instrument seeking views about the event as a whole. But interim questionnaires can be used to check that learning is taking place and that the training event is on course. These can include its use:

ELLRAY ASSOCIATES

'OPTIONS FOR TRAINERS' SEMINAR

COURSE VALIDATION

Please ring the scoring number which you feel is most relevant for you.

LEARNING

Learned a lot	6	5	4	3	2	1	Learned nothing

If you have scored either 6, 5 or 4, please state briefly what you have learned and how you intend to use it at work.

If you have scored either 3, 2 or 1, please state as fully as possible why you have given this score.

Name.. Date..........................

Title of course...

Figure 12.2 Justified end-of-course validation questionnaire

ELLRAY ASSOCIATES

'OPTIONS FOR TRAINERS' SEMINAR

SESSION VALIDATION

Please ring the scoring number which you feel is most relevant for you.

SESSION: USE OF PRACTICAL ACTIVITIES

Learned a lot	6	5	4	3	2	1	Learned nothing

If you have scored either 6, 5 or 4, please state briefly what you have learned and how you intend to use it at work.

If you have scored either 3, 2 or 1, please state as fully as possible why you have given this score.

SESSION: USE OF PRACTICAL ACTIVITIES

Learned a lot	6	5	4	3	2	1	Learned nothing

If you have scored either 6, 5 or 4, please state briefly what you have learned and how you intend to use it at work.

If you have scored either 3, 2 or 1, please state as fully as possible why you have given this score.

Name.. Date.........................

Title of course...

Figure 12.3 Justified session validation questionnaire

a) simply as a mid-course validation – 'Consider your learning to this point in the course'
b) at the end of each day – 'Consider your learning as far as today is concerned'
c) if the course is divided into discrete blocks of learning (communication, delegation, presentation and so on) – 'Consider the sessions, activities, exercises, videos and discussions relating to *x* subject'.

The interim use of the validation questionnaire can usefully be linked with the learners' completion of a Learning Log; this is described in the following chapter.

Open questionnaires In many ways the scoring type of questionnaire is too restrictive, although it does lead the delegate to give information on aspects determined by the trainer – a trainer-led situation. Many of the questions may be ones which the delegate is not particularly interested in answering, but because the question is there it has to be answered. The open type of questionnaire resolves this difficulty for the delegate, because he is given the opportunity to comment on matters which are of interest to him. In this type of validation approach the questionnaire consists of a number of questions of a fairly open nature, to which the delegate is invited to respond

- in the way in which he wishes to respond
- on the aspects which he finds particularly interesting.

It is usual to lead the delegates a little, but not to any great extent, by suggesting that they might wish to comment on various aspects of the course which made the most and least impact on them, and which they felt were important to them. They should be asked to be open and honest, and to make their responses as fully as possible. Naturally, ample time should be allowed for them to consider their responses and compose them, and it is often useful to precede the questionnaire by pairing the delegates for a period to discuss their views of the event.

Unless the organiztion demands that names should be added to any validation statements, the delegates should be given the free choice of whether to add their names or not. However, it is sometimes valuable to the trainer to know who has completed which questionnaire, not for any personal identification reason, but to

ELLRAY ASSOCIATES

V and E2

'OPTIONS FOR TRAINEES' SEMINAR

1. Which parts of the seminar did you find the most useful?

2. Which parts of the seminar did you find the least useful?

3. Are there any parts of the seminar you would omit?

4. Is there anything you would wish to see added to the seminar?

5. Any other comments.

Please add your name if you wish to do so.

Figure 12.4 Open questionnaire

compare, for example, responses from delegates with different types of jobs, from those who have been in particular syndicates during the event and so on. If this is requested, however, the reasons must be made clear in a very open way – an alternative might be to ask them to annotate their jobs, syndicates and so on rather than their names. An example of this type of questionnaire is given in Figure 12.4.

The main disadvantages of a questionnaire of this nature are:

- There is no guarantee that you will receive comments and feedback on the areas in which *you* are particularly interested
- The entries will be in *their words* and phraseology and this may cause you some interpretation problems
- Because the feedback is all in words, you will be unable to analyse the feedback numerically as you would with a scoring sheet.

The advantages can be summarized as:

- The delegate is free to comment on whatever he wishes, so the comments made will represent the significant factors retained in his memory = learning retention
- No inhibitions are placed on the delegate with questions which he *must* answer
- There are no problems of interpretation of questions other than the general ones, which the delegate is free to interpret in any case.

Totally open questionnaire This type of questionnaire takes the openness of the previous approach further and does not even pose general questions. The delegates are presented with what is effectively a blank sheet of paper on which they are invited to write whatever comments they wish to make about the training event. The range, content, level, extent and so on are left completely to them, the only guidance given on the sheet being a very general introduction/invitation to comment. Figure 12.5 demonstrates an example of this questionnaire.

The risks are obviously large. The comments made may be few or superficial; they may ignore the important aspects on which you wanted feedback – these omissions may be significant in themselves. Analysis will be even more difficult than with the previous open questionnaire, perhaps impossible compared to the

ELLRAY ASSOCIATES

V and E 1

'OPTIONS FOR TRAINERS' SEMINAR

Please make any comments which you feel are important or significant on any aspect of the seminar.

Figure 12.5 Totally open questionnaire

scoring questionnaires, but you will certainly discover what the delegates consider to have been important and on which they want to comment.

Some guidance may be given verbally when introducing and handing out the questionnaire, by suggesting (and only suggesting) that they might wish to make comments on such aspects as

- the course content
- the value or otherwise of specific sessions, activities, videos and so on
- what they liked/disliked and why
- what they learned and what they intend to do with that learning
- any comments, the more the better, about anything they wish.

These comments should certainly not be directive; nor should you be disappointed if the comments do not follow your guidelines.

Some trainers feel that the risk with such an open questionnaire is too great to live with. It *is* a risk, but in my training experience I have had only one delegate who failed/refused to make any comments – there were very good reasons in his mind why this happened. But the choice is in the trainer's hands. It you want detailed feedback on subjects determined by you, then the more structured approach is necessary. If you will accept the trainee/delegate-led feedback, then the more open questionnaires will suit your approach.

It is easy to talk about evaluation but much more difficult to put it into effective operation!

One of the main difficulties in any evaluation system of training not concerned with specific technical skills is the phenomenon known as response-shift bias. Traditionally a pre-course testing instrument is given to the student either before or at the start of the course. He is asked to rate himself on a number of factors relating to the training. For example, in interpersonal skills training he might be asked to rate himself, on a Likert-type questionnaire with rating scales of 0–10, on his skills in initiating ideas, supporting others, building on others' proposals, managing conflict and so on. At the pre-course test stage the student might have rated himself as 8 on the scale concerned with managing conflict. At the end of the course, an identical questionnaire would be administered and the student might have rated himself on this occasion as 8.5 for the same aspect. This would be in conflict with the observation by others and recognition by the student himself that during the course he had the opportunity to handle conflict and his skills had increased considerably. But the comparison between the two tests shows an insignificant increase.

What has probably happened, and this would be confirmed by interview with the student, is that once the training has been completed the student realizes that his yardsticks for completing the original assessment were invalid and the rating should have been, say, 3. There has been a shift in the student's frame of reference and it is this that is referred to as the response-shift bias.

A method of avoiding this bias is to introduce a different measure that attempts to retain the same frame of reference throughout. One approach to this is to ask the students at the end of the course to reflect back to the start of the course and re-rate themselves in terms of how they think they were *then*, in the light of what they have learned about themselves during the training. Before completing the *then* questionnaire they will have completed the normal end-of course measure. Some degree of contamination will still have been introduced as a result of subjectivity, but the measures will be more realistically comparable. Mezoff in the USA is developing this approach to evaluation and calls it the *pre-then-post* testing. He suggests that the traditional *pre-post* testing produces more conservative and underestimated measures of the success of a training programme. He considers that the *pre-then-post* method is equally applicable to leadership skills, interviewing skills, helping skills, assertiveness and human relations training as well as to more traditional approaches.

EVALUATING TRAINER EFFECTIVENESS

The evaluation approaches to this point have been concerned principally with the assessment of the effectiveness of the training and the implementation of that training, demonstrating the learning that has been achieved by the learners. But there is another factor in the training equation that has a significant bearing on the effectiveness of the process – the trainers. A training event might consist of moderate or even poor material, yet the event can be successful because of the trainer's skill. Conversely, excellent material can fail because of an inept trainer. The ideal must be good material and effective trainers. If the validation of the training shows a good level of effectiveness, this will *usually* reflect on the skill of the trainer, but this may not always be the case. Additional or separate assessment of the trainer effectiveness will be the only way to confirm which is the case.

We have considered the ways in which we can assess to what extent the training and the learning have been effective. Can we do this for the trainer? Considerable care must be taken in assessments of this nature as we are looking at the personal skills of individuals, rather than the impersonal act of training and learning.

Two approaches are immediately apparent. The first requires observation and assessment by an auditor – an external assessor or the internal training manager; the second relies on the comments of the learners or course participants.

It would seem that the second course of action – using the learning group – would supply the required information: after all, they are the ones that have been subjected to the trainer's activities. But there are several problems involved in using the learners:

- trainer assessment is a sensitive issue
- the learners may not be capable of assessing the skills of the trainer
- subjectivity might affect the real views.

Sensitivity Later in this chapter we will be considering the sensitive issue of the trainer reporting back on the learners. There is, of course, a similar sensitivity involved in the learners reporting on the trainers. This sensitivity may be reduced or at least aired as an issue by ensuring that the learners are made fully aware of what they are being asked, why this is happening, and what will happen to their comments.

Capability The course participants will have been in a learning situation and may have been so deeply involved in this that the skills of the trainer may not have been apparent to them. Sometimes a trainer has to require a learning group to perform in a way that the group does not like: this can have an effect on the attitude of the learners to the trainer's skills, even though the approach was the only one possible in the circumstances. At best, all we can hope for from the learners is a subjective assessment, often based on fragmented observation, and often based on non-understanding of the processes involved. Nevertheless, these learners are the people who have been on the receiving end of the trainer's behaviour and although fragmented, the group response can frequently add up to a coherent view.

Subjectivity The learners are not attending the course to assess the trainer – they are there to learn. The learning process may have been enjoyable, the trainers pleasant and sociable, and the feelings of the group at the end of the event may contaminate any assessment in favour of the trainer. Or the reverse might be the case, particularly if, although a 'good' trainer, that person was not particularly likeable or had not socialized as much as another, more popular trainer. After all, some trainers do seem to treat the training course as a means of ensuring their personal popularity. Another contaminating factor could be that the learner might be returning soon for another course with the same trainer!

The views of learners must therefore be treated carefully; the end-of-course euphoria (or the reverse), close or distant relationships with the trainer, and the proximity of going back home, resulting in either a positive or negative feeling, will all affect the objectivity of the assessment. Consequently there cannot be reliance on these views in isolation and supportive assessment should be sought.

ASSESSMENT QUESTIONNAIRES

Learner assessment One method of obtaining the views of the learners will be to seek these by means of a questionnaire. This will usually be issued at the end of the course, although, even more than with validation questionnaires, this may not be the most effective time for its completion. If a control mechanism for the return of questionnaires exists, it may be best to have the learners take the questionnaire away with them for return within 10 days to two weeks. This time lapse will allow euphoric and subjective feelings to rationalize and the resulting response may be more objective. As discussed earlier, simple tick lists should be avoided, rather the completer should be required to think about the questions. If the questionnaire is taken away from the course, it can be made more extensive than if it had to be completed before the learners left for home. Appendix 4 suggests a format for a questionnaire of this nature.

External assessment A more objective and qualified assessment should be obtainable from sources other than the learners, although these should support any other assessment. The most likely assessor will be the trainer's line manager (the Training Manager in many cases) or an external assessor brought in for this purpose. The questionnaire in Appendix 4 can be used by the external assessor; this will ensure that possibility of comparison with the learners' comments, or, more usually, a more detailed, function-specific checklist can be used as the assessor observes the trainer. Examples of these detailed questionnaires are given in *Assessing Trainer Effectiveness* (Rae, Gower, 1991).

Naturally, if a more detailed and uniform assessment is required, the external assessor could consider using performance criteria contained in the Training and Development NVQ competence standards, even though an NVQ is not being sought.

Self-assessment Trainers themselves should constantly be assessing their own effectiveness from their own viewpoint. The questionnaire in Appendix 3 can be converted easily to a self-assessment instrument and additional questions as required can be added, or the more detailed checklists suggested for the external assessor can be modified.

When the assessments – learners and/or external assessor and/

or self-assessment – have been completed, the results should be analysed carefully and the results discussed to see where the trainer might most usefully develop. This discussion might follow a series of courses or form part of an appraisal or mini-appraisal system. It would be most effective if observations were made of more than one course and more than one type of course or event – one swallow does not make a summer, particularly when the 'swallow' knows that it is under observation! But the ratings must not be treated as absolute and unalterable scores, because of the innumerable subjective aspects which depend strongly on personally biased views; but at least they provide a starting point for a discussion.

REFERENCES AND RECOMMENDED READING

Evaluation and Control of Training. A.C. Hamblin, McGraw-Hill, 1974.

How to Measure Training Effectiveness. Leslie Rae. Gower, 2nd edition, 1986.

Evaluation of Management Training. P. Warr, M. Bird and N. Rackham. Gower, 1970.

The Evaluation of Management Training. Matt Whitelaw. IPM Publishing, 1972.

Glossary of Training Terms. Department of Employment. HMSO.

Assessing Trainer Effectiveness. Leslie Rae. Gower, 1991.

Training Evaluation Handbook, A.C. Newby. Gower, 1992.

13 Training for training

There can be no doubting the truth of the oft-quoted statement that one of the prime responsibilities of a manager is the training and development of his staff. Of course, this must not be taken too literally since if it were, the manager would have no time to exercise his other functions. But the emphasis must surely be on 'responsibility'. The effective manager is skilled in using all the resources available to him, including people. One of the people resources he normally has available in a large organization is a training section of which he may himself be the Training Director. Depending on the size of the organization he may delegate this part of his responsibility to a training manager. Whatever the division, there is some sort of skilled training team available to him as a resource to fulfil his obligations to his employees.

At the other end of the scale are the organizations that are too small to sustain any form of structure for employee training. In these cases the enlightened manager has three choices – to buy in training expertise as required, to utilize external training organizations, or to fulfil a training role himself. In practice, use can often be made to a greater or lesser extent of all these options.

However, economic needs impose a limitation of choices and in the present climate many organizations have had to restrict their traditional training activities. In a constrictive climate, production and sales outweigh the apparent value of training. I say apparent because training must always have an intrinsically high value. If employees are not well trained, production, sales, marketing and accounts will suffer. However, money can only go so far and the manager can but hope that efficiency will not sink to too low a level without the degree of training that he knows is necessary.

Economic constraints of this nature have forced many organizations to reconsider their attitudes to training, and more enlightened management has come to recognize its direct responsibilities. This has led to the evolution of a greater number of manager-trainers. In the best cases, the manager-trainer takes his responsibilities seriously and ensures that he has sufficient of the basic skills and knowledge to fulfil at least the basic training needs of his employees. This means in essence that he has to learn the basic skills of training, and knowing when these skills are insufficient to cope with more advanced needs.

CHOICES OF TRAINING ORGANIZATION

The management of organizations with staff who will have training needs must make one or more of these choices:

1) to have an internal training department sufficiently large and skilled to satisfy the training needs of the organization
2) to use specialists and experts within the organization to train employees in their specialist fields
3) to buy in external trainers to produce training events when training needs are identified
4) to send employees on 'public' courses produced by training organizations
5) to use the coaching techniques described earlier whenever this is appropriate
6) to encourage the use of self-development techniques and facilities, again whenever this is appropriate
7) to develop internally the greater use of manager-trainers.

Apart from options 3, 4 and 6, these choices entail some degree of training for the trainers, and even options 3, 4 and 6 must be approached with intelligence and knowledge. The remainder require a greater or lesser involvement in the development of training skills and knowledge. In option 1 the trainers themselves must be trained to a sufficient standard to satisfy whatever level of training is required by the organization. The specialists cited in option 2 may be expert in their own fields, but this does not necessarily mean that they have the skills to impart learning. Such a situation requires that the specialists are given the skills of presenting material in a way that can promote learning rather than just the receiving of information. The coaching approach requires the coach to have the necessary skills. It also depends on the subject for which coaching is required, and though the technique is powerful it is not always appropriate. Option 7 is in many ways the most difficult to maintain and to provide for, as it demands both management time and training of the manager in at least the basic skills of the trainer. The most appropriate approach within this option is to give the manager-trainer these basic training skills; training needs beyond his capability may be catered for by a combination of some of the other options.

Obviously the level of training involvement of the manager-trainer will vary considerably according to the organization.

TRAINING OF TRAINERS

The Training of Trainers Committee set up by the Manpower Services Commission in November 1976 conducted a survey intended to define the basic requirements of trainers whether full- or part-time (including manager-trainers). The remit of this committee was to

- consider the roles, relationships, training needs and current training of those staff who have specific responsibilities for training and to make recommendations on

  (a) the pattern of training required for such staff
  (b) the provision of such training
  (c) appropriate means of its evaluation.

The committee's work was based on the concept that specialist training staff are not always necessary, but managers with an inherent training role *are*. However, the needs and practices of both were recognized.

One very important aspect of the committee's considerations was the identification of 'core competences' which were the basic aspects of specific knowledge and skills, and the common know-how of trainers.

Four specific roles were also identified for those involved in training:

- direct training
- organizing/administrating
- determining/managing
- consulting/advising.

DIRECT TRAINING

Competences in this area include knowledge of learning methods and styles, teaching methods and styles, presentational techniques, learning objectives and design of training. Also required are skills in determining appropriate learning programmes, designing sessions and programmes, techniques of instruction and teaching and use of training aids.

ORGANIZING/ADMINISTRATING

Skilled trainers are not restricted to simply walking into the classroom and conducting a session. They need to be involved in the organization and administration of the events in which they are participating. The skills and knowledge needed in these areas of responsibility include the knowledge of a wide range of training systems and resources, the skills of analysing training needs, and the ability to plan and organize courses and manage all the resources available.

MANAGING

Wider skills and knowledge of the management of training will be needed by some trainers, particularly senior trainers and trainers who are also in a management position. Budgeting, costing and evaluation must be strong areas of knowledge, and the skills must include the abilities to analyse and consider organization development needs, general management skills and problem-solving approaches.

CONSULTING/ADVISORY

Many 'trainers' are not solely concerned with running training courses. They can also be involved in consultancy and advisory relationships with individuals either for direct training activities or in a management development capacity. To act as a consultant adviser demands a wide knowledge of consultancy styles and the associated skills in interviewing, counselling, coaching and developing relationships.

The work of the Training of Trainers Committee has indicated the core knowledge of skills necessary for both direct trainers and managers with a direct responsibility for a practice in training. The identification made has opened the doors for a procedure for registration of organizations which can show that they satisfy the demanding criteria.

What do the requirements for training skills and knowledge mean to trainers and manager-trainers, whether these skills are measured against organizational needs or the criteria for registration under the training for trainers? Obviously there will be differences between these two types of trainer, constraints being imposed mostly by the amount of time available for training and development. Other participants in some aspects of training can include training managers and directors, who will need at the very least a considerable amount of knowledge of training requirements rather than actual training skills, in addition to their administrative abilities.

FULL-TIME TRAINERS

Let us look first at the more demanding group, the trainers who have a full-time involvement in the variety of training approaches.

Training staff can be recruited in a variety of ways. They may be experienced managers transferred from line jobs to training, having little or no experience of or skills in training; similar people who have had either some experience in training or related activities within or outside the organization; newcomers to the organization, coming with or without some training experience, or externally trained trainers from training schools or from other organizations. My own entry to full-time training was a mixture of these, as I had training and teaching experience outside my employer's organization, some training as a trainer, and line management experience. The background experience will naturally determine any further training necessary; the less the experience, the more the training required

As suggested by the Training of Trainers Committee, the new trainer requires a number of core competences to enable him to practise the skills demanded. We can summarize these areas as follows.

Knowledge	*Skills*
Learning styles	Job and task analysis
Barriers to learning	Identification of training needs
Basic methods of training	Practical design of courses
Product knowledge, i.e. the subjects for which training is required	Methods of session design and brief construction
The range of training and learning aids available	Preparation and use of visual aids
Methods of job and training needs analysis	Presenting and controlling training sessions
Design of training events	Discussion leading
Basic training validation methods	Preparation of session handouts

Typical training courses for new trainers will include all these aspects and will give the newcomer at least the basic skills to enable him to perform acceptably on his first training event. What the course will not do is produce a completely skilled trainer: this level can be attained only by practice and experience.

Commonly, the new trainer will take part in a training course in which he will eventually be directly involved, but in the first instance he will not act as a trainer. He will take part in the course as a student, this involvement having three main objectives:

- to be exposed directly to the actual training and to view this from the trainee's standpoint
- to observe the techniques, methods and approaches of the trainers who will eventually be his direct colleagues
- to have a greater appreciation of the material that he will himself be presenting at a later stage.

Often this participation takes place as part of the new trainer's induction to his job and before his attendance on a training for trainers course.

Following the new trainer's participation in his own training event, he can be progressively integrated into the training team, whenever this approach is possible, though it must be admitted that contingency requirements can get in the way. This is my own preferred approach to developing new trainers for whom I have been responsible.

The next stage normally introduced to the new trainer is again an inactive role as far as his direct participation in the course is concerned. He again attends the training course in which he will eventually be directly involved, not this time as a student, but as an observer. His objectives on this occasion can include:

- observing to a deeper level the styles and methods of the trainers so that he can start to assess how his own approach might develop
- assimilating, again to a deeper level, the material for which he will eventually be responsible, i.e. the sessions he will be leading
- making extensive notes of the sessions which he will lead so that he has the maximum amount of material from which to produce his own briefs or session notes
- assessing the reactions of trainees to various aspects of the session material and to the styles of the trainers.

Depending on the complexity of the trainee trainer's involvement in his eventual training role, and his apparent skill potential, this stage can be repeated. For example, if the trainer will have to lead in a number of sessions, he might look in depth at half the sessions during the first course he attends as an observer and not too deeply at the other sessions, simply soaking up the atmosphere. He would then attend the course on a second occasion as an observer when he would look at the remaining material. Of course, circumstances may not permit this leisurely, though desirable approach. Once the trainee trainer has attended his trainer course, he may have to be thrown in at the deep end and to write immediately his own session briefs and plunge into the next training course, preferably with the strong support of a colleague.

If time allows, the next stage of the trainer's progressive development is to take some of the sessions for which he will eventually be fully responsible. It is helpful if he does not have to take all his sessions straight away, if possible. Our trainer's development at this stage will be helped if full appraisal and guidance is given immediately following his performances by his trainer colleague.

From this point on, training in his basic approaches can only be through experience and practice. During this period concern must be for the trainees attending the course, since by necessity they may not be receiving full professionalism and expertise. This effect can be minimized with the support and appropriate interventions of an experienced colleague.

CUSTOMIZED TRAINER TRAINING

One of the problems of trainer training, perhaps encouraged by the increasing demands for professionalism and trainer certification, is a slavish agreement to the full range of training programmes. It is assumed that new trainers *must* be immediately exposed to all aspects of trainer training so that they become almost instant experts. In many cases this is far from the most effective format. The core skills described on page 243 include such items as learning styles and barriers, design of training events and validations, and skills aspects which include job and task analysis, identification of training needs and even design of courses. A glance at the syllabus of many trainer training courses can prove frightening in its comprehensiveness and complexity, certainly to an embryo trainer and also to the more experienced ones. The complete trainer, of course, must come fully to terms with all these aspects of training in the search for professionalism. But my continuing familiarization with more and more new trainers in a wide range of industrial and commercial concerns, large and small, suggests that training of this nature is 'Rolls Royce' training, where, with respect to that excellent car, 'Mini' training is what is really required.

Many new trainers once engaged by a company are faced with a number of demands and also constraints. They are entering in most cases, already well-established training departments which have equally well-established ranges of courses with determined material, structured programmes and even laid-down methods of presentation. A trainer entering this environment has little opportunity, or encouragement, to practise many of the knowledge and skill areas mentioned above. In fact, in most cases, attempts to experience these would be forbidden.

What is more the general picture is that the new trainer is told that he or she will be involved initially in a particular range of training courses which already exist. Having followed the introduction to these courses as described earlier, he/she will then take part, sometimes progressively, as the trainer or one of the trainers 'responsible' for the course.

The newly 'responsible' trainer will be told

- the objectives set for the course
- the objectives set for each session

- the programme for the course complete with running order, which trainers will be involved in which sessions and the timings of the sessions
- how each session will be run – inputs, discussion, activity and so on
- the content of each session
- THE brief or script for each session describing what will be included and how it will be presented
- which OHPs (already prepared) will be used in which session and at which stage in the session
- the availability of all the prescribed material for the course/sessions – pre-work (if any), handouts, tests, questionnaires and so on.
- whether sessions or the course will be validated and which forms of validation will be used in any case.

There is nothing intrinsically wrong for all this (and the list is not exhaustive) to be presented to the new trainer, because the course/sessions in the forms decreed may have reached these levels through considerable experience by other trainers. In addition, most new trainers know no better than that this is the normal practice; and welcome all these supports at a time when they are feeling very inexperienced, vulnerable, have little confidence and have little idea how they are going to perform in real training situations. But it is very obvious that if they have followed one of the comprehensive training courses, they could

- quickly forget the more advanced trainer requirements which they learned on the course, but which they will not be allowed to practise at work
- become dissatisfied with the insistence on following the laid-down path and want to try out some of the other techniques they learned about on the course
- become dissatisfied and critical of the type of training they have to do, seeing it as not being as good as it is claimed to be.

If the new trainer has received the 'Rolls Royce' treatment before being engaged by an organization, this will no doubt have stood him in good stead in obtaining the position. But if the organization sends the trainer on one of the comprehensive courses after engagement, but knowing the way they will be used, the training is far from cost-effective and some of the negative attitudes described above may become evident in the trainer.

What then *is* required? The answer depends on the range and scale of training the new trainer will be asked to do and for how long this will be likely to continue. If change is not envisaged, this can have a strong influence on the staged training of the new trainer. But if, although there is an existing programme, changes are likely or imminent, a different approach will be necessary.

In the first instance, what path should be followed? The question to ask is 'What knowledge and skills does the trainer need to perform the duties expected of him?' Let us take the extreme example described in detail above where the duties *and* methods are prescribed.

The knowledge required will include that of the content of the session and the script, with its stage directions for visual aids and handouts and so on. This will have to be learned in the new trainer's induction period – talking to the existing trainers, sitting-in on sessions and courses, learning the script and so on. At this stage the trainer does not need the 'luxuries' of learning styles, barriers to learning, training design and so on, and as suggested earlier, these could get in the way of the new trainer's development.

As far as skills are concerned, the main ones are

- group presentation skills – those of talking coherently in a manner which is acceptable to a group and helps learning rather than distracting from it
- group discussion skills – those of initiating and continuing to an effective end a discussion related to the session subject
- activity operation and feedback for experiential events – setting up the pre-prepared activities, controlling the trainees during the activity, and, most important, feedback/appraisal
- practical skills in the use of the visual aids available, including video player operation.

These are the 'core' skills necessary and are much less demanding than the fuller core skills mentioned earlier. But these are the areas of knowledge and skill needed so that the trainer can function effectively *now* within the constraints placed upon him.

Some trainers may say that this is unnecessarily restrictive, and this may be so, but very many new trainers are introduced in this way. Even more, they are required to stay in this environment for a considerable time.

The initial training event for the new trainer may, however, more realistically include at least an introduction to other skills. Even if the trainer is not willing or not going to be allowed to utilize these skills immediately, an early opportunity might arise and the trainer would have had some preparation. This is not suggesting that a very wide range of skills, for example, neurolinguistic programming, transactional analysis, behaviour analysis, organizational training needs analysis and so on, should immediately be added, but rather the more basic skills that will encourage the new trainer to develop.

Questioning skills will quickly become a necessity if the trainer is to develop from a strictly 'chalk and talk' presenter to one involving the group to a significant extent. These skills will include not only development of the types of questions to be used and their relevant use, but also what to do in common problem situations: the question does not produce a response; how to deal with responses received, how to respond to learners' questions, and so on.

Although in the scenario described earlier, the new trainer may be presented with the session objectives, design, brief and aids, few trainers will, or will be able to, restrain themselves within these constraints for too long. The trainers may not want, indeed may not be allowed, to change the session design and objectives. But they may be able to exercise some individually preferred modification, however limited, in some or all of the environmental factors, personalization of the brief, and the design, construction and use of aids that are more in keeping with their preferred styles. This is the reason why chapters including these subjects have been included in this edition.

The new trainer may be aware of the use of videos during an input session, but the rather more advanced and effective use of videos in place of sessions, the use of trigger videos, and the variations on the in-session use of videos may be strange country. Similarly, sessions on the use of other technological aids such as computers, interactive video and CCTV may encourage the trainer to consider movement from the straightforward approaches initially imposed. Of course the introduction of these types of skills and techniques must be weighed in the context of the organizational culture and freedom. But there are few trainers who are not allowed some developing latitude if they can show that (a) they can cope with the skills and (b) they will improve the training effectiveness.

A suggested programme, which has been proved effective in practice in a number of organizations follows.

A SUGGESTED TRAINER DEVELOPMENT PROGRAMME

The following, suggested programme is based on actual trainer development programmes in which I have been involved as either the designer or trainer or both. The several programmes were all different, principally because of the skill and experience mix on the courses – from a completely new trainer who had been appointed only that day to trainers having five years and more experience, but who had worked in restricted environments and had not received previous training. For example, one trainer of five years' standing, because of the type of training she had been performing had not used an OHP, but would, because of a change, soon have this pleasure!

The complete programme suggested is one which starts with an Open Learning Induction Pack which the learners and their managers receive on the appointment of the former and prior to the workshop programmes. The workshops programme is attended at the earliest opportunity following the appointment and completion of the Induction Pack. This consists of two basic core skills courses, separated by an interval of about two months, the basic skills being modelled on the basic requirements of TDNVQ Level 3. During the following months, one- and two-day modules are offered as required covering specific and more advanced training skills, until by the end of an 18-month period the new trainer will have covered most of the NVQ competences with the exception of some of the more global requirements.

The following suggested programme relates to the two-week course and is intended to run from just before lunch on the Monday to about noon on the following Friday of both weeks. Ideally, the course is residential and the learners should be prepared to work on most days from 9 am to about 7 pm. I have found committed, new trainers, although finding this tiring, do not feel that excessive demands are being made on them in the circumstances.

With a group of 10 to 12 learners, two trainers is the recommended cadre.

WORKSHOP ONE

Day one

1200–1300 Introduction to programme and learner introductions.

Lunch

1400–1445 Introduction continued. Learner expectations, description of Learning Logs activity and first completion of the self-assessment Three-Test.

1445–1700 The role of the trainer – selected material (includes break).

1700–1730 Trainer qualifications (if relevant).

1730–1900 Adult learning – barriers, learning recall, etc.

(The Learning Styles Questionnaire can be issued for evening completion, without any explanation other than instructions for completion and that the results will be discussed on the next day). The learners will be asked to complete their Learning Log for this first day during the evening.

Day two

0900–0930 Brief presentation of learning log entries in two parallel sub-groups.

0930–1030 Adult learning – analysis of learning styles and related activity.

1045–1215 Communication – methods, problems and barriers and activity.

1215–1315 Non-verbal communication – selected according to prior experience and learning of learners.

Lunch

1415–1445 Period for final preparation for mini-presentations.

1445–1630 Mini-presentations (group divided into two parallel-operating sub-groups).

1630–1800 Activities in training.

The learners will be asked to complete their Learning Log for this second day during the evening.

Day three

0900–0930 Brief presentation of Learning Log entries in two parallel sub-groups.

0930–1100 Questioning skills (selected activities).

1115–1300 Preparing a script (may include part preparation of learners' briefs for their 20-minute presentation if time is available). (Inclusion of some material will depend on (a) the time available and (b) the needs of the learners.)

Lunch

1400–1600 Visual aids including hands-on experience or sub-group presentations.

1600 onwards Preparation time for the 20-minute talks. This should be allowed to continue to any time in the evening that the individuals require, with workshop trainer support.

The learners should also be expected to complete their Learning Log during the evening.

Day four

0900–1015 Presentation skills.

1015–1045 Break

1045 to end, includes lunch break. 20-minute presentations in two parallel sub-groups. Two presentations before lunch, three or four after lunch depending on size of learning group.

If time is available, a discussion can be held to bring out the significant points that emerged during the presentations.

Day five

0900–1015 Listening skills.

1015 Break

1030 to end Conclusion – completion of final Learning Log, sheets two and three of the Three-Test, and of the personal action plan. If mechanism exists to follow-up learners, an end of workshop validation questionnaire can be issued for completion and return soon after the workshop. If there is no such mechanism, completion should be at this stage of the workshop.

WORKSHOP TWO

Day one

1200–1430 Re-introduction of the programme and discussion of the experiences during the period between the two workshops (includes lunch break).

1445–1700	Training objectives (includes break).
1700 onwards	Reminder about Learning Log and first day completion.
Day two	
0900–0940	Presentation of Learning Log entries and discussion in two parallel sub-groups.
0940–1200	Observation and feedback skills.
Lunch	
1300–1500	Role plays.
1515–1600	CCTV and its place in training.
1600–1730	Videos and their use in training.
1730 onwards	Learning Log completion.
Day three	
0900–1245	Discussion leading as a training technique.
1245 to end of day as determined by the learners (includes lunch and afternoon breaks).	
	Team presentation preparation.
Day four	
0900 to end	Team presentations.
Day five	
0900–1030	Technology and other techniques in training.
1030–1200	Validation, evaluation and action planning to closure.

When the trainer has remained in the organization for some time and can perform in this way very efficiently, either the trainer or the organization can then require an increase in knowledge and skill level. At this point, perhaps because of the introduction of new training needs in the organization, those needs will have to be identified, and task and job analyses performed. Consequently training will have to be designed, learning styles accepted and complete validation and evaluation programmes introduced and so on. It is hoped that the training department will have been informed in good time of the new demands and then trainers can receive the upgrading training to cope.

Much of this has its parallel in the movement away from the traditional form of training for supervisors and managers. The ineffective approaches were based on subjecting a newly appointed or promoted supervisor or manager to a course of training which included every aspect of knowledge, skill and attitude required by a supervisor or manager *in one course and all at the same time*. This approach was based on the view that because a supervisor/manager needed all these skills, he should have them from the start, *whether or not he would use them immediately, not taking account of what he already knew, and assuming that every supervisor and manager needed the same*. Fortunately, in most management and supervisory training (although still not all) it has been recognized that a more effective approach is a modular one related to the individual's needs and taking into account timing and change. Few individuals took away from the all-embracing course a fraction of what they had been 'taught' and at worst had not learned what they needed to because this had been crowded out. The training of trainers must take account of this experience.

DEVELOPMENT OF TRAINERS

The development progression described relates to the initial basic training of the trainer, providing him with the preliminary skills for probable training courses with fairly formal, structured types of courses and approaches. It would be completely unfair on the trainer to expect him to plunge into training of high complexity or training requiring much more than basic approaches at this stage in his development.

Development will depend on the expectations of the trainer's employer and the enhanced demands made upon him. He may stay in the more procedural training environment, may be required to facilitate developmental training, or to become an expert in human relations training. Whatever the nature of these progressive demands, there will be the need to develop the trainer and give him additional skills and knowledge, sufficient to fit him for those greater demands.

Whatever road the trainer's development follows most trainers will need exposure to more advanced training skills, even if the objective of this activity may be only to widen his horizons. Most trainers will need to increase their knowledge of and skill in constructing and operating case studies. A knowledge of the range of course validation and training evaluation methods will certainly be of value; so will skills in producing analytical instruments such as questionnaires and surveys, and so on. The list is almost endless in view of the wide range of training needs, approaches and methods. Opportunities must be made available to the trainer to take advantage of any of these developmental events which will enhance his value to the organization and give him greater job satisfaction and confidence.

Many avenues exist for the trainer's development in the way just described: some opportunities for training may be available internally, or through guided self-development by means of self-operated training packages, or the trainer may have to attend courses arranged as public events by the many organizations which offer a large variety of subjects. If there are a number of trainers they can provide special in-company courses. Whenever possible, the latter approach has many advantages as the courses can usually be tailored to suit the trainer group and company needs, an approach that can be difficult on a public course.

When does this trainer development cease? My own belief is – never. 'New' techniques and approaches are constantly appearing, whether they are variations on previous ones or actually innovative approaches. Whatever their bases, the trainer must test them and decide whether or not he is depriving himself of skills by not adding them to his repertoire of training tools. Human relations training is particularly prone to new approaches, since it is essentially an evolving area of training as psychological research becomes more evolved and can be applied to training. Typical examples of these practically applied approaches have been described earlier – Quality Circles, Action Learning, BMod approach to solving people problems and so on.

Present-day approaches to trainer training recognize these developmental needs within a planned rather than an accidental process. The two-week programme suggested earlier is intended to be the basic core training for the new trainer, but it becomes less than a true developmental process if a series of more advanced skill modules is not linked to it on a progressive basis. Depending on trainer needs these might be part of a planned programme or offered as modules to be attended when a new need is identified (preferably before it is actually needed).

PERSONAL DEVELOPMENT

The planned development of the new, and even the more experienced, trainer can be usefully supplemented by the introduction of two developmental instruments. I have used both of these successfully in several organizations with developing trainers. These are the Learning Logs and the Trainer Development Record (TDR). Both are valuable in helping and supporting the trainers in their ongoing development during and following a trainer development programme. In addition, they are concrete and demonstrable evidence of progress with many uses including the pursuit of NVQs or other professional awards and in career or development appraisal. In the latter cases, the 'evidence' will be of practical and valuable use to both the trainers and their line managers.

Learning Logs The Learning Log is primarily an instrument in which the learner-trainers record during the initial programme part of the development programme, the learning points from the training event that have become a significant part of their personal learning and which they want to be sure of recalling.

The log consists of an introductory, explanatory page followed by a number of sheets in sets of three, one set for each day of the training event. Set-sheet 1 can be used by the learner instead of or in addition to any note sheets that might be made during the training day of interesting, useful or significant learning points. Set-sheet 2 is used by the learners to sort and summarize the points from sheet 1 that they particularly want to recall, perhaps adding references to handouts and other information. Set-sheet 3 is a mini-action plan, detailing from sheet 2 entries about learning that the learner particularly intends to implement and how, etc. this action will be taken. The various sheet 3s can be used eventually in the formulation of the final action plan.

The second and third sheets are usually completed by the learners during the evenings of the course. This gives the learners the opportunity to reflect on the day's learning and what it means to them. This reflection and recording supports consolidation and recall of the learning points. As a further consolidation and recall support it is useful to use the first 45 minutes or so at the start of the next training day for the learners to give a short presentation based on their previous evening's log entries. The learners find that in addition to consolidating further their learning they are reminded of other learning points by hearing the presentations of their colleagues.

The format of the morning review of the log will depend on a number of factors: time available, the number of learners, the number of trainers and the type of training event.

If a training group consists of, say twelve learners, the group can be sub-divided into two groups that will meet separately and concurrently. If two trainers are available each sub-group can be supervised by a trainer who would support and guide the presentations. If only one trainer is available, the support may be limited to a peripatetic presence by the trainer with each group. At the end of the meetings, the sub-groups could be brought together in the full group to identify and discuss significant issues. An alternative, albeit one which requires more time and stronger control by the single trainer, is to have the presentations in one large group. The time can be reduced by encouraging the learners to comment briefly on their entries, extending only those that have not been mentioned to that point. This approach is not as valuable nor as satisfying as the small group approach, but it is better than no review at all if circumstances restrict the activity.

The pattern of log completion and implementation should be encouraged to continue beyond the training course, and certainly during the learners' development period and beyond, whenever learning takes place. I have a friend, an experienced trainer, who has maintained logs over several years – he has now about 1000 entries, most of which he took action on after making the entry.

Appendix 1 illustrates in an abbreviated form an exemplar Learning Log, set-sheets 1, 2 and 3 being shown with the sheet titles only. A log would normally be contained in a ring-binder with the introductory page, title sheets for the Workshops 1 and 2 of the two-week trainer development programme, each followed by five sets of three sheets for use on the course. Subsequent pages can be added for post-training event use.

Trainer Development Record The Learning Log is essentially a personalized, individual document. The Trainer Development Record (TDR) is also a document which is personal to the learner-trainer, but one which is also intended to encourage involvement of the line manager in the learner's development. A developing trainer can, in many circumstances feel that he or she is alone with no one to support them in their growing stages. Colleagues, if any, are usually too deeply involved in the practice of their own training responsibilities to have much time to spare. The learner's line manager *should* be there to offer this support, but frequently this involvement needs a helping hand to enable it to develop. The TDR can assist in this and, in the ideal situation, becomes the principal document in a regular discussion between the learner and the line manager.

Appendix 2 illustrates, again in an abbreviated form, the content of the monthly and quarterly records of a possible TDR. You will note that each document requires entries which look back over the previous period and record action and learning, and also those that relate to the next progress period and the action planned. The quarterly sheets summarize what has been learned to that stage and what has still to be done.

Consequently, the TDR which is intended in the first place to form a record of the first year in a trainer's development, can be seen as evidence of development intent and achievement. It can therefore be usefully retained (and indeed continued) as part of the trainer's portfolio of evidence towards awards for professional competence.

Part of the immediate post-trainer development programme should be an agreement between the learners and their line managers to meet regularly, say at monthly intervals, to consider the items of the TDR. In addition to fulfilling the process of the TDR, this contact ensures the active co-involvement of the trainers and their bosses at a personal, individual level – not a bad objective for a line manager and all his or her trainers, learners or otherwise!

THE PART-TIME TRAINER OR MANAGER-TRAINER

It is inevitably more difficult to define the training needs of the manager-trainer as so many more variations are possible than in the case of the full-time trainer. The range can extend from the manager with no time for training other than that of necessity as part of his responsibility to develop his staff, to the manager who has been selected as a part-time trainer by his company. Usually the latter has been selected because of either his learnt or innate skills as a trainer.

In the case of the part-time manager-trainer, much will depend on the objectives of the organization and its willingness to aid the development of the individual part-time trainer. An enlightened company will want to ensure that the individual's professionalism is developed to the fullest extent. If the manager-trainer is to have an extensive involvement in practical training he will require at the very least the basic core competences of the full-time trainer. It is likely that the manager-trainer's duties will include fairly basic training of the company's employees in terms of procedures, practices, systems and technologies. Consequently he will probably not be required to extend his skills into the more complex realms of human relations training. If the company feels that, after the trainer has gained some experience, his skills can be extended, further training can be given, usually by the manager-trainer attending relevant external events.

At the other end of the training spectrum, we have the manager whose company is unable or unwilling to employ training staff. In such cases the manager will have a dual responsibility – his basic responsibility to develop his staff and, depending on his own will to help in a practical way, a responsibility to ensure that his staff receive any training necessary.

The absolute minimum is that the manager takes an interest and involves himself in any training activities in which a member of his staff takes part. This interest should be taken whether the training takes the form of a training course or a self-generated form of learning. This approach has been discussed earlier, and as a minimum involvement the trainee should have a pre-course briefing session and a post-course debriefing discussion. But this must not be the end of the matter and the manager must take a longer-term interest. Most training courses encourage the production of a plan of action by the trainee at the end of the course. The active manager will use the action plan as a basis for the post-course action, regarding it as the start of his involvement with the trainee's further development, rather than as a one-off discussion. This will naturally involve the expenditure of time by both himself and the trainee: if the company requires development of its employees, it must also be prepared to accept and recognize this expenditure and adjust some of its objectives accordingly.

In addition to taking an active interest and involvement in a trainee's progress, the interested manager will need to coach as many of his staff as need this help, either from a remedial or a developmental point of view. This approach demands the expenditure of even more time, but the payoffs can only be of benefit to the manager and the organization, as well as to the trainee. However, coaching is a particular technique and there are numerous cases of more harm than good resulting from an unskilled approach to coaching and more harm than if nothing had been attempted. The skills of coaching include not only the knowledge of how to produce a coaching plan, but also the ability to consult, counsel, advise, guide and interact effectively with others. Few have these skills naturally and the company that has a sincere desire to involve its managers to an effective level of employee development must encourage them to gain these skills and practise them. Obviously coaching must not only occur at the managerial level and few managers will have the time to take part personally in coaching activities with all the staff who need help. The answer to these constraints is delegation, with the active involvement of the supervisory level. Either the manager can train his supervisors, once he has developed his own skills, send them to learn coaching techniques, or perhaps a number of managers with the necessary skills in coaching and training can be used as trainers of the supervisors in-company.

Apart from interest, involvement and coaching, training and development approaches will encroach considerably into the time of the manager without changing his role and developing him as a part-time direct trainer. But in times of economic constraint when an organization may have to rationalize its costs of internal or external training, there must be a clear policy on the extent to which it can support internal initiatives. If a negative approach is decided, the company must accept either that more money must be expended on attending public courses or that skills within the company will be in danger of regressing.

However, if a more positive internal approach is agreed, in addition to training in coaching skills being given to managers and supervisors, both these management levels must be given what can be described as absolutely basic core competence. Basic skills will include the identification of training needs and the knowledge of how these can be satisfied; presentational and discussion-leading skills and similar skills. Minimal training of this nature will enable managers to bring groups of employees together for internal learning events and give a reasonable chance of effectiveness. A costing exercise for any company considering this approach must include definition of such factors as the cost of training the managers and allowing time for events to be mounted internally, balanced against the cost of sending individuals on public courses or engaging an external consultant to work on a temporary basis within the organization – or worse, not having any training at all, with the likely adverse consequences.

TRAINER COMPETENCES

The identification for wider use of competences standards and measures of performance criteria is currently an active subject of research in a range of ideas (see pages 13–23 for a description of the TDLB competence standards for training functions).

In June 1984, the Manpower Services Commission and the Institute of Training and Development (now the Institute of Personnel and Development) published jointly the *Trainer Task Inventory*. This was based on original research by Terry Morgan and Martin Costello for the Air and Travel Industrial Training Board. The inventory is a comprehensive, structured job analysis questionnaire concerned with all the tasks carried out by trainers. Job holders are asked to state in a simple way whether they can or cannot do the various tasks listed. The inventory is highly flexible for use by a range of different types of trainers in that items which are not relevant can be deleted, and items added if not mentioned. There are likely to be few serious omissions in the 252 tasks listed.

The inventory is also sufficiently flexible to be used in the simple 'do', 'not do' approach, or it can include an organizationally developed competence scale, albeit subjective in many cases. One example of this, which I have used, is to use*. The absence of

* will show that the trainer/trainer-manager has no knowledge or skill in this area, or so little that it is not useful to record; one * shows that the trainer has some knowledge and skill of the task, but not sufficient to be of practical value; ** shows that the trainer has a reasonable skill and knowledge of that area and could, with limitations, use these in training; *** shows that the individual has a wide knowledge and skill in the area.

If necessary or desirable, this simple method of marking can be modified in a number of ways. Ticks can be used instead of *; a system can be developed to show the competences in knowledge and skills separately – a tick for knowledge level, * for skill level and so on.

The inventory is divided primarily into four main sections:

- helping people to learn or develop
- helping people to solve performance problems
- helping people to anticipate needs and problems and to formulate policies
- general functions of administrating, managing, knowing the business, and self-development.

Each Section is broken down into Work Areas – 7 in Section A, 5 in B, 2 in C and 4 in D. These define broad areas of work more specific, however, than the sections. For example, the five Work Areas in Section B are:

1) identifying performance problems – gathering information
2) identifying performance problems – processing information
3) selecting and designing intervention strategies
4) implementing an intervention
5) evaluating an intervention.

At the final level of analysis, each Work Area has a number of Tasks (the 252) listed under it. These lists range from 4 through 28 tasks in the various Work Areas.

For example, the tasks in Work Area 2 (identifying training/learning needs – processing information) of Section A are:

1) Analyse surveys
2) Apply statistical tests to survey data

3) Identify skills and knowledge requirements of jobs
4) Discuss training priorities with management
5) Assign priorities to identified training needs
6) Review nominations to applications for training/learning events
7) Identify training population
8) Write reports to line managers
9) Study training programmes produced by manufacturers
10) Consider training methods and programmes used by other operators.

USE OF THE TRAINER TASK INVENTORY

The inventory has a wide range of possible uses, some of which are:

- to be a guide to the areas of training and education needed for people entering the profession
- to determine or evaluate the content of training programmes
- to decide the scope of the training department
- to structure individual jobs
- to describe a job in precise terms
- to assess current competences
- to use as a basis for appraisal
- to plan development of an individual or group
- to use as a basis for a job description/job specification used in recruitment
- to produce a CV
- to assist individuals in the self-assessment of their own development needs.

At first sight the inventory looks daunting, but it is relatively simple and quick to complete and experience has shown that it can be a valuable tool in the control and development of training in a variety of ways.

CHOICE OF EXTERNAL HELP

Reference has already been made to the use of trainers or consultants external to the company, so that employees can attend public courses mounted by such individuals or organizations. Alternatively these consultants can be invited into the company to conduct training activities on an in-company rather than public basis. The cost of training of this nature can be high, usually higher than training provided in-company by the company's own trainers, if the organization is large enough to support such a division. The client, that is to say the company, must also be in a position to assess whether it is getting value for money if it buys in skill and expertise. This latter assurance can be difficult, particularly as there are so many individuals and organizations advertising their availability. With as many options as this, the range of skill would be expected to vary considerably, and it does.

The first step in seeking external help must be a specific identification by the organization itself of the training needs of the employees it wishes to develop. The jobs they are required to do are analysed and from this and comparison of what is required and what actually happens, the training needs can be identified. Then the organization must construct specific and detailed terminal objectives for the training so that once it has been performed, the company can have some measure of whether it has been successful.

All training organizations or consultants produce some form of brochure describing the services they offer, or will provide information of this nature. Advertisements appear regularly in professional training and management journals which give brief details of what the training organization can provide. Whatever the source of information, the client has the right to have the maximum amount of detail about the provisions and, if everything is not immediately available, searching questions must be asked. Such questions will relate to the extent to which the trainer can satisfy the identified training needs. It is advisable to obtain the answers in writing so that there can be no problems at a later stage.

Training organizations can advertise their services in a variety of ways. Mention has been made of advertisements in professional journals, either in the form of inclusive advertisements or brochures which come with the journal. But information about sources of training can be obtained in other ways. Professional bodies such as the Institute of Personnel and Development, the British Institute of Management and so on can often give information and advice. Where still available the relevant Industrial Training Board or its registered voluntary equivalent can also provide this service and often more practical help. Regional Management Centres and similar educational establishments provide direct training and are usually willing to make training advice available. A very useful source of information is the *National Training Index,* subscription to which gives both information on training organizations and consultants and the services they offer, and also appraisal information on the courses by individuals who have attended them. But by far the most satisfactory method of obtaining information, particularly concerning the value of the training provided, is to ask people who have undergone the training themselves or similar companies who have used particular trainers.

Once the range of possible providers is identified, the available information must be studied carefully and compared with the training objectives that have been determined. If there is reasonable agreement, then possible organizations have been found; if there is not total agreement, but other factors are acceptable, it may be possible to negotiate some variation, particularly if the consultant is to work in-company.

There must be a direct dialogue with the selected trainer or trainers with the intention of confirming which provider will satisfy the needs, or if the training is to be in-company, that he fully understands the special needs and can vary his approach to satisfy them. The effective consultant whose services are being contracted should be able to offer a considerable degree of variation. It is common practice, as in most cases of purchasing services, to ask for proposals from a number of possible providers, and most will be willing to make a personal presentation of their proposals. One aspect of which to take care is in the area of cost variation; trainer skills are more difficult to assess than the quality of materials included in a practical provision tender.

Before the final decision is made, it is advisable to obtain from the provider most likely to be accepted detailed information about session objectives, content and methods, rather than the more general subject headings usually provided initially. A detailed synopsis of what would be done should be readily available from an efficient provider. But beware. Have you the skill to interpret and assess the information given? It may be clothed, with no devious intent, in training terms and jargon. Can you understand all the implications of what is offered? If there is any doubt, ask the provider for an explanation of anything about which you are not completely clear and do not accept the explanations unless you are satisfied. It is often useful to ask a friend with training knowledge and experience to vet the proposals and identify the questions you should ask.

In addition to clarifying and confirming the training details just mentioned, you will need to be aware of other aspects, particularly if the provider is to perform the training in-company. Many learning subjects can be approached in a general manner with little or no emphasis on the special needs of the organization, but others must be linked closely to the company's procedures, methods or cultures. In such cases it will be necessary to know whether the provider is sufficiently informed about the industry or company and its special needs. If he is not, the trainer must conduct some research and preparation: this will add to the cost of training and will need to be negotiated in addition to the training itself.

What will be the method of evaluating the success or progress of the individuals taking part in the training? To what extent will the employing organization have to or need to do some form of this evaluation, or will this be taken care of by the provider? This may be another aspect for prior negotiation.

Finally, ensure that it is clear that the trainer who is personally acceptable and has been discussed as the individual who will provide the training, is guaranteed to appear for the actual event. This is particularly important when negotiating with a large training organization, and it would certainly be desirable to build into the contract some cover against failure in this respect as well as the other more obvious guarantee clauses.

Much of the descriptive literature provided by training organizations includes lists of organizations whose members have attended their training events. Such information can be useful, but must be treated with some caution as these organizations may have had training objectives that differ from yours, their employees may have attended different courses than the one you are considering, or the course in which you are interested may have been attended by people at different levels than the ones for whom you have identified the training need.

The constraints of training may appear many and severe, and the economics may make you question very strongly whether you should do anything at all, but when considering whether training can be afforded, consider even more carefully whether you can afford not to have training.

REPORTING-BACK ON THE LEARNERS

This is a contentious subject but one with which many trainers have to contend. Should a report on the learners be given to their managers after the end of the programme?

In some organizations this decision is taken out of the hands of the trainers with statements that either a report is definitely required (and in what form) or such a report is not required (and perhaps may not be welcome).

In other organizations, the trainers are given no guidance and the decision is left to them. The solution is not clear-cut, but in the absence of organization guidance, usually nothing is reported. Nevertheless, there are cases when the trainer has to make this kind of decision without guidance. If one of the learners is seen to be so incapable of learning or performing that something *should be said*, should it in fact become an exception? Other situations can include those where discipline might be a problem. If a course participant has been a difficult or troublemaking member of the course, but not sufficiently so to make immediate discipline necessary, the trainer is faced with the problem of whether or not to report this to the participant's line manager. If nothing is said, the fact that the other members may have had reduced learning opportunities is being ignored. The individual may later be sent on another course with similar behavioural dysfunction. A report-back would at least ensure that the person is 'disciplined' back at work and would either attend further courses with an improved behaviour or receive training in another way. But the moral question raised by the trainer, *in the absence of specific instructions*, is whether they have the right to report on an individual who may be their junior, peer or even senior in the organization.

The question of discipline is one which should be clarified by the organization and, in relation to training, can vary to a considerable extent. One organization used to require pre-course reading, the performance of this being tested at the start of the training event. If it was seen that this had not been done, the individual(s) was sent back to work and the relevant line manager was informed. Draconian? But if the success of the learning depended on this action being taken, its correctness becomes more acceptable.

A more common disciplinary situation can occur during a course. The troublemaker described above may take his or her actions further to the extent that the course and the learning of the other members is being disrupted. What does the trainer do? The first step is to have a quiet word in private with the offender. If this is not successful, a further reference to the training manager may be the next step. But if appeals to the individual do not work, more drastic action has to be considered. One option is that the individual is asked to leave the course and return to work where the reason for the return will have to be explained to the line manager by the individual. Another is prior reference for guidance to the relevant line manager by telephone – this may result in a request to send the person back to work, or to be called to the phone to discuss the situation.

Many trainers will, fortunately, continue their careers without the occurrence of a problem of this nature, but, because it can happen at any time, it is always best to be forewarned about what you can do or what you have to do.

On the general question of reporting-back on course performance, the trainer must remember, however, that most of the learners passing through the event will be experiencing many situations for the first time. Is it possible to make an objective comment on a person under such an environment over a short period of time (say two or three days)? I believe that (a) although the trainer can form an opinion, a fully objective assessment is very difficult to make and (b) surely it is the responsibility of the learner's manager to assess ability.

Whatever the decision or requirement, if at all possible the learners should be made aware of what is happening; failure to do this can give rise to suspicion which in turn leads to over-participation or withdrawal depending on the nature of the learner. A participant may take a lead in many of the course activities, be the one to volunteer, and be what appears to be a very active learner, but this may be done superficially to encourage the trainer to think that the person is an ideal learner. Certainly, because of the participation, some of the learning will stick, although much will have been temporary learning only. At the other end of the spectrum, someone attending the course may take so much exception to the intended report-back that they will be a rebellious 'participant'.

It may be suggested that you do not tell the learners that they are to be reported on – this will obviously be with the conscience of the trainer, but it certainly goes against the present philosophy of openness in employment and relationships. Also the trainer's credibility is gone forever if the learner eventually discovers that a report has been made – this could certainly affect any future training events in which both the trainer and the learner have to interact.

REFERENCES AND RECOMMENDED READING

Improving Training Effectiveness. Ed. Roger Bennett. Gower, 1988.

The Management of Learning. Ivor K. Davies. McGraw-Hill, 1971.

Planning and Running your Exhibition Stand. Nathan Hoshen. Management Update, 1988.

A Handbook of Training Management. Kenneth R. Robinson. Kogan Page, 1981.

Managing the Training and Development Function. Allan D. Pepper. Gower, 1984.

The Skills of Management. A. N. Welsh. Gower, 1980.

A Consultancy Approach for Trainers, Keri Phillips and Patricia Shaw. Gower, 1989.

Ten Tips for Trainers. Video. Melrose, 1994.

Memories are Made of This. Video. Melrose, 1994.

The Trainer Development Programme: A Manual for Trainers. Leslie Rae. Kogan Page, 1994.

How to Design and Introduce Trainer Development Programmes. Leslie Rae. Kogan Page, 1994.

Choosing and Using Training Consultants. Diane Bailey and Clare Sproston. Gower, 1993.

Appendix 1 A learning log book

KEEPING A LEARNING LOG

The objective of attending a learning event is to learn something you can use. A complex event can contain a number of ideas, concepts, activities, etc. that you might wish to implement at work. It can be difficult, particularly over an extended period, to remember all that you considered, perhaps even some important ones.

A Learning Log:

- gives you a permanent document in which to record these ideas as they occur
- helps you at a later stage think about what you have experienced and learned, particularly the key ideas you want to retain
- helps you consider at leisure which aspects you want to implement and how you are going to do this
- is a reminder for you about your intentions when you get back to work
- is a permanent record of your progress and development and of what you have learned.

If the other notes you may have taken and the handouts issued during the training programme are combined with this log, you have a full record of your training to which you can refer at any time.

Your Learning Log should be completed frequently during the event – preferably during periods which may be allocated for this purpose – or during the evening following the training day. Do not leave its completion any longer than this, otherwise there is the danger that some useful and/or important ideas or learning may be lost.

From your ongoing notes section, review these notes and select the ideas, techniques, suggestions, activities that you feel could be important or significant for you.

In the second section of the log, describe these selections in as much detail as necessary so that you will be able to recall them later.

In the third section, preferably with a priority listing, describe, from your list in the second section, what you are going to implement or otherwise take action on:

- WHAT are you going to do?
- HOW are you going to implement or action it?
- WHEN AND/OR BY WHEN are you going to implement it?
- WHAT resources will you need?
- WHO can or needs to be involved?
- WHAT implications are there for effects on others?

THE CONTINUED USE OF THE LEARNING LOG

ON THE TRAINING PROGRAMME

At the start of the day following the one for which you have completed your log you will, in a small group, be asked to describe the entries you have made. This presentation will:

a) help you clarify your thoughts on the area presented
b) help you in the recall process
c) widen the views of the remainder of the group who may not have seen the implications of the areas you have highlighted
d) raise the opportunity for clarification of doubtful points to be given.

AS A CONTINUOUS PROCESS

A Learning Log is not intended for use only on training programmes. We are learning all the time, in every type of situation and a log can help us capitalize on these opportunities. If you read a book and there are ideas that you want to remember and implement, enter these in the log. If, in discussion with others, ideas are suggested that you feel may be of use to you, remember them and enter them in your log at the first opportunity. Keep referring to your log constantly to remind you of activities that you have not yet implemented.

Your line manager in his/her process of your continuing assessment, will not only find your log entries valuable in assessing your development, but could also be impressed by your intent and persistence.

Remember that if eventually you decide to seek the award of the Training and Development National Vocational Qualification (TDNVQ), this record can form a useful part of the portfolio you will need to produce for this award.

WORKSHOP ONE

****

SECTION ONE

RUNNING RECORD OF ITEMS OF WHICH YOU WISH TO REMIND YOURSELF

****

SECTION TWO

DETAILED DESCRIPTIONS OF YOUR SELECTED ITEMS

****

SECTION THREE

IMPLEMENTATION DECISIONS

WORKSHOP TWO

****

SECTION ONE

RUNNING RECORD OF ITEMS OF WHICH YOU WISH TO REMIND YOURSELF

****

SECTION TWO

DETAILED DESCRIPTIONS OF YOUR SELECTED ITEMS

****

SECTION THREE

IMPLEMENTATION DECISIONS

Appendix 2 A trainer development record

1. MONTHLY REVIEW SHEETS

MONTHLY REVIEW AND ACTION PLANNING

What have I done this month?

What have I learned as a trainer this month?

How can I use/have I used what I have learned?

In what way am I operating differently now to a month ago?

What development goals do I have for the next month?

Action plan for next month

Signed: Learner .... Line manager .... Date ....

2. QUARTERLY REVIEW SHEETS

QUARTERLY REVIEW AND ACTION PLANNING

Quarter 1

What have I learned as a trainer this quarter?

In what way am I operating differently now?

What development goals do I have for the next quarter?

What might hinder me in achieving these?

What might I do to reduce or obviate these hindrances?

What might help me in achieving my goals?

Signature .... Date ....

QUARTERLY ASSESSMENT

Quarter 1

	Need further training or action (T or A)	Competent
PLANNING AND ORGANIZING TRAINING		
1. Identify, analyse or respond to specific training needs	....	....
2. Take account of policy, operational and other developments	....	....
DIRECT TRAINING ACTIVITIES		
1. Establish learning objectives	....	....
2. Analyse individual training needs of the learners	....	....

and so on

Signed: Learner .... Line manager .... Date ....

ACTION PLAN FOR SECOND QUARTER

What core skills development objectives have been agreed for the next quarter?

What activities are planned to meet these?

How will progress be measured?

How will progress be reviewed?

What else will I need to do?

Signed: Learner .... Line manager .... Date ....

Appendix 3 Assessment of the trainer by the trainees

This appendix contains a questionnaire that can be used for the trainees or learners to assess the apparent skill of the trainer(s) involved in their course. It must be used carefully with the caveats discussed in Chapter 12.

TRAINER ASSESSMENT

COURSE ....

Please complete the following questions by placing a tick or other mark against each question under the heading that most nearly represents your view. In some cases you will be asked why you have given that rating – please answer as fully and honestly as possible.

It will help the trainer and his/her manager in the trainer's development if you would complete the questionnaire fully and honestly. There is no intention to use it in any way as a discipline document and it will support other assessments of the trainer so that the training can be made as effective as possible.

	To a large extent	Partly	Hardly at all
1. To what extent was interest created from the start? Why have you given this rating?	....	....	....
2. How much was this interest maintained? Why have you given this rating?	....	....	....

	To a large extent	Partly	Hardly at all
3. How was it maintained? Please describe briefly.	....		
4. To what extent were the objectives of the course declared and explained? Why have you given this rating?	....	....	....
5. To what extent was the training just telling?	....	....	....
6. How much variety was there in the course? Why have you given this rating?	....	....	....
7. To what extent was the group involved? Why have you given this rating?	....	....	....
8. To what extent were practical activities used?	....	....	....
9. How well were these conducted and controlled? Please describe briefly. Why have you given this rating?	....		
10. To what extent was discussion used? Why have you given this rating?	....	....	....
11. How much were visual and audio-visual aids used? Why have you given this rating?	....	....	....

	To a large extent	Partly	Hardly at all
12. To what extent were these relevant? Why have you given this rating?	....	....	....
13. Were the aids of good quality? Why have you given this rating?	....	....	....
14. How much use of summaries was made?	....	....	....
15. To what extent was the language used understandable? Why have you given this rating?	....	....	....
16. To what extent was enthusiasm exhibited? Why have you given this rating?	....	....	....
17. How much opportunity was there for the group to ask questions?	....	....	....
18. How far were these dealt with satisfactorily? Why have you given this rating?	....	....	....
19. How much did the trainer's 'platform presence' distract your learning? Why have you given this rating?	....	....	....

	To a large extent	Partly	Hardly at all
20. To what extent was he/she responsible for what you learned? Why have you given this rating?	....	....	....
21. Please feel free to add any other comments here	....		
	....		
	....		
	....		
	....		
	....		
	....		
	....		
	....		

Appendix 4 A guide to additional resources

There are many resources available to trainers to help them in the design and implementation of their training events – books on training and specific skills subjects, films and videos, collections of activities, training packages and so on. There is insufficient room to list all these in this book and the reader is referred to the relevant source books and publishers. However, the following pages offer a representative selection to start new trainers in their search for supportive material.

The list of books is limited because all the chapters of this book end with a list of references and recommended reading.

SELECTED BOOKS

Title	Author	Obtainable from	Comments
The Kogan Page Practical Trainer Series Current titles: COMPETENCE-BASED ASSESSMENT TECHNIQUES COST-EFFECTIVE TRAINING DESIGNING COMPETENCE-BASED TRAINING EFFECTIVE FEEDBACK SKILLS HOW TO DESIGN AND DELIVER EQUAL OPPORTUNITIES TRAINING HOW TO DESIGN AND DELIVER INDUCTION TRAINING PROGRAMMES HOW TO DESIGN AND DELIVER QUALITY SERVICE TRAINING HOW TO DESIGN AND DELIVER RETIREMENT TRAINING HOW TO DESIGN AND IMPLEMENT TRAINER DEVELOPMENT PROGRAMMES HOW TO DESIGN AND INTRODUCE APPRAISAL TRAINING HOW TO TAKE A TRAINING AUDIT HOW TO WRITE AND PREPARE TRAINING MATERIALS THE IN-HOUSE TRAINER AS CONSULTANT THE LONE TRAINER MANAGING TRAINING ONE-TO-ONE TRAINING AND COACHING SKILLS	Various	Kogan Page	A series of softback booklets dealing with specific subjects Reader-friendly, they produce a useful desk library for trainers. The titles are generally self-explanatory.

Title	Author	Obtainable from	Comments
A PRACTICAL APPROACH TO GROUP TRAINING SELECTING AND USING TRAINING AIDS TRAINING FOR TOTAL QUALITY MANAGEMENT TRAINING NEEDS ANALYSIS IN THE WORKPLACE VALIDATING YOUR TRAINING.			
The McGraw-Hill Training Series THE BUSINESS OF TRAINING DEVELOPING EFFECTIVE TRAINING DEVELOPING MANAGERS AS COACHES EVALUATING TRAINING EFFECTIVENESS FACILITATION THE HANDBOOK FOR ORGANIZATIONAL CHANGE HOW TO DESIGN EFFECTIVE TEXT-BASED OPEN LEARNING HOW TO DESIGN EFFECTIVE COMPUTER-BASED LEARNING IMAGINATIVE EVENTS VOLUMES I AND II LEARNING THROUGH SIMULATIONS MAKING MANAGEMENT DEVELOPMENT WORK MANAGING THE TRAINING PROCESS MEETINGS MANAGEMENT MANUAL RESOURCE-BASED LEARNING SALES TRAINING TEAM BUILDING	Various	McGraw-Hill	A series of softback books dealing with a range of training and development subjects, both strategic and tactical. The titles are generally self-expalanatory.

Title	Author	Obtainable from	Comments
TRAINING FOR PROFIT			
TRAINING TO MEET THE TECHNOLOGY CHALLENGE			
WORKSHOPS THAT WORK			
Management Pocketbooks	Various	Melrose	A series of small, pocket-size booklets, produced in a format of mainly bulleted headlines and graphics. Good and easy reference.
THE BUSINESS PRESENTER'S POCKETBOOK	John Townsend, 1990		
THE INSTRUCTOR'S POCKETBOOK	John Townsend, 1991		
CHALLENGERS! (HOW TO HANDLE DIFFICULT PARTICIPANTS)	John Townsend, 1994		
THE TRAINER'S POCKETBOOK OF READY-EASY-TO-USE EXERCISES	John Townsend, 1993		A collection of 40 mainly simple, but useful icebreakers, spot-checks, activities, team building exercises, tests and quizzes.

SELECTED FILMS AND VIDEOS

Title	Time	Obtainable from	Comments
THE FLOOR IS YOURS NOW	24 mins	Gower	Completely updated remake of *The Floor is Yours*. Describes presentation techniques for new trainers and occasional speakers, demonstrates 22 main teaching points and up-to-date techniques. Includes use of OHP slides, flipcharts, video; channelling nervous energy; the importance of rehearsal; objective setting; eye contact and body language and so on.
THE AUDIENCE IS YOURS NOW	25 mins	Gower	The sequel to 'The Floor is Yours Now' and it highlights and demonstrates the techniques of presenting to audiences. The programme focuses on the main areas of audience interaction: communicating the message, inviting and responding to questions, dealing with interruptions, and maintaining control throughout the presentation. It looks at some of the potential pitfalls awaiting an unsuspecting presenter and how to deal with them – the ultimate determination of how successful a presentation will be.
MEMORIES ARE MADE OF THIS	16 mins	Melrose	One of the few videos directed specifically at trainer training, although it relates equally to general presentation skills. It covers in an impactive mixed live and animated sequence, communication, the problems of memory and recall and methods of improving these.
TEN TIPS FOR TRAINERS	35 mins	Melrose	Another recent video directed specifically at the training of trainers skills. Ten useful tips are presented by John Townsend with discussions, image sequences, etc.

Title	Time	Obtainable from	Comments
TEN TIPS FOR TRAINERS *continued*			Subjects covered include starting and ending with a bang, planning and designing training, using flipcharts and OHP slides effectively, presentational skills, and handling difficult participants.
MAKING YOUR CASE	20 mins	Video Arts	Uses the *Alice in Wonderland* trial scene to demonstrate the problems and pitfalls commonly experienced by presenters who have not thought through the requirements for presenting an effective case.
SEE WHAT I MEAN	26 mins	Gower	This video is designed to train presenters in the techniques of choosing the most appropriate visual system for the event – flipcharts, whiteboards, OHP, large screen video and so on. It uses the story of an inexperienced presenter learning to use the various visuals available.
DON'T JUST TELL THEM	20 mins	Gower	The use of basic visual aids when presenting information to others is demonstrated. Gives tips on the use of chalkboards, magnetic boards, flipcharts, models, slide projectors, OHP. For the person who is inexperienced in the use of basic visual aids.
SPEAKING EFFECTIVELY TO ONE OR ONE THOUSAND	20 mins	Gower	Shows managers/trainers how to speak in public in exactly the same way as they would talk to an individual rather than be intimidated by large audiences. The content describes the control of the nervous speaking reactions such as dry mouth, racing pulse and sweaty palms.

Title	Time	Obtainable from	Comments
APPLAUSE	20 mins	Cally Curtis Co.	Seven steps to effective presentation are offered to improve any speaker's self-confidence. The video stresses the need for thorough preparation – the key to presentation success.
YOU'LL SOON GET THE HAND OF IT	29 mins	Video Arts	A variety of situations are used (manual, clerical and technical) with a series of comedy sketches to put over the essential points and illustrate the main pitfalls in teaching a trainee.
VISUAL AIDS	27 mins	Gower	Deals with most of the visual methods a trainer can use showing the right and wrong way to use them and illustrates the 'Do's and Don'ts'.
BODY LANGUAGE	3 videos each 20 mins	Gower	Three videos are contained in this programme in which Allan Pease, an Australian authority on body language and TV personality presents extracts from his productions. He helps in recognition and use of subconscious body language to advantage. The various uses of gestures and other non-verbal communications are described and demonstrated, in addition to looking at their origins.
BODY TALK	28 mins	Wyvern Business Training	Two videos are included in this package and also two supporting booklets – one as a trainer's guide, the other giving the full script of the main video. The main video uses a case study presentation to demonstrate the body language faults and remedies for a proposal presentation the three players have just made. The support video is typical of the Wyvern approach in that it presents a number of short 'trigger' scenes for discussion and key point reinforcement.

Title	Time	Obtainable from	Comments
THE POWER OF LISTENING	26 mins	CRM/McGraw-Hill	This film takes a look at those things which prevent us from listening as well as we should – a necessity for trainers who often assume they are good listeners, but are not always so.
YOU CAN'T DO IT ALL	20 mins	Gower	Although not a direct training of trainers video, this is an example of the new 'breed' of video which is presented not as a video alone, nor with a supporting booklet alone. The package contains the video which is constructed specifically as a training video, emphasizing the learning points by interrupting techniques. The supporting booklets – one a trainer's guide and one a participant's handbook – extend the range of the video into a complete training package. The trainer's handbook, in addition to extending the learning points shown in the video, also describes additional points, but above all suggests a complete training programme using the video as an integrated part. The content of the video is concerned with the barriers to delegation and in a realistic case study shows the development of a supervisor who is 'trying to do it all himself' (and failing). The package covers not only the barriers to delegation, but also the processes used by a skilled delegator.

SELECTED TRAINING ACTIVITIES

Title	Author	Obtainable from	Comments
GOWER and CONNAUGHT ACTIVITIES	Various	Gower and Connaught Training	This is an extensive and developing series of training activities and exercises which are available for use on a variety of training programmes. Materials are provided to run each activity successfully – trainer's notes and guidelines, aims and objectives, role play briefs, summary sheets, handouts, discussion questions and group exercises, appraisals and so on. They are presented in a loose-leaf format whose pages can be reproduced without further permission.
50 ACTIVITIES FOR DEVELOPING MANAGEMENT SKILLS Volumes 1 to 9			
A MANUAL OF MANAGEMENT TRAINING EXERCISES	John Payne		
20 ACTIVITIES FOR DEVELOPING MANAGERIAL EFFECTIVENESS Volumes 1 and 2	Lewis, Kelly and Armstrong		
GOWER and CONNAUGHT TRAINING SPECIFIC SUBJECT TRAINING ACTIVITIES	Various	Gower and Connaught Training	This is a further extensive and developing series of activity collections, but in this instance the activities are collected into mainly single subject collections, e.g. sales, stress, etc. Most of the titles are self-explanatory and some examples are those following.
20 ACTIVITIES FOR DEVELOPING SALES EFFECTIVENESS	Patrick Forsyth and Marek Gitlin		
50 ACTIVITIES FOR MANAGING STRESS	Dr Roy Bailey		

Title	Author	Obtainable from	Comments
50 ACTIVITIES FOR TEAM BUILDING	Mike Woodcock		
50 ACTIVITIES FOR UNBLOCKING ORGANIZATIONAL COMMUNICATION	Dave Francis		
50 ACTIVITIES FOR SELF-DEVELOPMENT	Dave Francis and Mike Woodcock		
Trainers interested in these collections should contact Gower/Connaught, Aldershot for up-to-date information.			
FENMAN TRAINING COLLECTIONS	Various	Fenman Training (formerly Wyvern Business Training)	Collections of activities and workshop manuals on specific subjects. The range includes:
35 WAYS TO START A TRAINING EVENT	Leslie Rae		
THE ASSERTIVENESS SKILLS PACK	Joanna Gutmann		
SESSION SHAKERS	Sarah Cook		
PRESENTATION SKILLS ACTIVITIES	Mike Fenwick		
Trainers interested in the full Fenman range should contact Fenman Training, Ely.			

Title	Author	Obtainable from	Comments
KOGAN PAGE TRAINING COLLECTIONS	Various	Kogan Page	Two activity ranges are produced by this publisher: (a) training manuals on specific subjects and (b) collections of resources.
(a) Training manuals:			These detail training courses in the subject and include input session material, handouts and OHP slide masters.
NEGOTIATION SKILLS	Wendy Carter		
COMMUNICATION SKILLS	Wendy Carter		
NEGOTIATION SKILLS	Rob Baston		
(b) Activity sourcebooks:			These are similar to the ring-binder, specific subject collections of Gower but are in bound book format.
ICEBREAKERS	Ken Jones		
INTERPERSONAL SKILLS TRAINING	Philip Burnard		
TEAM BUILDING	Glenn Parker and Richard Kropp		
ROLE PLAYS	David Turner		
TRAINING FOR CHANGE	Sue Bishop and David Taylor		
LEADERSHIP TRAINING	Elizabeth Christopher and Larry Smith		
Trainers interested in the full Kogan Page range should contact Kogan Page, London			

Title	Author	Obtainable from	Comments
McGRAW-HILL TRAINING COLLECTIONS	Various	McGraw-Hill	This publisher has a more restricted range of activity collections than the other sources, but includes:
WORKSHOPS THAT WORK	Tom Bourner, Vivien Martin, Phil Race		
IMAGINATIVE EVENTS, Volumes 1 and 2	Ken Jones		
MEETINGS MANAGEMENT	Leslie Rae		
THE TRAINER'S TOOLKIT		Melrose Film productions	Although described as a 'toolkit', this is a collection of 17 activities and role plays taken from several Melrose training packages. A collection of resources over a wide range of activities.
Trainers may also wish to refer to the article 'Activities for Trainers' – bane or boon', Leslie Rae, *Training Officer*, December 1993, vol. 29, no. 10.		Other publishers produce collections of activities and manuals for specific subjects. These include such organizations as Longman, Pfeiffer and so on. Publishers' lists should be referred to for up-to-date information on the ranges available.	
SELECTED TRAINING PACKAGES			One of the most significant developments in the provision of training resources has been the increased (and increasing) availability of complete training packages. These packages offer trainers ready-made material with which to conduct training sessions, groups of training sessions or complete courses. The packages which, in the best examples, are very flexible and allow the trainer to modify according to his or her requirements, range from

Title	Author	Obtainable from	Comments
SELECTED TRAINING PACKAGES *continued*			simple text programmes describing how the programme can be run, through videos with supporting text programmes or text programmes with supporting videos, to complete packages which can contain text instructions, videos, interactive videos, computer programs and so on or a varying mixture of these. The following is a selection of such packages.
GOOD QUESTION		Wyvern Business Training	In this programme two videos and a supporting booklet are provided. The first video is a traditional one in which, through the activities of different people in a company, the most appropriate ways of questioning people in recruitment, discipline, counselling and appraisal are considered. This video can be run straight through and be followed by a general discussion on the content. The second video contains a series of short cameos, some extracted from the main video, others based on the theme of the main video. These cameos are intended to be used as discussion initiators and pick out significant areas of the main theme, saving the trainer having to determine which questions to ask to arouse discussion. In addition, the accompanying booklet offers other areas for discussion, questions to ask and associated activities to concentrate the learning.
YOU CAN'T DO IT ALL YOURSELF		Gower	This package is essentially a training video for delegation, but because of its novel treatment and the supporting material, is much more than just a video. The package contains a video which demonstrates the development of a supervisor's skills in delegating and highlights the barriers to delegation. The construction of the video is such

Title	Author	Obtainable from	Comments
YOU CAN'T DO IT ALL YOURSELF *continued*			that it can be stopped realistically at a number of points to permit discussion of 'the story so far'. On the other hand it can be played straight through with discussion delayed until the end of the video. To assist in the trainer's decision on how to use the video, it is supported by a *Trainer's Handbook* which • consolidates the barriers shown in the video • describes a number of other barriers not included in the video • describes in detail the recommended process of delegation, a process mentioned only briefly in the video • suggests a programme with various options, which the trainer might wish to use for a complete training programme on delegation. Participants' handbooks are also included in the package. These concentrate principally on the process of delegation.
CONSTRUCTIVE NEGOTIATION	Bill Scott	Gower	This is an in-house programme developed on the subject of negotiating and represents one of the more complex and complete training packages available. It consists of: • a trainer's guide leading the trainer through a complete course on the subject of negotiating, but giving options on which parts to use as required in various situations • four video cassettes which show dramatized negotiations and which are used at relevant stages in the recommended course

Title	Author	Obtainable from	Comments
CONSTRUCTIVE NEGOTIATION continued			• a set of 15 OHP transparencies which can be used in conjunction with the trainer input sections of the programme • masters of the case study briefs available for photo-copying • eight participants' workbooks for use in the practical work of the programme • a copy of Bill Scott's book *The Skills of Negotiating*. Other options within the package include ways of offering a course in five modules each lasting about half a day. In this way the full course can be run over 2½ consecutive days or in the modular form spaced over five weeks.

Index

The Techniques of Instruction

Roger James

What do effective instructors do that makes them effective? In this ground-breaking book, Dr James examines the whole process of instruction from the point of view of skill development to discover which are the best techniques and why. He shows:

- how to produce the best trainee performance possible in the shortest possible time
- how to structure practice sessions to maximize learning
- how to analyse the task involved so as to design the most appropriate exercise
- how to deal with the "slow" trainee
- how to boost the trainee's confidence
- how to instruct "at a distance".

Although based on extensive research, the material in the book is presented in non-technical language and draws on a wide range of examples. The result is a comprehensive guide to the practice of instruction which will be of immense value to anyone involved in training, teaching or coaching.

Contents

Preface • The role of the instructor in training • Training technology • Are instructors useful? • The instructional process • The learning machine • How people develop skill • Open and closed skills • Developing speed and accuracy of movement • The three stages of skill development • Designing skill practice conditions • Preparing for instruction • Delivering instruction • Talking to trainees • Helping the trainee to avoid errors • Correcting trainee errors • Instructing when you can intervene • Instructing when you cannot intervene • An instructor's toolkit • Index.

1995 200 pages 0 566 07550 4